MW00686198

222 Secrets of Hiring, Managing, and Retaining Great Employees in Healthcare Practices

Bob Levoy

JONES AND BARTLETT PUBLISHERS

Sudbury, Massachusetts

BOSTON   TORONTO   LONDON   SINGAPORE

World Headquarters

Jones and Bartlett Publishers	Jones and Bartlett Publishers	Jones and Bartlett Publishers
40 Tall Pine Drive	Canada	International
Sudbury, MA 01776	6339 Ormindale Way	Barb House, Barb Mews
978-443-5000	Mississauga, Ontario L5V 1J2	London W6 7PA
info@jbpub.com	CANADA	UK
www.jbpub.com		

Jones and Bartlett's books and products are available through most bookstores and online book-sellers. To contact Jones and Bartlett Publishers directly, call 800-832-0034, fax 978-443-8000, or visit our website, www.jbpub.com.

Substantial discounts on bulk quantities of Jones and Bartlett's publications are available to corporations, professional associations, and other qualified organizations. For details and specific discount information, contact the special sales department at Jones and Bartlett via the above contact information or send an email to specialsales@jbpub.com.

Copyright © 2007 by Jones and Bartlett Publishers, Inc.

All rights reserved. No part of the material protected by this copyright may be reproduced or utilized in any form, electronic or mechanical, including photocopying, recording, or by any information storage and retrieval system, without written permission from the copyright owner.

The author discloses that he has no relationship or financial interest in any of the resource materials, products, or organizations listed in this book.

The author has made every effort to ensure the accuracy of the information herein. However, appropriate information sources should be consulted, especially for new or unfamiliar procedures. It is the responsibility of every practitioner to evaluate the appropriateness of a particular opinion in the context of actual clinical situations and with due considerations to new developments. The author(s) and publisher disclaim all responsibility for any liability, loss, injury, or damage incurred as a consequence, directly or indirectly, of the use and application of any of the contents of this volume.

Library of Congress Cataloging-in-Publication Data
Levoy, Robert P.
  222 secrets of hiring, managing, and retaining great employees in healthcare practices / Robert Levoy.
     p. cm.
  Includes index.
  ISBN-13: 978-0-7637-3868-6 (casebound)
  ISBN-10: 0-7637-3868-9 (casebound)
  1. Employees—Recruiting. 2. Personnel management. 3. Employee retention. 4. Employee selection. I. Title. II. Title: Two hundred twenty two secrets of hiring, managing, and retaining great employees in healthcare practices.
  HF5549.5.R44L45 2007
  658.3—dc22
                          2006025214

6048

Production Credits
Executive Editor: David Cella
Editorial Assistant: Lisa Gordon
Production Director: Amy Rose
Production Editor: Tracey Chapman
Associate Marketing Manager: Laura Kavigian

Manufacturing and Inventory Coordinator: Amy Bacus
Composition: Arlene Apone
Cover Design: Anne Spencer
Printing and Binding: Malloy, Inc.
Cover Printing: Malloy, Inc.

Printed in the United States of America
10 09 08 07 06   10 9 8 7 6 5 4 3 2 1

Dedication

In loving memory of Morton Roberts, M.D.

Contents

> **HIRING**

RETAINING

Introduction

The challenge of finding, managing, and retaining great employees is greater today than ever before. The job market is tight—especially in many niches of the healthcare professions. Basic skills are in short supply. Recruiting and hiring is a minefield. And employees today simply don't respond to the motivations of yesterday.

Yet some healthcare providers always seem to find and keep top performers who work hard, enjoy what they're doing, and pull together to achieve operational efficiency, patient satisfaction, and practice growth.

This book will provide a blueprint of what they have done and what you can do to make it happen in your practice.

Real Practices, Real Solutions

In the course of my career, I've had the privilege of conducting more than 3,000 seminars and in-service programs for a wide range of healthcare providers throughout North America and overseas.

As part of the market research for these programs, I have visited countless practices, multi-specialty groups, and institutions of varying size, where I've had the opportunity to interview leading practitioners, practice administrators, and managers as well as employees themselves.

Among the questions I've posed to those with supervisory responsibilities are the following:

- When interviewing job applicants, which techniques and questions have been most useful in identifying top performers?
- In an environment where there are more healthcare jobs than qualified workers, and in many cases higher salaries available elsewhere, how do you retain top performers?
- What are the keys to keeping employee motivation in high gear?
- What are the keys to improving staff performance and productivity?
- What have been your toughest human resource management problems, and how did you solve them?
- What lessons have you learned about the hiring, managing, and retention of great employees that may help others avoid costly mistakes?

The answers to such questions became the framework for this book.

Terminology and Unique Features of This Book

This book is written for a diverse audience in the healthcare professions. Because of the wide range of specialties and organizations involved, I've used a few shortcuts.

The acronym *HCP* (healthcare provider) is used to designate the person responsible for hiring, managing, and retaining employees—recognizing that in your organization, it may be a practice administrator, office manager, or someone with an entirely different title.

The term *great employees,* as used in the title of this book, refers to those who have an emotional commitment to their jobs and to the organizations for which they work. Great employees are more willing to provide the extra measure of dedication, care, and effort on behalf of patients as well as co-workers—that represents the difference between *acceptable* job performance and *outstanding* job performance. This "discretionary effort" is what employees *choose* to do as opposed to what their job descriptions *obligate* them to do. The book will explain what makes it happen in some organizations and not in others.

The word *practice,* used as a noun throughout the book, refers to the setting in which healthcare services are provided—again recognizing that yours may be a hospital, HMO, multi-specialty group, ambulatory clinic, long-term care facility, or some other type of healthcare organization.

The expression *high performance practice* refers to one with above-average patient satisfaction, referrals, productivity, profitability, and practice growth—a subject about which I've written several books. One of the common threads among these outstanding practices is that they have the right people, in the right jobs, doing the right things, at the right time—which, in turn, has led to this book about hiring, managing, and retaining the "right" people.

Among the unique features of this book are the following:

➥**Action steps:** These tell you how to easily implement the ideas presented in this book.

➥**Hard learned lessons:** These represent the priceless, real-world wisdom that people have acquired about the hiring, managing, and retention of great employees.

➥**From the success files:** These stories from actual practices validate many of the concepts presented in this book. The philosopher Bertram Russell said, "The very best proof that something can be done is that others have already done it."

➥**Reality checks:** These inserts are intended to "keep it real."

Blind Spots

In the back of the eye where the optic nerve enters, is an area about 1.5 mm in diameter called the blind spot. What makes it unusual is that it is not affected by light and has no sensation of vision.

To experience the blind spot, hold this page at arm's length; close your left eye and look directly at the dot on the left. Then bring the page slowly toward your face. For a brief interval, when the page is about 10 to 12 inches away, the right dot will suddenly vanish from view, only to reappear as the page is brought still closer toward you.

●   ●

Management blind spots occur when healthcare providers fail to see the impact their words and behavior have on employees. Many HCPs, for example, are plagued by employee morale, motivation, and turnover problems and can't account for it. They often blame the employees, the economy, or some other entity they can't control— when in many cases, such problems are their own doing.

➡**Hard learned lesson #1:** "Many ailing organizations have developed a functional blindness to their own defects," observed John W. Gardner, Lyndon Johnson's Secretary of Health, Education and Welfare. "They're not suffering because they cannot *resolve* their problems, but because they cannot *see* their problems."

It's been said that the first step in solving a problem is *recognition.* It is my hope that this book will help you recognize any problems pertaining to the hiring, management, and retention of employees that you may have overlooked, underestimated, or perhaps created without realizing it. In addition, I'll share 222 strategies that high performance HCPs have utilized to put their employees' morale, motivation, productivity, and loyalty into high gear.

➡**Reality check:** The information given in this book is not intended as legal advice or as a substitute for legal consultation regarding the general hiring process or the management of specific situations.

With that caveat in mind, let's turn to the first step: getting the right people on board.

Bob Levoy

The Importance
of Staff

E veryone who works at Summa Health Systems in Akron, Ohio, carries the following wallet-sized card (see page xviii) with them. Besides being a powerful statement of their values and beliefs, it's also a way to remind both newcomers and long-time employees that the hospital is judged by their performance.

These same principles apply to any size healthcare facility—from a large, multi-specialty institution to a solo practice

Ambassadors for Your Practice

Employees' behavior and comments outside office hours also carry significant weight. It affects how their friends, neighbors, and relatives feel about the practice or institution for which they work. In many cases, people's only knowledge of a healthcare practice, ambulatory clinic, hospital, or long-term care facility is through its employees. What employees say about their jobs and the people with whom they work can be extremely positive if they're committed and enthusiastic—or deadly if they're miserable in their jobs.

➥**Hard learned lesson:** As a healthcare provider, the importance of your staff cannot be overemphasized.

"You are Summa. You are what people see when they arrive here. Yours are the eyes they look in to when they're frightened and lonely. Yours are the voices people hear when they ride the elevators and when they try to sleep and when they try to forget their problems. You are what they hear on their way to appointments that could affect their destinies. And what they hear after they leave those appointments. Yours are the comments people hear when you think they can't. Yours is the intelligence and caring that people hope they find here.

If you're noisy, so is the hospital. If you're rude, so is the hospital. And if you're wonderful, so is the hospital. No visitors, no patients, no physicians, or co-workers can ever know the real you, the you that you know is there—unless you let them see it. All they can know is what they see and hear and experience.

And so we have a stake in your attitude and in the collective attitudes of everyone who works at the hospital. We are judged by your performance. We are the care you give, the attention you pay, the courtesies you extend.

Thank you for all you're doing."[1]

Reference

1. Boyatziz R, McKee A. *Resonant Leadership*. Boston, MA: Harvard Business School Press; 2005.

"Of all the decisions a manager makes, none are as important as the decisions about people because they determine the performance capacity of the organization."

—Peter Drucker, management consultant, university professor, and author of 35 books

Chapter One

HIRING

Getting the Right People on Board

There's no such thing as the perfect, universal employee. For starters, some jobs require prior qualifications; others offer employees the necessary training after they're hired. In addition, different positions are typically filled by people with different styles and personalities. It obviously helps to have an outgoing personality for a front-desk job that involves constantly meeting patients and fielding phone calls. A shy, retiring person, by contrast, might be more comfortable working backstage and always dealing with the same people. Finally, as discussed in Chapter 5, different practices have different cultures.

As pointed out by Robert Levering in his book, A *Great Place to Work,* "No company is perfect for everyone. . . . Companies with distinctive personalities tend to attract—and repel—certain types of individuals."[1]

This chapter includes a host of qualifications sought by others—which you may have overlooked or perhaps underestimated in your search for the right employees for your practice.

1 Action Step #1

The initial step in hiring an employee who is right for your practice is to prepare a written job description of the duties and responsibilities that the position entails. Such profiles will help simplify the hiring process, ensure that employees know what is expected of them, and provide supervisors with a guideline during performance reviews.

When Joe Waechter, administrator for the Medical Center Radiology Group in Orlando, Florida, started writing job descriptions, he contacted the Medical Group Management Association (MGMA) in Englewood, Colorado (http://www.mgma.com). "There he was matched with a practice similar to his own. Using that practice as a resource, he was given some job descriptions to use as templates for his own practice."

Waechter also recommends using your current employees as a resource for creating job descriptions. "Ask them what they do. They may only write a line, or it may be pages and pages, but it is a starting point," he says. "Supervisors can then glean from those employee descriptions what is necessary and what is not."

Once Waechter and the supervisors complete the job descriptions, they have the current employees check them. "That way, if they think these are inaccurate portrayals of what they do, they can let us know," he said.[2]

2 Identify "Musts" and "Preferreds"

The second step in the hiring process is to list the qualifications the ideal job applicant must have to do the job. Start with this list of "musts." Put in writing the kind of experience, knowledge, skills, education, or whatever the candidate *must* have. Also specify the areas of pertinent responsibility the person must have handled in the past.

Paul Angotti, president of the consulting firm Management Design LLC in Monument, Colorado, urges physician leaders to develop detailed job descriptions when hiring a practice manager. To aid them, he gives physicians a list of 40 management tasks—more than most managers would be asked to tackle—and asks them to mark which ones they want their new manager to handle.

"You need to define what you want the person to do in excruciating detail so you'll know what to look for in the person's skill set and experience," Angotti says.[3]

Keep in mind that once they're finalized, the "musts" are inflexible and nonnegotiable. They are absolute minimum requirements.

"Preferreds," on the other hand, include things that would be helpful and desirable but not absolutely essential to success on the job. If the list is lengthy, assign relative weights to them before you begin interviewing. Afterward, they will help you choose from among the candidates who have all of the "musts."

The consensus of human resource professionals with whom I've spoken is that there should be no more than six to eight "musts." More than that number means you have either included some "preferreds" or you've eliminated most of the population.

Listing job requirements in this way will save you a lot of time. Either a job applicant has all the "musts" or he or she doesn't qualify for the job. It's that simple.

3 Establish an "Employee Success Profile"

During the seminars I conduct on this topic, I sometimes walk around the room and ask audience members why they fired the last person they did. Typical responses include "bad attitude," "unreliability," and "lacked people skills." Seldom does anyone say that a person was fired for lack of technical skill.

Ironically, technical skill is almost always the first thing listed in job advertisements and descriptions. This contradiction frequently leads to problems because although technical skills can be taught, a good attitude almost never can.

"In our selection process, kindness, caring, compassion and unselfishness carry more weight than years on the job, an impressive salary history and stacks of degrees," says Hal F. Rosenbluth and Diane McFerrin Peters, CEO and director, respectively, of New Ventures for Rosenbluth Travel and co-authors of *The Customer Comes Second*. The formula for their company's success, they add, "is that we have more nice people than our competition. Niceness is among our highest priorities because nice people do better work."[4]

➡️**Action step:** The next step in hiring the right employees for your practice is to establish an "Employee Success Profile" for your practice. Begin this process by identifying the personality and behavioral traits that are common among your best employees. It will help you understand the type of people who thrive in your practice environment.

Add in others from your "wish list" or include some of the traits mentioned in this chapter.

Then select the five that you consider most important and rank order each of them with "1" being the most important character trait and "5" being the least important.

➡️**Reality check:** Another factor to consider is how those patients with whom your staff interacts will perceive them. A highly efficient, no-nonsense receptionist, for example, may lack the people skills needed for your type of practice.

4 Involve Your Staff

Circulate the list of personality and behavioral traits to all staff members and ask each person to check the five traits he or she considers most important for a given job in your office. Discuss the results at a staff meeting and reach a consensus. Doing so will expedite your search for the right person.

There are several advantages to involving your staff in this process. For one, it makes them realize their ideas and opinions are important. It boosts their morale. It may alert you to traits you've overlooked or underestimated. And perhaps most significant, this list of high priority traits represents a consensus among employees themselves. As such, it applies a certain amount of peer pressure to each person to live up to these same standards. In other words, if "being on time for work," for example, is considered an important trait, then "being late" lets everyone down—and provides added incentive for everyone to be on time.

➡️**Hard learned lesson:** The more compatible a new employee is with your present staff, the better everyone's morale, motivation, and teamwork will be.

The balance of this chapter deals with personality and behavioral traits that others deem important. It may help to clarify or reinforce your thoughts on the subject.

5 Qualities of Exceptional Employees

The following are some of the qualities that Dr. Steven L. Rasner, Cherry Hill, New Jersey, believes lead to exceptional employees:

- "Perceives himself or herself as a 'winner.' Look for clues that speak of one's pursuit of individual excellence."
- "Eagerness to learn. Not all candidates have lifestyles or a desire that will embrace continued education. Make it clear that your office seeks candidates who embrace the magic of learning."
- "Needs to work. Staff members who need to work historically have been more interested in the team values we profess and the commitment needed in and out of the office to attain high levels of achievement."
- "An infectious smile. People who are internally happy often carry a glow that reveals itself in a relaxed, natural and almost infectious smile. Someone once said that the morale of your office will only be as good as your worst attitude. Keep the winners—pass up the frowns."[5]

6 A Friendly Staff

One of the first things patients notice about a practice is the ambiance. An upbeat, friendly staff is a huge plus for a practice, especially in today's high-volume, often impersonal healthcare environment. And it's never an accident.

Friendliness is usually easy to spot. One of the signs is the number of times a job applicant *smiles* during the interview.

Vincent Stabile, vice president of people at JetBlue Airways, says, "We don't train people to smile. We hire people who smile. I look at people and try to ascertain their default position. If their natural default is pleasant, courteous, smiling, that's likely to be a person who will provide the customer service we want. If someone is unhappy or frowning, or has to put on a front to engage with people, that's not going to be the right kind of person."[6]

➡**Hard learned lesson:** "A highly-skilled, know-it-all matriarch or pessimistic introvert," says Dr. William G. Dickerson, Las Vegas, Nevada, "is more destructive to your practice than an optimistic and enthusiastic trainee."[7]

7 High Tolerance for Contact

Part of every HCPs job—and even more so, their employees' jobs—involves what sociologist Arlie Russell Hochschild calls "emotional labor." It refers to the kind of work where "feelings" such as cheerfulness, warmth, and sympathetic concern are an important part of job performance—and expected by the patients with whom they interact.[8]

Having to display such emotions with one patient after another, day after day (whether or not they feel like it), is taxing—especially if patients are demanding, unappreciative, uncooperative, or otherwise unhappy about being in a healthcare setting.

Above all, such repetitive encounters require what's called a high tolerance for contact. Those who lack it and find it uncomfortable and psychologically draining to deal with a steady flow of patients can become moody, irritable, or even hostile toward patients. Needless to say, this takes its toll on patient relations and practice growth.

"This simple concept of emotional labor," says Karl Albrecht, author of *At America's Service,* "explains why all of us as customers, see so much toxic behavior on the part of frontline service employees who are supposed to be giving us good service. The person we're tempted to describe as lazy, indifferent, uncaring, and not qualified for a service job may actually be in the advanced stages of burnout because of contact overload. In other words," he writes, "a great deal of negative behavior on the part of frontline service people is *normal behavior* [sic]. That doesn't mean we have to approve of it or consider it acceptable, but it does mean we need to understand it and deal with it in human and humane terms."[9]

➡**Action steps:** We need to learn more about identifying people who are more resilient to the demands of emotional labor and help those who are less resilient find work more suited to their orientation.

➡**From the success files:** American Airlines has a policy to help employees if they are ever stressed to the verge of losing control while dealing with difficult customers. Agents have the option to walk away from their positions and ask anyone to take their place—no questions asked. American would rather have an employee who is having a bad day get the help and relief he or she needs than to risk a negative customer experience.[10]

8 The Most Important Trait

Dr. Charles Blair, a management consultant in Charlotte, North Carolina, searches for employees with the following traits, beginning with what he considers the most important:

1. Loyalty
2. Stability
3. Enthusiasm
4. Judgment
5. Intelligence
6. Technical ability

Surprised that the top ranked characteristics are so subjective? "Creating a conscientious, effective and efficient team," Blair says, "depends more on those personality traits than on IQ, computer literacy, or credentials."[11]

Samuel H. Esterson, founder of Esterson & Associates Physical Therapy in Baltimore, Maryland, and author of *Starting & Managing Your Own Physical Therapy Practice,* writes that "the characteristics I deem important for hiring anyone to work in my clinic are the following ones:

- Outstanding customer (patient or referring physician) service
- Excellent coping skills and ability to deal with stress and frustration (such as patients in pain)
- Excellent communication skills (verbal and written)
- Excellent technical skills
- Attention to detail"[12]

9 Empathy

"Working with a large healthcare provider, Gallup had a chance to study some of the best nurses in the world," say Marcus Buckingham and Curt Coffman, co-authors of *First, Break All the Rules.* "As part of our research, we asked a study group of excellent nurses to inject 100 patients and a control group of less productive nurses to perform the same injection on the same population of 100 patients. Although the procedure was exactly the same, the patients reported feeling much less pain from the best nurses than from the rest. Why? What were the best nurses doing to lessen the pain?

"Apparently, it all came down to what the nurse said to the patient right before the needle punctured the skin. The average nurses introduced themselves with a brisk, 'Oh, don't worry, this won't hurt a bit,' and then plunged in the needle with businesslike efficiency.

"The best nurses opted for a very different approach. They were just as efficient with the needle, but they set the stage rather more carefully. 'This is going to hurt a little,' they admitted. 'But don't worry, I'll be as gentle as I can.'"

"The best nurses," say Buckingham and Coffman, "were blessed with empathy. They knew the injection would hurt, and each of them, in their own style, felt compelled to share that knowledge with the patient. Surprisingly, this confession eased the patient's pain. To the patients, it seemed as though the nurse was in some small way, going through the experience with them. The nurse was on their side. The nurse understood. So when the needle broke the skin, somehow it didn't feel as bad as they thought it would."[13]

➡**Reality check:** Inpatient satisfaction research by the Gallup Organization has shown that a patient's interaction with hospital staff members is the primary predictor of that patient's evaluation of his or her overall hospital experience. Nurses, in particular, have a strong influence on inpatient experiences. This is clear from the individual items on Gallup's patient satisfaction surveys that turn up as key predictors of overall satisfaction:

- Concern shown by staff
- Staff treated you as a person, not a medical condition
- Staff made you feel safe and secure
- Nurses anticipated needs
- Staff communicated effectively
- Nurses helped calm fears
- Nurses responded to requests [14]

10 The Likability Factor

Some staff members are extremely personable and instantly likable; others are less so. And oh, what a difference it makes in the rhythm of the office, the image of the practice, patient satisfaction, and everyone's "mood" at the end of the day.

A likable personality is a priceless asset, some say "necessity," in any service occupation, healthcare very much included. But it's frequently underestimated by HCPs or completely overlooked during the hiring process.

What is a "likable personality"? Bobbie Gee, former image and appearance coordinator for Disneyland, says likable people:

- Smile easily
- Have a good sense of humor
- Are great listeners
- Know common sense etiquette and use it
- Compliment easily and often
- Are self-confident
- Engage you in conversation about yourself
- Can laugh at themselves
- Are approachable[15]

When interviewing job applicants, pay special attention to their personalities. Do they have the above-mentioned traits or others you deem important? Ask current employees to judge how likable and friendly they are. It will raise everyone's awareness of the "likability factor" and its importance to a successful practice.

➡**Reality check:** The likability factor also works in reverse.

In his book, *Kids Don't Learn From People They Don't Like*, author/educator David Aspy writes that when students don't like a teacher, they develop a resistance to learning from him or her. Students, it seems, do best with teachers they *like*.[16]

Our surveys indicate the same is true in the workplace. When employees like the HCPs and office managers with whom they work, there tends to be less absenteeism and turnover, better morale and motivation, and more teamwork and productivity. And they speak openly about how much they love their jobs.

➡**Action step:** Take another look at those traits of a likable personality. Do any of them need a little polishing on your part?

11 The Spirit of Service

High performance professional practices that have a reputation for great service have a quality that consultant Karl Abrecht calls the *spirit of service.* "It's an element of giving," he says, "a spirit of generosity that makes people give something of themselves in addition to just doing the job. It's going beyond the bare minimum or the standard actions. It's being attentive to the *person* behind the need, and responding to the person more than just responding to the need. It's being there psychologically and emotionally as well as being there physically."[17]

➥**From the success files:** When the Four Seasons Hotel opened in Chicago, management was looking for employees with a "friendly nature" and a "sense of teamwork." For 545 job openings, over 15,500 applicants were screened.

The reason the search took so long, said John Young, recently retired VP Human Resources for the Four Seasons, was "We don't want people who think serving others is demeaning. We don't want people who say in a crisis, 'That's not my job' but rather those who say, 'How can I help?' We don't want people who roll their eyes and give a long sigh when a guest requests something but rather those who'll say, "No problem'—and just do it. We want people who feel good enough about themselves to be able to focus their attention on the needs of others."

"It's a long and expensive procedure," Young said, "but it pays off in high employee retention and productivity. If you hire well, you seldom have to fire. And it sends a morale-boosting message to all employees, long term and new, that we recognize from the beginning how important they are."[18]

➥**Hard learned lesson:** You can't write this Spirit of Service into a job description. There's no "script" for it. Nor do "incentives" really work. The reason is because it comes from within.

Interviewed on another occasion, John Young said: "We don't look for applicants who can be trained to make people feel important. We want applicants who genuinely *believe* that people are important."[19]

12 The Civility Factor

Yankelovich Partners Inc., one of the premier market research firms in the United States, specializes in studying consumer behavior and attitudes, often the best predictor of future marketplace behavior. Their signature product, *Monitor®,* is an ongoing survey of 2,500 consumers, 16 years of age and older, from all parts of the country who are interviewed in their homes for two hours. They're asked hundreds of questions about their values, beliefs, and behaviors on a wide variety of topics. For example: "What is most important to you regarding customer service—that is, the way you are treated by a business or its employees when purchasing products or services?"[20]

The results in descending order:

Courtesy	25%
Knowledgeable	21%
Friendliness	13%
Listens to you	13%
Efficiency	10%
Thoroughness	8%
Promptness	5%
Availability	5%

What's interesting about these findings is that *efficiency,* often the focus of HCPs' efforts to improve the profitability of their practices, is significantly less important to consumers than courtesy, friendliness, and simply listening to them.

Britt Beemer, author of *Predatory Marketing,* isn't surprised by these statistics. "Efficiency is not a replacement for customer service," he says. "It's only a small part of building relationships with customers. This blind focus on efficiency perfectly describes the breach between what customers want and what companies think they want."[21]

"The overriding message of these findings," Barbara Kaplan, a partner at Yanklelovich Partners Inc., told me, "is that people want to be treated with *civility*. If they're not, they can and will go elsewhere."

The "civility factor," as I now call it, should be an important consideration when deciding whom to hire and what the priorities of your practice will be.

➥**From the success files:** In a 2003 nationwide study of hospitals published by AARP's *Modern Maturity,* North Shore University Hospital in Manhasset, New York, was selected as the number one hospital in America.[22]

A survey is sent to patients' homes following their visits to the hospital's emergency department. It asks for feedback about their visits; interactions with admitting personnel, doctors, and nurses; and how (if they were accompanied) their family or friends were treated. Only three to five questions are asked about each of these encounters, requesting patients to "rank their experience" on a scale of 1 to 5 (very poor to very good).

What's significant is that every cluster of questions about interactions included a question about *courtesy*—as the first question (e.g., courtesy of the nurses, doctor, person who took your blood, radiology staff, person who took your personal/insurance information, and the courtesy with which family or friends were treated).

➥**Hard learned lesson:** "One of the lessons to be learned about service," say consultants Karl Albrecht and Lawrence J. Bradford, Ph.D., "is that the longer a business has been in existence, the more likely it is that it has lost sight of what is important to customers."[23]

13 Traits That Are Often Overlooked

The following is a list of some commonly overlooked traits that HCPs attending my seminars have deemed important when hiring employees:

- Does the applicant appear to have a systematic and logical approach to work?
- How verbal and articulate is the person?
- What is the applicant's energy level?
- How effective is the person's overall presentation and impact upon others?
- Does he or she project a degree of personal warmth in interactions with others?
- Does the person seem willing to cooperate and collaborate with others in order to achieve mutual goals?
- How tactful and diplomatic does the applicant seem to be?
- Does the applicant have a positive manner and attitude?

- Is the person rather rigid, inflexible, and highly opinionated in his or her viewpoints?
- How competitive is the applicant?
- Does the applicant display initiative, drive, and resourcefulness or is he or she the type of person who must be closely supervised?
- Is the person a self-starter or one who needs to be prodded into action?
- Is the applicant a goal-oriented individual who applies himself or herself in a serious, conscientious, and purposeful manner?
- Did the applicant leave former jobs for reasonable, sound, and logical reasons?
- Has there been progress in the person's compensation?
- How ambitious and career oriented is the individual?
- Is the applicant involved with an ongoing program to improve his or her knowledge and skills?
- How well does the candidate respond to stress and pressure?
- Does the applicant seem persistent and persevering or does he or she give up easily when encountering obstacles and difficulties?
- How effective is the applicant in dealing and working with others?
- Does the applicant speak favorably of past employers and teachers or does he or she display a high degree of negativity in discussing relationships with these people?
- Does the person show patience with others?
- What is the person's "view of the world"?

"Nothing better indicates a candidate's confidence than his or her view of the world in general," writes Robert Half, president of the recruiting firm Robert Half International Inc. "Are they optimistic or pessimistic?" he asks. "Do they view the proverbial glass as half empty or half full? People with a positive viewpoint are infinitely more likely to be happier, more productive and more efficient. They are easier to motivate, quicker to learn and adapt to a variety of situations, and in general, have greater potential to become top-notch employees."[24]

Some of these traits may provide clues as to why employees with good skills and experience have not done well in your practice and what to look for when hiring new team members.

14 Do Your Own Hiring

"Checking out a job candidate's basic skills and credentials is pretty boring stuff," says OBG specialist Francis A. Lombardo, Winchester, Massachusetts, "but doing it yourself is the only way to be sure your employees feel as you do—about patients, and about life. You want to hire people who like the type of doctoring you do, whether it's pediatrics, geriatrics, or ENT. You want them to be up to the pace and the special stresses of your practice, and to enjoy working with your type of clientele, whether it be upper-crust society or, as in my office, heavy on welfare and minority patients."

"For my OBG practice," Lombardo says, "I prefer to hire women who've had a baby or two, so they can relate to my patients. I'd never hire an assistant who didn't feel as I do about childbirth, birth control or abortion, and I wouldn't want an aide who felt obliged to scold teen-age patients who come to me for the pill, or might offend a pregnant 40 year old."[25]

Identifying the traits of the people who would be right for your practice is the first step in the hiring process. Finding them is the next step.

References

1. Levering R. *A Great Place to Work.* New York: Random House; 1988.
2. Putting Expectations in Writing Can Help Productivity. *Physician's Marketing & Management*, June 1997, 75.
3. Redling R. In Search of . . . . *Physicians Practice*, October 2004.
4. Rosenbluth HF, Peters DM. *The Customer Comes Second.* New York: William Morrow; 1992.
5. Rasner SL. Hire Right. *Dental Practice Report,* October 2000, 37–44.
6. Tahmincioglu E. Keeping Spirits Aloft at JetBlue. *Workforce Management Online*, December 2004. http://www.workforce.com/archive/article/23/90/36.php
7. Dickerson WG. Frontdesklessness and the Quality Practice. *Dentistry Today*, March 1993, 82–85.
8. Hochschild AR. *The Managed Heart.* Berkeley, CA: University of California Press; 1983.
9. Albrech K. *At America's Service.* Homewood, IL: Dow Jones-Irwin; 1988.
10. Nelson B. Stressed? Some Proven Coping Strategies. *CMI*, March 2003, 32.
11. Blair C. *Blair/McGill Advisory.* Charlotte, NC: August 1995, 4.

12. Esterson SH. *Starting & Managing Your Own Physical Therapy Practice.* Sudbury, MA: Jones & Bartlett Publishers; 2005.
13. Buckingham M, Coffman C. *First, Break All the Rules.* New York: Simon & Schuster; 1999.
14. Blizzard R. Patient Satisfaction Is a Hospital's to Lose. *The Gallup Poll,* December 28, 2004.
15. Gee B. *Creating a Million-Dollar Image for Your Business.* Berkeley, CA: PageMill Press; 1991.
16. Aspy, D. *Kids Don't Learn From People They Don't Like.* Amherst, MA: HRD Press; 1978.
17. Albrecht K. *The Only Thing That Matters.* New York: HarperBusiness; 1992.
18. Brown SA. *Total Quality Service.* Scarborough, Ontario: Prentice Hall Canada; 1992.
19. Reichheld F. *The Ultimate Question.* Boston: Harvard Business School Press; 2006.
20. Most Important Factor in Service. *Yankelovich Monitor Minute,* June 22, 1997, Table 17.25.
21. Wood N. So You Want a Revolution. *Incentive,* June 1998, 41–47.
22. http//:www.northshorelij.com
23. Albrecht K, Bradford LJ. *The Service Advantage.* Homewood, IL: Dow Jones-Irwin; 1990.
24. Half R. *Finding, Hiring and Keeping the Best Employees.* New York: John Wiley & Sons; 1993.
25. Lombardo FA. How to Keep Your Staff Smiling and Your Office Humming. *Medical Economics,* October 11, 1992, 179–185.

Chapter Two

HIRING

Creative Recruitment Strategies

"There are more health care jobs than qualified workers," say Wendy Leebov and Gail Scott, authors of *The Indispensable Health Care Manager.* "Staffing shortages abound. Other providers are competing like mad for your people. Young people are not entering health care professions in sufficient numbers. The annual turnover percentage in most health care organizations has increased to double digits. The problem," say Leebov and Scott, "isn't limited to hospitals. Doctors' offices, ambulatory clinics, long-term facilities, and home health agencies are experiencing similar pressure. Demographics are increasing the number of people who need health care, as baby boomers age and older people live longer."[1]

This chapter reveals some of the creative ideas that HCPs are using to recruit desperately needed employees.

15 Build an Appealing Employment Brand

"Employment branding is the process of placing an image of being a 'great place to work' in the minds of the targeted candidate pool," says Dr. John Sullivan, author, speaker, and advisor to senior management for *Fortune* 1,000 firms. "It is a concept borrowed from the business side of the enterprise. Product branding is designed to develop a lasting image in the minds of the consumer so they start to automatically associate quality with any product or service offered by the owner of the brand. An employment brand does the same thing in that it creates an image that makes people want to work for the firm because it is a well managed firm where workers are continually learning and growing. Once the image is set, it generally results in a steady flow of applicants."[2]

➡**Action steps:** How, then, do you create an appealing employment brand for your practice? "Start with an accurate assessment and high-light your strengths," says Elizabeth Amorose, project director at the Carbone Smolan Agency (CSA), a New York–based marketing firm that specializes in recruitment strategies.

To determine your employment brand, Amorose encourages clients to develop a list of the top 5 to 10 messages they feel candidates must know. These should include any special advantages employees might gain by working for your organization, such as opportunities for advancement, the chance to help in an important cause, the opportunity to develop highly prized skills, the respect of working for an industry leader, or the ability to reap generous benefits and perks.[3]

➡**Reality check:** Gone are the days when HCPs sold job applicants strictly on salary and benefits. Today's employees want a great place to work—especially those in healthcare where, as pointed out in the beginning of this chapter, there are more jobs than qualified workers.

The next chapter includes the action steps to make your practice a great place to work and to become what is known as an Employer of Choice.

16 Consider Alternative Recruiting Channels

Finding the right people for your practice who have positive attitudes, exceptional people skills, and are able to leap tall buildings in a single bound isn't easy. If the usual recruiting channels aren't producing qualified candidates, consider these alternatives:

- "Go to your successful hires and ask them 'What initially attracted you to us,' and 'What are the factors that make you want to stay with us,' 'Where did you hear about us?'" advises Training Systems, a training and HR consulting firm based in Frankfort, Illinois. "You'll find that a significant number of your employees heard about you from the same sources, such as: current or former employees, their friends or the local newspaper. This is immediate feedback. It will help you to stop wasting money on advertising in the wrong areas. You'll find out what is important to the staff: salaries, working relationships, working environment or flexibility for example."[4]
- If the salary plus benefits you're offering is lower than the going rate in your area, that might explain the small pool of applicants. A higher salary may produce more and better qualified applicants. Nothing is more important to patient satisfaction and practice growth than having the right people on board. In the long run, the investment will pay off.
- For front desk and administrative positions in your practice, look outside your profession for candidates. If you want people with strong "people skills," for example, consider job applicants from banks, hotels, airlines, and retail stores where they most likely have received extensive training.
- Sharon Bearor, nursing manager of Coastal Women's Healthcare, a Scarborough, Maine, OB/GYN office with 27 nurses, looks for possible recruits at job fairs and health fairs. "Whenever I meet nursing students," she says, "I ask them what they're doing. If they're looking for something different, I take their names and résumés.[5]
- The premier recruitment method for many office managers is word of mouth. "I go by referral only," says Susan Genrich, office manager for Selden Medical, a solo family practice in Selden, New York. "I created a network of office managers, and we use each other for

staffing purposes. And I ask my nurses if they know anyone who's job hunting."[6]

- If one of your *patients* has all the traits you're looking for
in an employee, consider recruiting him or her. You might
ask, "I'd love to have someone with your personality
working here. Do you know of anyone?" The person may
be interested in the job or know someone who might be. I
know many healthcare team members who were hired in
exactly this way.

- If you've tried these strategies without success, it may be
time to take a second look at the reputation your practice
has *as a place to work.* What, for example, do your
employees say about your practice when they gather with
their friends at weekend barbecues and describe what it's
like to work there? Are they saying what you want them to
say? Do you come off as an "Employer of Choice"? If not,
then you'll need to ascertain the underlying problems and
resolve them.

➡**From the success files:** "It has been our experience that our Web
site is wonderful for attracting new, high-quality staff members," says
Dr. Kambiz Moin, Manchester, New Hampshire. "In our newspaper
ads, we encourage applicants to visit our Web site in order to learn more
about our office and help them make a more informed career decision."[7]

17 Use a Recruiting Bonus

One of the conclusions of a Bernard Hodes survey, in partnership with
Advance Magazines, of 1,045 employees in nursing fields and 1,721
respondents in allied health disciplines is that people are finding jobs
through friends. "Among occupational therapy practitioners for example, employee referrals are the top source of hires and number one
way people say they both look for and find jobs."[8]

➡**Action steps:** Consider offering a substantial recruiting bonus to
any staff member who recommends an individual who, following a
90-day probationary period, is subsequently hired.

Your present office staff may have friends or acquaintances who
are looking to resume their careers or who have been "downsized" out

of a job. Although they are well qualified, they may not otherwise answer classified ads. Besides, your already satisfied employees can "talk up" a job opening much better than a half-inch ad placed among hundreds of others. Furthermore, if an employee you respect likes someone well enough to recommend him or her, the odds are better than average that the new person will fit in with your staff.

At the outset, ask your current employees to think about the specific aspects of your practice they most like. When they talk about their jobs with potential employees, they should have an inventory of things to discuss beyond whether they like it or not. This will serve two purposes: It will give existing employees something specific to discuss when they are talking with potential employees, and it will also boost their motivation because it will remind them of why they enjoy working in your practice.

Make it clear that the same high standards and selection process will be used to evaluate job applicants recommended by staff members. Stating this policy up front helps avoid any obligation you may feel to hire someone you don't consider the best choice for your practice.

➡**From the success files:** "Our staff members recruit some of our best employees," says allergist/immunologist Robert J. Holzhauer, Rochester, New York. "We sometimes pay incentive bonuses to those employees whose 'recruits' make it through our four-month probationary period."[9]

➡**Reality check:** A recent survey by Referral Networks, a New York City–based company, offers some insights into what motivates employees to make referrals. The news is good: Monetary incentives are not what drives the process. Forty-two percent of the 2,300 employees surveyed said they referred because they wanted to help a friend find a good job. Twenty-four percent said they wanted to help the company. Another 24 percent said they were motivated by a reward.[10]

18 Three Options

"There are only three ways to get more [medical] help," says Marilyn Moats Kennedy, founder of Career Strategies, a consulting firm in Wilmette, Illinois, specializing in healthcare workplace issues. "The first is to recycle them. When people leave, wait six months, then call them and say, 'I wonder if you like your new job as well as you thought you would? We still miss you at the practice. How about coming back?'"

A variation of this line of questioning is to simply ask: "What would bring you back?"

"The second way to recruit," says Moats, "is targeting the women who retired to raise their children and those children are now in high school or college. Many people who were RNs don't want to go back to work because they think they'll have to take lower-level positions. But if you start a retraining program that hospitals and practices would support, you would reconnect the people that have the very work ethic that practices are so hot to get. This program would involve intensive training that gives them a sense of accomplishment from the start. They could go to school every day or go to school part-time and work part-time. And what they need is total immersion into the workplace—like a body shock. This age group of RNs between 45 and 50, is energetic too. They are the last untapped labor pool in the country and the only way to bring new people into the market and stabilize them is this type of retraining. Someone is going to pay these people to go to school. The question is not *if* but *when*—and many hospitals are already doing it. Practices could do it as well."

"The third way to recruit is to hire retirees. In the next five years, a huge number of people are going to blast out of government jobs. They will be 55, but they'll be competent people."[11]

19 Train from Within

An obvious alternative to recruiting new employees with the proper qualifications and experience is to promote someone from within and provide training for the job.

Both approaches, however, can be costly and risky. In promoting, for example, you run the risk of demanding too much from an unqualified employee, while in recruiting you could alienate current staff members and damage office morale.

"Jim Brazil, M.D. a dermatologist in Olympia, Washington, said that when he started looking for a replacement office manager for his solo practice, he considered an internal candidate—the billing supervisor—but finally decided to offer the job to an outsider. He said the choice was the best move for the practice, but the internal candidate, who was upset by the decision, later left. That left a void that was filled by promoting a billing clerk."

"It's easier to hire from within if you have a big enough staff," Brazil said. "But in a small office, it can be a problem."[12]

➡**Action steps:** Consultants suggest always starting with an internal search. But because every practice is different and every situation is different, the most important factor is the HCP's comfort level with that potential employee.

20 Utilize Part-Time Employees

If you answer "yes" to one or more of the following questions, your practice may benefit from hiring part-time employees:

- Have you had difficulty finding qualified, full-time office personnel?
- Does your practice have peaks and valleys of activity?
- Does your staff lack the time to implement ideas that would generate practice growth?
- Do your employees have child- or eldercare obligations that impinge on their work schedule?
- Has burnout become a problem for any of your employees?
- Has employee turnover been a problem in your practice?

➡**Reality check:** In many areas of the country, part-time employees are the fastest growing segment of the labor force. Among the many benefits of hiring them are the following:

- Greatly increases the pool of applicants including those who may have left the profession to start a family and now want to return to work on a part-time basis.
- Provides a tremendous recruitment edge when other practices offer the same compensation—but no part-time option.
- Helps smooth the peaks and valleys of workflow and improve patient service at the busiest times.
- Improves productivity and morale. Because of a reduced workweek, part-time employees bring increased energy to the job. They're also able to better focus on their work and usually miss fewer days.

- "Part-timers have better attendance records than full-timers, who can burn out in hectic practices," says Kathryn Moghadas of Associated Healthcare Advisors in Casselberry, Florida.[13]
- Retains older employees who have valuable skills and experience. Surveys indicate many members of this age group would extend their working life *if* they could work part time—rather than choose between full-time work and retirement.
- Reduces labor costs during slow times when full-time employees are not needed. Also, as a general rule, employers are not required under current law to provide fringe benefits for employees who work fewer than 1,000 hours a year. Check your state's requirements.

➡**Caveats:** Part-time employees may feel like outsiders or "second class citizens." To foster a connection, schedule staff meetings at times when they can attend, keep them informed about policy and protocol changes, and provide frequent performance feedback.

Another caveat, says consultant Barry Pillow with Healthcare Consulting in Lynchburg, Virginia: "Make sure a candidate for part-time work really wants to work part-time. Some will take the job and leave when a full-time position opens up someplace else. Others will try to convince you that you need a full-time employee for the job, when you really don't."[14]

➡**From the success files:** Dr. Stuart Gindoff, managing partner of the Eye Center South in Sarasota, Florida, reports, "We have four part-time employees and are extremely satisfied with the arrangement. One reason: the saving in overhead costs. For example, our part time employees realize they won't be paid sick time, do not accumulate vacation time and won't be paid when the office is closed for a holiday (unless it is a regularly scheduled workday). It's also understood their status does not require a contribution on our part to a retirement fund."

"Another major advantage," Gindoff adds, "is that we're able to have more than one employee trained to do a specific job. Should illness or unexpected absences occur, substitutes can be called."

"Is *consistency* a problem?" I asked.

"For the most part, it's not been a problem," he replied. "However, if there's a visible difference between two part timers doing the same job, then it's the supervisor's (or doctor's) responsibility to straighten things out."

"We've successfully used part time personnel for the last several years," Gindoff says. "If we didn't have such a trained ophthalmic labor shortage in our area, we'd hire even more."[15]

21 Maintain Alumni Relations

Rather than lose touch with former staff members, Dr. Phillip E. Bly, Indianapolis, Indiana, started an alumni-relations program so employees who have shared work experiences over the years can stay in touch. He coordinates periodic get-togethers of current and former staff members. The group usually meets for a luncheon in a private dining room at a local country club or hotel. On other occasions, the employees and their spouses gather for a picnic, a swim, bowling, or a Christmas party. The get-togethers are fun, Bly says, and provide some unexpected fringe benefits to his practice. For example, most of these former employees remain with the practice as patients, bringing along, in some cases, their spouses and children. Many continue to be active referral sources for the practice. On occasion, when Bly is short-handed, the former employees fill in on an emergency basis and are glad to help out. In fact, some of them say that being back in the practice is like "old home week."

If your alumni list is large, it may be necessary to delete some names after several years or to rotate the names, inviting alumni to your practice functions in groups.

➡**Reality check:** In a *Harvard Business Review* article titled, "Cultivating Ex-Employees," the authors Anne Berkowitch and Cem Sertoglu said that hiring a former employee costs organizations about half as much as hiring someone new.[16]

22 Recruit Older Employees

"During the next 15 years," predict Ken Dychtwald, Tamara Erickson, and Bob Morison in the *Harvard Business Review,* "80 percent of the native-born workforce growth in North America—and even more so in much of Western Europe—is going to be in the over 50 cohort. In the next decade or so, when baby boomers, the 76 million people born between 1946 and 1964, more than one-quarter of all Americans, start hitting their sixties and contemplating retirement, there won't be nearly enough young people entering the workforce to compensate for the exodus. The Bureau of Labor Statistics projects a shortfall of 10 million workers in the United States in 2010, and in countries where the birth rate is well below the population replacement level (particularly in Western Europe), the shortage will hit sooner, be more severe, and remain chronic."

"The proportion of workers over 55 declined from 18 percent in the 1970s to under 11 percent in 2000—but it's projected to rebound to 20 percent by 2015," say the authors. "In other words, we've recently passed what will prove to be a historic low in the concentration of older workers. Just when we've gotten accustomed to having relatively few mature workers around, we have to start learning how to attract and retain far more of them."[17]

➡**From the success files:** In the late 1990s, when online bookselling was sweeping the nation, Borders Books took a hard look at the demographics of its customer base. From that research, it discovered that 50 percent of the books bought in the United States were purchased by consumers over 45 years old. To reach out to those customers and differentiate itself from the impersonal online booksellers, Borders created a formal hiring and retention initiative aimed at older workers, says Dan Smith, senior VP for human resources. "We found that they better related to our customers," he says.

Today, 16 percent of Border's workforce is over the age of 50, up from 6 percent in 1998, when it started its recruitment effort. The book retailer has found other advantages to having older workers in its stores. According to Smith, the turnover rate for workers over the age of 50 is 10 times less than for those under 30. Borders has seen its turnover drop 30 percent since it began its effort to recruit older workers. "These workers have a great passion to be connected to the community, and our bookstores provide them with that venue," Smith says. "Also, since the work is often part time, it's a great fit for them."[18]

23 Recognize the Misconceptions

"The biggest barriers to the employment of older workers are myths about productivity, safety and costs of employing these workers," says Catherine D. Fyock, author of *America's Work Force is Coming of Age*.[19]

"Yet none of these rumors have proven to be substantial," says Charlene Marmer Solomon, writing in the *Personnel Journal*. "For instance, AARP states that workers between the ages of 50 and 60 stay on the job an average of 15 years, and their attendance is as good as or better than other groups. Safety also should be of limited concern, according to the AARP. In most occupations, mature workers have a lower accident rate, with workers 55 and older accounting for 13.6 percent of the work force but for only 9.7 percent of on-the-job injuries."

"Finally," Solomon says, "there's little proof that older workers cost more to employ. For instance, the belief that older workers cause increased health-care costs—one of the most tenacious myths—have proven to be unfounded by several studies. In particular, one by Yankelovich, Skelly and White Inc., showed that health-care costs between 30-year old males, women with dependents and 65-year old retirees are about the same. It also proved that 55-year olds are the least costly of all groups. And, in a number of surveys, according to Fyock, respondents revealed that even if health care costs were higher, the advantages of employing mature workers offset any additional cost because of lower absenteeism and turnover."[20]

24 Recruit Employees from Diverse Backgrounds

"Many health care organizations are currently suffering shortages of a wide range of health care workers, from nurses to pharmacists to technicians," states a 2006 report from the American Hospital Association entitled "White Coats and Many Colors: Population Diversity and Its Implications for Health Care." "Although the reasons for these shortages are multiple and complex, it must be admitted that a failure on the part of health care professions and health care employers to reach out to potential employees who are members of minority groups is one of the primary factors."

"This means that efforts to attract young people to the health professions must start at an early age," says the AHA report. "That outreach must include people with less-than-perfect English skills; health care must compete with other sectors for immigrants and others new to the job market; and recruitment must take place in a broader array of sites than the traditional ones. This includes reaching out to potential employees while they are still in secondary or even primary school."[21]

➡**Reality check:** "It is one thing to recruit a diverse work force," says the 2006 report from the American Hospital Association, "but it is another thing to retain its best members. Among the efforts required to retain the best workers are a top-down, sincere organizational commitment to nondiscrimination in recruitment, retention, and advancement; a zero-tolerance policy regarding discriminatory behavior; and continuous training of all staff in proper behavior in a multicultural and multilingual environment. These efforts not only help to promote a harmonious work force, but also improve patients' experiences."[22]

Chapter 16 includes a discussion of diversity training.

25 Consider Outsourcing

"Many physicians hire someone outside the office to handle billing and transcription, but you don't have to stop there," says Tyler Chin in an article for *AMNews*. "Just about anything can be outsourced—from watering plants, copying medical records, filing and coding to practice management, technology, collection, payroll, employee benefits administration and even nursing."[23]

"Outsourcing can save money and offer access to a higher level of professional expertise and service that doctors couldn't afford to hire or find on their own, observers say. It also can let doctors shift the hassles associated with a specific function to somebody else, freeing them to practice and generate revenue, says Dr. Michael Weinstein, a gastroenterologist at 12-doctor Metropolitan Gastroenterology in Washington, D.C.[24]

➡**Reality check:** Outsourcing, however, is not for everyone. "In business today, in order to survive, make ends meet and pay the bills, every service has to be evaluated based on whether or not we can perform that service at a lower cost with more reliability and quality in-house or out-of-house," says family physician Joseph Leming, president of the four-doctor Primary Care Family Practice in Colonial Heights, Virginia.[25]

26 Hard Learned Lessons About Recruiting

- "Be patient," says Dr. Steven L. Rasner, Cherry Hill, New Jersey. "Putting together a staff can take years. No matter what method you use, sometimes it's not going to be the right time and you will have to fill the role with the best available candidate—not the best candidate. If the person you hired fulfills your definition of excellence, fine. If not, you eventually will be in a position to hire a top candidate."[26]
- Keep in mind that older workers are as varied as any other large segment of the population. They include people who are in mid-life career changes, early retirees, older retirees, displaced workers, and people who may have never worked outside the home before. Each group has its own motivations to work and benefits needs.
- Placing want ads in the newspaper can only bring in a relative trickle of applicants. Even great Web pages tend to have only a marginal impact compared to the most powerful recruiting tool of all: having your healthcare practice known throughout your community as an Employer of Choice. Once you have that enviable reputation as a "great place to work," it will make it a lot easier to find quality employees.

The next chapter focuses on this topic.

References

1. Leebov W, Scott G. *The Indispensable Health Care Manager*. San Francisco: Jossey Bass; 2002.
2. Sullivan J. Building an Employment Brand. Electronic Recruiting Exchange. July 23, 1999. www.erexchange.com
3. Brandon C. Truth in Recruitment Branding. *HR Magazine*, November 2005, 89–96.
4. http://www.trainingsys.com/tips/recruit0102.html
5. Weiss GG. How to Find and Keep Top-Notch Clinical Staff. *Medical Economics*, March 8, 2002, 36.
6. Ibid.
7. Five Ways to Make Your Web Site a Profitbuilder. *Blair/McGill Advisory*, July 2003, 4.
8. Raphael T. Health Professionals Share Their Candid (and Mixed) Feelings About the Field, August 9, 2005. http://www.workforce.com/section/00/article/24/13/49.html

9. Holzhauer RJ. Secrets for Recruiting and Retaining Employees. *American Academy of Allergy Asthma and Immunology News*, August 2004.
10. Lachnitt C. Employee Referral. *Workforce*, June 2001, 67–72.
11. Treat 'Em Right. *Physicians Practice Digest,* July/August 2001.
12. Norbut M. Every Practice's Hiring Dilemma: Train from Within or Recruit, August 11, 2003. www.amednews.com
13. Murray D. Get the Most from Your Staff. *Medical Economics*, July 26, 1993, 54–64.
14. Ibid.
15. Personal communication.
16. Berkowitch A, Sertoglu C. Cultivating Ex-Employees. *Harvard Business Review*, June 1, 2002, 20–22.
17. Dychtwald K, Erickson T, Morison B. It's Time to Retire Retirement. *Harvard Business Review*, March 1, 2004, 49–57.
18. Marquez J. Novel Ideas at Borders Lure Older Workers. *Workforce Management*, May 2005, 28.
19. Fyock CD. *America's Work Force Is Coming of Age: What Every Business Needs to Know to Recruit, Train, Manage and Retain an Aging Work Force.* Lanham, MD: Lexington Books; 1990.
20. Solomon CM. Unlock the Potential of Older Workers. *Personnel Journal*, October 1995, 55–66.
21. Friedman E. White Coats and Many Colors: Population Diversity and Its Implications for Health Care. American Hospital Association, 2006.
22. Chin T. The Doctor Is Outsourcing: To Hire or Not to Hire? August 11, 2003. http://www.ama-assn.org
23. Ibid.
24. Ibid.
25. Ibid.
26. Rasner SL. Hire Right. *Dental Practice Report*, October 2000, 37–44.

Chapter Three

HIRING

Become an Employer of Choice

" **T**here is a tidal wave of change occurring within today's work force due to dynamic demographic changes," says Robert K. Critchley, author of *Doing Nothing Is Not an Option!*, "yet many organizations and their leaders are oblivious to the consequences and are not implementing necessary strategies for future survival."

Referring to the previously mentioned prediction by the Bureau of Labor Statistics that by 2010 there will be a shortfall of 10 million workers (see Chapter 2, Secret 22), Critchley warns, "Creative employment strategies and practices must be embraced to retain and motivate workers of all ages."[1]

This chapter deals with a strategy to make your practice especially attractive to prospective employees.

🄬 Make Your Practice a "Great Place to Work"

As the need for well-qualified, high-performing employees intensifies, savvy HCPs vie to position their practices as the right place for the kind of people they want. They strive to become known as an Employer of Choice or, in simpler terms, as a "great place to work."

Having this reputation is invaluable in a tight labor market. It's what employees say about your practice when they're with their friends and describe what it's like to work there. If that word-of-mouth is highly favorable, job applicants will be predisposed to it.

➡**From the success files:** "Even before her interview, Doris Barnett had a good feeling about Dr. Jim Kaley's practice," says Laura Pelehach, managing editor of *Dental Practice Report.* "The ad in the paper stressed a fun work environment and good benefits. She liked that, but even more, she liked what she had been hearing about the Greensboro, North Carolina orthodontist's practice."

"'I was told that you either have to wait until someone dies or moves away before you have a chance of working there,' says Barnett, a former insurance company secretary and one of 40 candidates vying for the secretarial spot."

"On the rare occasion when he is in the market to hire, Dr. Kaley generally has his pick of quality employees. He has a reputation in his community as a good orthodontist and good employer, which appeals to candidates like Barnett. But the truth of the matter is, he doesn't often have to worry about hiring. Most of Dr. Kaley's employees have been there at least 10 years, some for almost 25 of the 29 years he's been practicing. He likes his staff. That's no small feat," says Pelehach, "considering many dentists still grapple with high turnover."[2]

The major benefits of being an Employer of Choice:

- Your practice will be more attractive to prospective employees. Not only will you have more applicants to choose from, but also the overall quality of applicants will tend to be better than practices that are not recognized as Employers of Choice.
- Your practice will also tend to have higher levels of staff morale, motivation, and productivity; less absenteeism and

turnover; enhanced loyalty; more efficiency; and as a result, greater profitability.

➥**Reality check:** "Hospitals for the most part have not focused on being good employers," says Connie Curran, a Chicago-based consultant. "They've focused on being good caregivers and good corporate citizens. But nobody has anything in their mission about being the employer of choice."[3]

➥**Hard learned lesson:** "The only things that evolve by themselves in an organization are disorder, friction and mal performance," said management guru Peter F. Drucker. "In other words, a competitive, well-managed, high performance, profitable Employer of Choice organization is an intentional outcome—it doesn't just happen."[4]

28 Don't Overlook the Appeal to Patients

Being an Employer of Choice will also make your practice more attractive to patients. This appeal is critical in a relationship-based practice (versus a high-volume, more impersonal healthcare environment). Patients like to deal with the same people on a long-term basis. This relationship continuity builds stronger bonds and gives patients a greater sense of comfort, confidence, and trust.

➥**Reality check:** "A division of Daimler-Chrysler discovered they were getting correlative results from customer and employee surveys. When the employees were happy, the customer satisfaction scores were high. When the employees weren't happy, the customer satisfaction scores were lower. There was such a correlation that the company decided to stop spending money on customer surveys and concentrate on the employees instead."[5]

➥**Hard learned lesson:** Make sure your reputation on the inside drives the reputation on the outside—not the other way around.

29 What Makes a Great Place to Work?

Robert Levering, author of *The 100 Best Companies to Work for in America* and co-founder of The Great Place to Work Institute based in San Francisco, defines a great place to work as one where the employees trust the people they work for, have pride in what they do, and enjoy the people with whom they work.

When asked "Is there anything unique or unusual about this company that makes it a great place to work," employees at some of the "100 Best" companies said the following:

- "The door to management is always open. They listen."
- "My boss is a great leader. She can make hard but fair decisions, and she always seems to do the right thing. She values differences in people."
- "I feel as though I make a difference. My job allows me latitude to make decisions and implement them in order to get the job done. At the end of the day I can look back and see what I have been able to accomplish with a great feeling of satisfaction."
- "Every morning I wake up I am more than excited to get to work and do the best I can for a company that really appreciates it."
- "This is a great place to work because people care about each other. It doesn't seem so much like work when you are surrounded by people who care for you as an individual."
- "I spent most of my career in a company which focused on efficiency and profits—employees were only a 'means to the end.' However, I have had the fortunate opportunity to join this company late in my career. This is truly a place that puts people first, manages from the heart, and cares for the community."[6]

➡**Reality check:** "It's not easy to become known as a great place to work," says Janelle Barlow, author of *Branded Customer Service.* "To make *Fortune* magazine's list of the '100 Best Companies to Work For,' for example, is a daunting task. This past year approximately a thousand qualifying companies started the application process. Only 350 completed it. The process includes a 57 question survey of at least 350 randomly selected employees. This accounts for two-thirds of the total rating, with the balance coming from an assessment of credibility, respect, fairness and pride."[7]

30 Put People First

SAS Institute in Cary, North Carolina, the world's largest privately held software company, has for eight consecutive years been listed in the top 20 of *Fortune*'s "100 Best Companies to Work for in America," and was inducted into the list's "Hall of Fame" in 2005. In addition, SAS has been listed 13 times by *Working Mother* as one of the "100 Best Companies for Working Mothers."

SAS's strategy is to do everything it can to become an Employer of Choice. Here's a partial list of the benefits it provides:

- The best on-site childcare center in the state.
- Employee conveniences like on-site car detailing, massage, dry-cleaning pickup and delivery, and a hair salon.
- Cafeteria with piano music.
- Art on every wall.
- Health clinic.
- No limit on sick days.
- Eldercare coordinator.
- Financial planning for college and retirement.
- "Break stations," which are stocked with breakfast pastries, fruits, six varieties of snack crackers, and soda, juice, coffee, and tea.
- Every floor has free M&Ms served in bowls that are replenished every Wednesday. (The company goes through an estimated 22 tons of M&Ms annually.)

"Even the simplest perk," writes Jennifer Schu in *Workforce* magazine, "is part of a highly-developed business strategy designed to attract and retain employees, and to reduce the cost of turnover. How can SAS afford such largesse?"

"'Knowledge-based companies need knowledge workers,' says CEO Jim Goodnight. 'Looking at . . . services that keep employees motivated, loyal and doing their best work as merely an expense and not an investment is, I think a little shortsighted.'"

"Stanford University researcher Jeffrey Pfeffer has studied SAS extensively," reports Schu. "He estimates the company saves over $70 million per year as a result of its low turnover. 'You can pay that money to employees in the form of benefits, or you can pay head-hunters and corporate trainers to fund the revolving door of people coming in and out,' Goodnight says. 'To me, it's a no-brainer.'"

"'I think our history has shown that taking care of employees has made the difference in how employees take care of our customers,' Goodnight says. 'With that as our vision, the rest takes care of itself.'"[8]

➡**Reality check:** You may not have the budget to provide the many benefits that SAS does for its employees. Consider however, the following flexible work arrangements.

31 Offer Alternative Work Arrangements

Work/family conflicts are some of the most pressing issues faced by today's employees. Among them are the issues of childcare and eldercare—both of which have a tremendous impact on employee productivity and retention.

Among mothers with children younger than a year old, 53.8 percent were in the labor force during 2005, according to the Current Population Survey, Bureau of Labor Statistics.[9]

As people live longer and deal with a variety of health issues, eldercare responsibilities are also becoming more common. The National Alliance for Caregiving (NAC) and AARP has reported that nearly one in four households, about 22.9 million nationally, is involved with eldercare.[10]

➡**Reality check:** Studies show that staff members with such care-taking responsibilities tend to come to work late, use the telephone excessively for personal calls, have more absenteeism, and quit their jobs more readily. The buzzword to accommodate such employees in what *BusinessWeek* calls The New World of Work, is *flexibility*.

If you are experiencing a shortage of skilled job applicants and/or high employee turnover, give some consideration to alternative work arrangements. For example, the following are now being offered by an increasing number of employers:

- Flextime (flexible work hours)
- Compressed work week (work longer days in exchange for a shorter week)

- Job sharing (divide one full-time job, for example, into two part-time jobs)
- Telecommuting (work at home with computer, fax, and modem)
- Paid "personal days" to be used for any purpose
- Paid maternity/paternity leave

Alternative work arrangements (discussed at length in Chapter 7) can ease the conflicts many employees have between home and work, reduce turnover, and enhance on-the-job performance. They can also be appealing to prospective employees in a tight labor market. Include them in classified ads.

32 Care for Caregivers

A recent study showed 82 percent of working caregivers have come into work late or left early as a result of caregiving. The average age of the employed caregiver is late 40s to early 50s. Some are the primary caregivers for a sick or handicapped child. Others are taking care of a terminally ill spouse. Many more are tending to an older adult.

"One of the greatest workplace needs of these employees is flexible hours and time off," says LeAnn Thieman, author of *Chicken Soup for the Caregiver's Soul*. "Other considerations should include providing information about available support services, such as eldercare services, adult daycare, respite care or home health assistance."

"Caregiving employees should be the ones that employers focus on retaining," Thieman says, "as their determination and commitment apply to both home and work lives. Supporting them is a win/win proposition."[11]

➡Resources
- The National Family Caregivers Association (www.nfcacares.org)
- The Area Agency on Aging (www.loaa.org)

33 A Flexible Sick-Leave Policy

What happens when employees are needed at home to care for a sick child, spouse, or other family member? Do they call in "sick" and take the day off? Do they come to work—yet remain distracted by the at-home situation? The answer depends on several factors, one of which is the flexibility of your sick-leave policy.

An employee benefit that is becoming more widely offered extends conventional sick leave to include other times when family members are ill. Called "family sick leave," it eliminates the need to fake an illness and then lie about it. In the end, it doesn't cost you any more.

Typically, family sick leave is computed at the rate of one-half day for each month worked (after a 90-day probationary period), up to a total of six days a year. What about unused sick days? Increasingly, employees are being paid for them. Doing so provides an incentive to get to work for those undecided about making the effort.

An alternative way of dealing with unused sick days is to accumulate them in a "paid leave bank" up to a maximum 20 to 30 days per employee. These days can then be used for such emergencies as a major illness or surgery, allowing employees to take the time needed for recuperation without losing pay.

Offering to pay for unused sick days is a way to reward loyal employees and to discourage those who view sick days as legitimate extra days off.

➡**Reality check:** Employees who treat sick days as free days and take every one of them while others come to work can severely disrupt morale in the practice. Loyal employees end up putting in more time, so their rate of compensation drops below that of less dedicated employees. It's a situation that could lead to office friction.

Sick-day compensation incentives also serve as a way to reward those who do come in whether they are 100 percent well or not. The reimbursement is not so large that it motivates truly ill employees to drag themselves into the office and perform below standards or get everyone else sick. But it is enough to encourage most staffers to come to work even if they have a headache or some other minor problem.

➡**Tested tip:** When first interviewing job applicants, you can get a sense of their attitude toward sick-day absences by asking such questions as:

- **What do you think constitutes a good attendance record?**
- **What do you consider to be good reasons for missing work?**

See Chapter 15 for a discussion of paid-time-off (PTO) programs.

34 Make Work Enjoyable

By making work enjoyable, says consultant Matt Weinstein, Ph.D., author of *Managing to Have Fun at Work,* you help create the kind of organization to which your employees will want to make a long-term commitment and where turnover and burnout will be minimal. The intentional use of fun, he adds, can have an enormous impact on team building, stress management, employee morale, and the way patients are treated.[12]

Research has shown that people who enjoy the company of co-workers tend to develop a bond with them and a sense of responsibility towards the group. This results in higher morale, less tardiness, and less absenteeism.

An enjoyable environment at work also helps employees to deliver "service with a smile."

➡**Action steps:** Workplace fun doesn't need to be planned. Most of the fun that happens in high-performance healthcare practices is spontaneous. Here are some ideas to get you started:

- "Give yourself and your staff permission to have fun with each other and with patients," says consultant/author Dr. Paul Homoly, Holt, Michigan.[13]
- Let employees bring homegrown, homemade, or store-bought food to work on a rotating basis. Snack food is fun and promotes camaraderie. Establish a budget for the purpose.
- Even better, contract with a local produce distributor to supply your office with fresh fruit when in season. A fruit snack is a healthy treat and an energy boosting alternative to coffee break foods. Start with once a week to see how it goes. An added benefit: It will make employees feel they're special and they work in a special place.
- Place a dry erase board in a central location where anyone (doctors or staff members) can write a compliment or thank you to anyone else.
- Fresh flowers from the garden or delivered by a florist are always uplifting and well worth the investment.

- Have in-office lunches—catered or otherwise. These are great for staff meetings, celebrations, and bad-weather days.
- Have a staff lounge where employees can take a break, renew their spirits, have a snack or group luncheon, or simply let their hair down. Decorate with humorous posters, cartoons, and anti-stress toys. A microwave oven is a must. Exercise equipment is another option.
- In Southern California, two massage therapists visit each nursing unit at Loma Linda University Medical Center on a rotating basis to relieve tense muscles and furrowed brows. They work 30 hours a week tending to the "kneads" of stress-weary staffers on all shifts.[14]
- Have parties for employee birthdays, anniversaries, going away, or "welcome aboard" occasions or, perhaps, for no reason at all. Make these festive occasions. Consider flowers or balloons, coffee and cake, perhaps a catered lunch. Exchange gag gifts.

➡**From the success files:** "Roger Wang, a solo family practitioner in Santa Ana, California, celebrates employee birthdays in the office. He also invites his staff, which includes a receptionist/office manager, nurse and X-ray technician, and their families out to lunch every couple of months. When he receives candy, wine, fruit and other gifts from patients, he shares it with the entire office so they know they are part of the team."[15]

You don't need to do elaborate things. Such activities need only provide a change-of-pace, a way to unwind if only for a few minutes, a way to celebrate and appreciate each other.

35 The Power of Celebrations

"Celebrating makes people feel like winners and creates an atmosphere of recognition and positive energy," say Jack and Susie Welch, co-authors of *Winning*.

"Imagine a team winning the World Series," they say, "without champagne spraying everywhere. You just can't! And yet companies win all the time and let it go without so much as a high five."

"Work is too much a part of life," the Welchs add, "not to recognize moments of achievement. Grab as many as you can. Make a big deal out of them. If you don't, no one will."[16]

"Do you know why most employees leave their jobs?" asks a newsletter from Lawrence Ragan Communications Inc. "Because they get in a 'rut' and are, in a word, bored. Sweep employees out of their ruts by launching 'guerilla celebration' attacks. Have bagels and coffee waiting for employees on a random Tuesday. Keep employees off balance about what you're going to do next. It's the sort of thing that separates one company from another—and convinces employees to stay put when they are thinking about leaving."[17]

There's no denying that celebrations with plenty of public pats on the back are a great way to make your staff feel like they're on a winning team. What can you celebrate? Ask your staff for ideas. Here's a short list of possibilities:

- Employee anniversary milestones
- The achievement of practice goals
- Your practice's anniversary
- The busiest day, week, or month since the beginning of the year
- To mark the end of a project or major effort such as the installation of EHR, practice Web site, major change in appointment scheduling, or remodeling of the office

➡**From the success files:** "Group recognition builds team loyalty and can be celebrated at the department, group, team or committee level," states a newsletter from the Baptist Health Care Leadership Institute. "Some of the top reasons for group celebration at Baptist Health Care, Pensacola, Florida, include: anniversaries (e.g. the open heart team celebrates a birthday every January 8th), group successes or accomplishments, patient satisfaction scores, meeting target goals, finishing a project, or giving encouragement. Celebrations occur spontaneously or as a planned event. Celebrations may take place during or after work hours, at a staff or committee meeting, at retreats, hospital functions, or department head meetings."[18]

➡Action steps: When things go well in your practice, make a point of celebrating the victory—and the people who made it possible. Recognize and thank everyone involved for their effort. It will nourish team spirit. Make people proud to be part of your practice. Burnish your reputation as an Employer of Choice.

➡Hard learned lesson: "Recognition and celebrations," say Ron Zemke and Chip R. Bell, co-authors of *Service Wisdom,* "are ways of reaffirming to people that they are an important part of something that matters. These little ceremonies can be significant motivators for people in any organization, but especially so in a service organization, where 'pride in the product' is essentially pride in personal performance."[19]

Among the benefits:

- Promotes teamwork because people feel bonded with one another
- Creates energy; people feel renewed, their batteries recharged
- Builds people's self-esteem by recognizing their contributions and achievements
- Showcases and reinforces desired norms of behavior
- Helps people through transitions and changes
- Makes work more fun

See Chapter 9 for more about the recognition and positive reinforcement of individual achievements.

36 Care for Your People

"You must show care for your people," says Marcus Buckingham, author of *The One Thing You Need to Know . . . About Great Managing, Great Leading, and Sustained Individual Success.* "I would like to be able to replace this skill," he adds, "with one that is more hard-edged, more tangible, but there's no getting around the data. A multitude of research studies confirm that employees are productive when they feel someone at work cares about them. Actually the research confirms more than the causal link between caring and productivity. It also reveals that employees who feel cared about are less likely to miss workdays, less likely to have accidents on the job, less likely to file workers' compensation claims, less likely to steal, less likely to quit, and more likely to advocate the company to friends and family. No matter how you choose to measure performance, being cared about seems to drive it."[20]

➠**Action steps:**

- Take an interest in the lives of your employees outside of work: hobbies, sports, family events such as anniversaries, birthdays, graduations, and the like. These discussions need not be lengthy. Even a brief remark such as "I hope your daughter does well in tonight's gymnastic competition" lets the person know you cared enough to remember it.

- Show concern for employees on extended leave due to illness or injury. Ongoing personal contact reassures employees they are valued, haven't been forgotten, and are missed on the job. Phone calls, hand-written notes, and when appropriate, personal visits to employees during extended leaves of absence are thoughtful gestures that will be greatly appreciated and long remembered.

- Provide training to give employees the skills they need to advance their careers and increase their value to the practice. Such training (discussed in Chapter 16) sends the message that your employees are valuable enough to invest in.

- Time off—especially around the holidays—is highly appreciated. If your practice is especially busy during the holidays, arrange, if possible, alternative work schedules. Your employees will be grateful all year long.

➠**From the success files:** "From time to time, we offer our staff some unexpected paid time off to participate in events that are important to them, such as a child's school play or a family occasion," says Javier Vazquez, a practice manager in Harlingen, Texas. "We can't do this for every event, and of course we have to be equitable, but we find it well worth the effort to make this work whenever possible. Try this statement," he recommends: "'You need to be there for your family. Get out of here and enjoy your time.' Your employees will thank you with extra productivity, a more positive attitude and a willingness to go the extra mile for you, just as you did for them."[21]

Reality check: A Bernard Hodes 2004 survey, conducted in partnership with Advance Magazines, that included 1,045 employees in nursing fields and 1,721 respondents in allied health disciplines found that in many cases, expectations are not being met. "Registered nurses, licensed practical nurses and nurse practitioners were disappointed in some things they found after taking their jobs. Prior to coming on board, more than 40 percent expected their employers to be caring. More than 30 percent expected their employers to be flexible. Many also believed their employers were dedicated to employee development. Once they arrived, they found something quite different. Not even 10 percent of nurses say that their employers are caring, flexible, open to employee feedback or dedicated to employee development."[22]

37 Employees Are #1

➥**Hard learned lesson:** Don't cave in to patients who abuse, insult, and intimidate your employees. Recognize the incredibly deflating message it sends employees if you side with an abusive patient while ignoring the rights and dignity of your own staff.

➥**From the success files:** "My office manager told me that Brenda, one of our calmest, most experienced secretaries, was very upset by the rudeness of a particular patient," says family practitioner John Egerton, Friendswood, Texas. "It wasn't the first time this patient had been overly demanding and rude to a receptionist. We wrote the patient a letter immediately, giving him notice that he would have to find another doctor. We have a no-tolerance policy on rudeness—and that includes patients as well as staff."

"Staff members appreciate that we stand behind them if a patient hassles them," says Egerton. "We encourage them to tell a belligerent patient that they are here to help, but that they do not have to put up with abuse. If the abuse continues, they have our permission to put down the phone or walk away from the reception desk."[23]

Imagine the level of commitment that emanates from such a willingness to dismiss a patient who hassles a member of your staff.

HCPs who have taken this step tell me they get a variety of responses. Some of these patients realize they've been out of line, apologize for their behavior, and become model citizens. Others take the hint and leave.

As a speaker, I've asked countless audiences of HCPs and staff members if anyone has ever *regretted* dismissing patients who were disruptive or troublesome in some other way. These are patients, best described by Dr. Rudy Dunnigan, Ashland, Kentucky, as "high maintenance patients who require excessive attention; chronic complainers who always find something to gripe about; and patients with high expectations and low compliance."[24]

The only regret I've heard from audience members about such dismissals (and it's expressed frequently) is, "I wish we had done it *sooner.*"

➥**Action step:** "Do yourself and your patients a favor," says Dr. James H. Hastings, Placerville, California. "Politely dismiss those patients who create stress for you and your staff. These patients distract you from giving 100 percent to patients who appreciate your services."[25]

➥**Reality check:** Lawyers advise that you should check with your malpractice insurer before taking any steps related to dismissing a patient. There are important issues regarding abandonment that need to be considered—including those that exist within the confines of a managed care plan's provider panel.

38 Help Employees Find Community in the Workplace

I've talked with many healthcare employees who have said that the people in the offices where they work are "like my second family."

That is what John B. Izzo, Ph.D. and Pam Withers refer to as a "sense of community" in their book, *Values Shift: The New Work Ethic and What It Means for Business.* It's similar also to what Dr. Abraham Maslow called a "sense of belonging" in his Hierarchy of Needs (see Chapter 8).

And it's priceless in the workplace.

Work is now seen by many employees as a major source of friendships, fun, camaraderie, and connection, say Izzo and Withers. Included are many who live alone or whose home lives are stressful. A *Fortune* magazine poll found that one of the main reasons people continue to work even when they don't need to financially is for social reasons—to connect with other people.[26]

➥**Action steps:** Many of the ideas discussed in this chapter are designed to enhance a sense of community in the workplace: caring about people, celebrations, and the efforts to make work enjoyable are among them.

➥**Hard learned lesson:** If people feel they're part of a workplace," says Bill Catlette and Richard Hadden, authors of *Contented Cows Give Better Milk*, "then they're going to have more resistance to leaving. They're not just leaving a job, they're leaving a community, and it takes a little bit more of a tug for that to happen."[27]

References

1. Critchley RK. *Doing Nothing Is NOT an Option! Facing the Imminent Labor Crisis*. Belmont, CA: South-Western Educational Publishing; 2004.
2. Pelehach L. Today's Employees Are Changing . . . Are You? *Dental Practice Report*, November 2001, 18–24.
3. Greene J. Attracting Nurses: Why Magnet Hospitals Succeed. *Trustee*, April 2003, 20–23.
4. Ahlrichs NS. *Competing for Talent*. Palo Alto, CA: Davies-Black Publishing; 2000.
5. Herman RE, Gioia JL. *How to Become an Employer of Choice*. Winchester, VA: Oakhill Press; 2000.
6. Great Place to Work Institute. What Do Employees Say? http://greatplacetowork. com/great/employees.php
7. Barlow J, Stewart P. *Branded Customer Service*. San Francisco: Berrett-Koehler Publishers; 2004.
8. Schu J. Even in Hard Times, SAS Keeps Its Culture Intact. *Workforce*, October 2001, 21.
9. United States Department of Labor, Bureau of Labor Statistics, April 26, 2006. http://www.bls.gov/news.release/pdf/famee.pdf
10. Aschkenasy J. Eldercare Grows Up. *Financial Planning*, September 2005, 125–128.
11. Thieman L. Caring for Caregivers. *Incentive*, March 2005, 49.
12. Weinstein M. *Managing to Have Fun at Work*. New York: Simon & Schuster; 1996.
13. Homoly P. Opportunity Knocks. *Dental Economics*, August 2001.
14. Weber DO. The Toll on Hospital Workers, Part 2. *HHN Magazine*, July 19, 2005.
15. Walpert B. Tips for Finding and Keeping a Good Receptionist. *ACP Observer*, January 1998.
16. Welch J, Welch S. *Winning*. New York: HarperBusiness; 2005.

17. Quick Tips. *Employee Recruitment & Retention* (newsletter), sample issue (no date), Ragan's Management Resources, Chicago, IL.
18. Reward and Recognition. http://www.baptistleadershipinstitute.com/Articles/ Articles.aspx?ContentID=100002
19. Zemke R, Bell CR. *Service Wisdom.* Minneapolis, MN: Lakewood Books; 1989.
20. Buckingham M. *The One Thing You Need to Know . . . About Great Managing, Great Leading and Sustained Individual Success.* New York: Free Press; 2005.
21. Vazquez J. Surprise Your Staff with Extra Paid Time Off. *Journal of Family Practice Management*, November/December 2005.
22. Raphael T. Health Professionals Share Their Candid (and Mixed) Feelings About the Field, August 9, 2005. http://www.workforce.com/section/00/article/ 24/13/49.html
23. Egerton J. On Rude Patients. *Medical Economics*, June 4, 2001, 101.
24. Dunnigan R. Stop and Smell the Eugenol. *Dental Economics*, January 2003, 14–18.
25. Allen J. Shortening the Learning Curve. *AACD Journal*, Winter 1997, 49–55.
26. Izzo JB, Withers P. *Values Shift: The New Work Ethic and What It Means for Business.* Vancouver, BC: FairWinds Press; 2001.
27. Retention Gurus Say Their Business Case Is Stronger Than Ever. Workforce Management Online. http://www.workforce.com/archive/article/23/87/09. php?ht=retention%20gurus%20retention%20gurus

Chapter Four

HIRING

Secrets of Savvy Interviewing

Have you ever hired someone who turned out to be very different than the person you thought you hired?

➥**Reality check:** Job seekers have become increasingly savvy and better prepared for job interviews than ever before. There are countless books and Web sites to help them look good on a job interview and get the job they want. There are outplacement specialists and "get-that-job gurus" who prime job hunters with stock answers, without reference to facts or personal inclinations. Their basic advice: "Give answers that make you look good."

When this deception works, they're hired. It's only after considerable time and money is spent on a probationary period (or sometimes longer) that the mistake is discovered.

With that in mind, I've asked countless HCPs, practice administrators, and human resource specialists in a wide range of professions and businesses to share the tested tips and interview questions they've found most helpful in judging job applicants. This chapter includes many of their insights and hard learned lessons about this topic.

39 Establish Rapport

It's one of the most common errors in interviewing: the failure to establish rapport. As a result, no substantive discussion takes place; nothing is learned about the applicant's priorities, expectations, or job-related needs; and the interview never gets off the ground.

Don't be misled or turned off by an applicant who appears nervous, thinking he or she may not be able to cope with a stressful job. The interviewing process itself can cause nervousness and it may have little bearing on a person's ability to perform a job.

The first task, therefore, is to put the job applicant at ease. The interview should be a pleasant informal conversation in which the person has an opportunity to talk freely and spontaneously to someone who is genuinely interested. The following guidelines are recommended:

- Set the right environment. The interview must be conducted in a place that's strictly private. Nothing interferes more with the free flow of information than the feeling that what's being said may be overheard by others. Offices without doors or open areas inhibit many people from talking openly. Neither should people be constantly interrupting or appearing at your door. If possible, instruct your receptionist to "please hold all but emergency calls." This will make the job applicant feel important and that the job being discussed is important. In fact, this small gesture, more than any other, will set a positive tone for the interview that follows.
- In your quest to learn as much as possible about a job applicant's suitability for your practice, don't cross over the line by being too interrogational or intimidating. You might *lose* a candidate you want to hire.
- Keep in mind that you cannot force job applicants to level with you. If they feel intimidated or defensive, they will be less likely to respond truthfully to your questions. One way to soften your questions is to ask permission before discussing a given aspect of a person's life. For example,

you might say, **"Would you mind if we were to talk about . . . ?"**

• If a job applicant is reluctant to answer one of these questions, move on rather than belabor the point.

➡**Reality check:** Admittedly, there's a thin line between questioning and interrogating a job applicant. In most cases, it comes down to tone of voice and body language (i.e., *how* you say *what* you say).

The following is a sampling of tested interview questions that go beyond skills and past experiences—along with the reasoning behind them. Use them selectively and modify them to suit the needs of your practice.

40 Use Tested Interview Questions

The purpose of the following questions is to ascertain if job applicants are as capable, determined, and sincere as they say they are. They're all open-ended, allowing candidates to divulge as much, or as little, as they want. Look not only for answers that parallel your view of the "ideal" employee, but also, as stressed in the next chapter, for answers that are a good fit with the culture of your practice.

➡**Tested tip:** As an ice-breaker at the start of an interview, use a question such as, **"Can you tell me something about your last job (e.g., what you did, with whom you worked, etc.).**

The objective is to relax the job applicant, put him or her at ease with an easy-to-answer question, and pave the way for further questioning.

Unlike many of the standard interview questions, the following are not as easy to answer with stock, preprogrammed responses. Hopefully, job applicants will answer them in an honest and straightforward manner.

What do you like most about your current job?

Almost as important as what job applicants include in their answer to this question is what they leave out. If they say, "I like that I can work independently and do my own thing," you need to carefully consider how good a fit they would be for a job requiring a lot of teamwork.

➡**Tested tip:** To draw applicants out on this and subsequent questions, use follow-up questions or requests such as, **"Why do you say that?"** or **"That's interesting. Tell me more."**

What *else* do you like about your current job?

This follow-up question is almost more important than the first question because, if people have a rehearsed answer to the first question, you're more likely to get a truthful answer with successive inquiries [e.g., short commute, flexible hours, matching 401(k) plan, or a host of other perks or benefits that may be lacking in your practice].

What are you looking for in your next job that's missing from your present one?

It's going to be difficult for a job applicant to know the best answer to such a question, let alone the one that will most impress you. If the person is honest, he or she may say "more autonomy on the job" or "management responsibilities" or something else that will be ideal (or less than ideal) for your practice.

What aspects of your last job did you like least?

Again, it will be hard for anyone to guess what you're looking for. He or she may say, "asking patients for money" or "overtime" or "filing insurance claims" or something else that would rule this person out for the job you're trying to fill.

What aspects of your last job did you like best?

Hopefully, there will be good fit with the open job in your practice.

Tell me about the best boss you ever had.

The answer may indicate whether or not the person would mesh well with your management style. Suppose the job applicant says she liked her last physician employer because she gave her full responsibility for certain tasks. Would that work for you? If not, she'd probably resent your close supervision just as much as you'd resent her unwillingness to take direction.

Tell me about the worst boss you ever had.

The answers, like those to the previous question, may offer a clue to the potential fit with your practice. If the description sounds anything like you, the person will not be happy working with you.

Did you enjoy working for your former employer?

This question can sometimes unmask malcontents: people who have a history of not being able to get along with employers. You're not necessarily looking for a candidate to rhapsodize about his or her former employers, but you want to be wary of anybody whose criticism is excessive. Someday, the candidate could be saying similar things about you.

On a scale of 1 to 10, how organized are you?

If you're looking for someone to do appointment scheduling or billing, for example, you'll want someone who says 8, 9, or 10. (Replace "organized" with other traits.)

What job-related situations have you found most stressful?

The answer to this question may give you an insight into the job applicant's tolerance for stress—which may be relevant depending on the level of stress in your practice.

What do you consider your greatest strengths? (Don't be modest.)

Depending on your type of practice, "good" answers might include: I love old people. I'm great with kids. I learn quickly. I speak three languages. I have infinite patience.

➡**Tested tip:** Any of these answers could be anticipated and well-planned (especially if you have a geriatric, pediatric, or multi-cultural practice). Take such answers a step further by asking, **"Please give me an example."** These are the five most important words in an interviewer's arsenal and they can't be used enough. There is nothing worse than ending an interview and finding an extraordinary comment in your notes—for which there is not a shred of supporting evidence.

Have you ever seen a receptionist (or whatever position for which the person is applying) use especially poor judgment? If so, please tell me about it.

I've heard job applicants recall, for example, how ineptly medical office personnel have dealt with apprehensive patients, complaints from patients about insurance coverage, incoming calls from referring physicians, among other situations that affect the reputation of a practice. Their answers and the way they expressed them revealed a lot about their values and desirability as employees.

Do you like a job where you are given a lot of responsibility or a more highly structured one with more supervision?

Most people have a preference. And the more closely your management style matches the needs of a prospective employee, the happier you *both* will be.

In which of your jobs did you learn the most?

A blank stare says a lot.

In your last job, did you receive the recognition and appreciation you felt you deserved?

The answer will help you better understand the person's job-related needs.

How do you feel about asking people for money?

You want to make sure the person you hire for payment arrangements and follow-up collection work doesn't have misgivings about the task. A surprising number of people do.

Surveys show the best bank collectors exhibit low sensitivity and trust, coupled with an assertive personality. A possible interview question would be: **"What's the most difficult thing you've had to tell a person and how did it make you feel?"**[1]

It doesn't serve your goals if you find a person with a great résumé but who can't handle the emotional realities of the job.

What am I likely to hear, positive and negative, when I call your references?

This question gives job applicants an opportunity to brag about their strengths and achievements at previous jobs. It also enables them to tell their side of any negative story you might hear (or one they *think* you might hear). I've heard reports of some startling admissions.

➡ **Tested tips:**
- Use the preceding questions and others that follow in this chapter selectively. Don't overwhelm job applicants.
- If you're interviewing several job applicants, be sure to ask the same questions of each person; for example, their backgrounds, what they would bring to the position, their long-term career objectives, and so forth. Their responses to similar questions will put you in a better position to compare the job applicants.

41 Hire Service-Oriented Employees

The service-oriented attitude (as discussed in Chapter 1) is particularly important in healthcare practices.

"How can a supervisor increase the chances of hiring someone who will really care about the patients in a medical practice?" asks Dr. Stanley M. Fineman, senior partner at Atlanta Allergy and Asthma Clinic in Atlanta, Georgia. "The process starts with the job interview," he says. "How the applicant responds and acts are critical, but there are several questions that can be helpful in finding personnel who are truly service-oriented."[2]

Among those suggested by Dr. Fineman are the following:

- **How did you become interested in nursing?**
- **Have you ever had a bad experience as a patient in a medical practice? What happened?**
- **If you could have improved anything about the way your previous employer went about work, what would you have changed?**

➥**Hard learned lesson:** "When an employee leaves a busy medical practice," Fineman says, "there is frequently pressure to hire a replacement as quickly as possible. Taking care to find the right person, someone who is service and patient oriented, is invaluable. With service-oriented employees, the quality of patient satisfaction should improve."[3]

42 The Must-Ask Question

"If I had just one area to probe in an interview," says Jack Welch, former chairman and CEO of General Electric, "it would be why a candidate left his or her previous job, and the one before that."

"Was it the environment? Was it the boss? Was it the team? What exactly made you leave? There is so much information in those answers. Keep digging and dig deep," Welch says. "Maybe the candidate just expects too much from a job or a company—he wants a boss who is entirely hands-off or teammates who always agree. Maybe he wants too much reward too fast. Or maybe she's leaving her last job because she has just what you want: too much energy to be held back, so much ability to energize she wants to manage more people, too much edge for a namby-pamby employer, and such a strong ability to execute she needs more challenge."

"The key," Welch adds, "is to listen closely. Get in the candidate's skin. Why a person has left a job tells you more about them than almost any other piece of data."[4]

43 Talk Less. Listen More.

Many HCPs make the mistake of doing most of the talking during job interviews. They mean well—often providing pertinent information about the position or about the practice—but in doing so, fail to learn what they need to know about job applicants. Jim Kennedy, author of *Getting Behind the Resume: Interviewing Today's Candidates*, says that when assessing a job applicant, you should listen about 80 percent of the time.[5]

➡**Reality check:** In taping job interviews for training purposes, it's not unusual for HCPs to discover (to their surprise) that they have dominated the conversation.

Equally important, if not more so, is *how* you listen. To be meaningful, it must be done in a skillful and understanding way called "active listening."

➡**Action steps:**
- Pay attention when the job applicant speaks.
- *Look* like you're paying attention. Looking, for example, at a patient's chart or worse your watch, implies less-than-total interest on your part. Someone worth listening *to* is worth looking *at*.
- Get involved while listening. Don't be a deadpan. Lean forward. Nod your head as the person speaks. Respond to his or her cues and facial expressions. Periodically say "uh-huh," "that's interesting," or other words to show you're listening.
- Listen for feelings. Try to understand each person's story from his or her vantage point.
- Provide feedback—particularly when elaboration is desired. You might say, for example, **"I can understand how you feel about that."** A sympathetic statement like this will encourage the person to go further and reveal more.

- Many interviewers interfere in their own information-gathering process by being too quick to fill a gap in the conversation. But often, a candidate's initial response to a question is the preprogrammed one. "After the applicant responds to your question, count to five slowly before asking the next question," say Franklin C. Ashby, Ph.D. and Arthur R. Pell, Ph.D., authors of *Embracing Excellence.* "By waiting five seconds, you'll be surprised how often an applicant adds something—positive or negative—to the response to the previous question."[6]
- If you imply (by your silence) that the answer is somehow inadequate, the candidate may continue and reveal the real answer—especially with some encouragement such as, **"Go on"** or **"Tell me more."**

➡**Hard learned lesson:** Silence can be your ally. Allow it to happen. You'll be amazed at what you can harvest from it.

44 Ask Scenario-Driven Questions

"At least one time during the interview process, ask the candidate a difficult-to-answer question," advise Neil Baum, M.D. and Gretchen Henkel, co-authors of *Marketing Your Clinical Practice Ethically, Effectively, Economically.* "In any medical practice, circumstances will arise that require the staff to think and respond quickly. Failure to react quickly can adversely affect the health of patients and might even lead to litigation."[7]

If the candidate has worked in a medical office or has healthcare experience, Baum suggests a question such as, **"What would you do if a patient called with a medical emergency and the physician couldn't be reached or located immediately?"**[8]

Other scenario-driven type questions might include:

- **How would you handle it if a patient began arguing with you in front of other patients about the cost of his visit?**
- **What would you say to a patient who requested that his records be sent to another physician?**

The answers in this case are less important than whether or not the person can think on his or her feet.

45 Uncover a Job Applicant's "Inner Traits"

After considering job skills and experience, many HCPs tend to appraise job applicants according to appearance, communication skills, sociability, or personality. Although these are important traits for a healthcare practice, they're not enough.

Equally if not more important are a person's *inner traits*: intelligence, achievement drive, attitude toward work, and the ability to get along with others to name a few. These factors determine whether a person with the right job skills and experience will be right for your practice.

Beth Israel HealthCare, a Boston-based network of healthcare services, seeks people with a strong team ethic, says Laura Avakian, vice president of human resources. "The people who are most likely to commit to us are people who have participated in group environments," she says. "We'll ask for examples of teams they've been on, like church choirs, or coaching soccer teams."[9]

Here are more tested interview questions to help elicit information about these inner traits. As with the previous questions, use them selectively.

- **In your last job, in what accomplishments did you take the most pride?**
- **In your last job, when you finished your work ahead of schedule, what did you usually do?**
- **In your last job, if you were asked to do something that wasn't part of your usual duties, how did you feel about it?**
- **Have you learned any new skills or explored some new field of interest, even a hobby, since leaving school?**
- **What is your long term employment or career objective?**

As a final question, consider asking:

- **Is there anything you would like to bring up that we haven't talked about?**

See if the job applicant asks about the job content, what your expectations might be, or why the last person left.

➡**Tested tip:** Evaluate a potential employee's energy levels by inter-viewing him or her at different times of the day.

➡**Hard learned lesson:** "Pay attention to the final five minutes," says Dr. Steven L. Rasner, Cherry Hill, New Jersey. "Announce casually that 'We're just about out of time.' Many candidates will save their most important comments or questions until the very end, so give them the chance to help you see what's important. You may hear a question such as 'Do we ever have to work weekends or overtime?' The closing minutes can offer the clearest insights to your candidate's concerns."[10]

As previously mentioned, long pauses or no answers to any of the above questions can be quite revealing.

46 Use Behavior-Based Questions

Hiring a good employee is more than finding a person with work experience that matches your opening. And it is more than finding a person you intuitively like. If you make hiring decisions based solely on work experience and personality, you set yourself up for turnover problems. There is a better way. Widely used in industry, behavior-based interviewing aims at projecting job applicants' future perfor-mance based on how they handled past work situations.

It's difficult for job applicants to fake answers to behavior-based questions or to prepare for them in advance. As a result, you're more likely to get an accurate picture of applicants, whether or not they'll be a good fit with your practice, and how they will perform on the job.

Conducting behavior-based interviews reveals skills, competen-cies, and character. "This is the most important part of the interview," says Carol Quinn, author of *Don't Hire Anyone Without Me!* "Your ideal candidate will have an 'I can' attitude, will not allow obstacles to stop him or her and will be constantly motivated. The so-so, below-average applicant makes excuses and blames others."[11]

Quinn suggests following the OSAE series of questions—ques-tions that get the candidate to reveal an Obstacle Situation, Action, and End result. OSAE works like this:

- First pose an Obstacle Situation (OS) that relates to the job you need to fill. For example, **"Describe a situation that required great patience on your part."**

- Then ask an Action (A) question: **"How did you deal with it?"**
- Next, find out the End result (E): **"What eventually happened?"**[12]

The following OSAE questions can be useful in getting applicants to speak candidly about themselves and will help you determine if what they have done in the past will be a good fit for your practice.

There are no right or wrong answers to behavioral questions— only responses that may or may not be relevant to the job for which you're hiring.

- **"Tell me about a time when you set specific work goals for yourself. How did things turn out?"**
- **"Tell me about a work emergency or crisis of some kind in which you were involved? What was your role? What did you do?"**
- **"We've all felt stress in our work lives. Tell me about work-related situations that cause stress for you. How do you typically handle such stress?"**
- **"In your past job(s), what kind of co-workers rubbed you the wrong way? How did you respond?"**
- **"Tell me about a challenge you faced in a previous job. How did you respond?"**
- **"In your most recent position, what did you learn? How did you apply this learning?"**
- **"What experience have you had with people of different ethnicities, ages, or physical ability levels?"**
- **"In the past, have you had a preference for working mainly with men or women? Explain your answer."**
- **"Tell me about a time when you felt you went beyond the call of duty in helping a patient (customer/client/co-worker)."**

One of the qualities that Southwest Airlines look for is a sense of humor. In the interview process, prospective employees are typically asked, **"Tell me how you recently used your sense of humor in a work environment. Tell me how you used your humor to defuse a difficult situation."**[13]

(Replace "sense of humor" with other personality traits of interest.)

➡**Reality check:** As revealing as the replies to such questions might be in evaluating a job applicant, not all candidates are going to be comfortable in answering them. Use such questions with discretion and move on to other matters as the situation warrants.

The following are some additional questions to consider when interviewing job applicants for management positions with supervisory responsibilities:

- **What types of staff performance problems did you encounter in your previous job(s)? How did you correct these problems?**
- **What type of experience do you have in dealing with interpersonal problems between subordinate staff members?**
- **Have you conducted staff meetings? How did you gauge the success of the meetings?**
- **Have you ever disciplined or fired an employee? What caused the problem? How did you feel about it? What could have been done to prevent the situation?**
- **Did you do any hiring in your past job(s)? What qualities are most important in making a hiring decision? Why?**
- **What type of successes have you achieved in managing staff to attain specific goals? What obstacles did you overcome? How did you do it?**

➡**Tested tip:** If you need more information and want to draw out your applicant's answers, ask these probing questions:

- **"Please clarify what you mean by . . . "**
- **"How did you feel when that happened?"**
- **"Looking back at your experience, how do you see things now?"**
- **"Did you consider other options at the time?"**
- **"Did the outcome of your actions satisfy you?"**

➡**Tested tip:** "Ask for specifics that demonstrate experience and skill," says Christine Hippie, vice president of training and organizational development with the human resources firm Total Compensation Services in Baltimore, Maryland. "Let's say your practice is very fast-paced. Don't ask, 'Have you ever had to do a lot of things at the same time?' Instead ask, **'How many rooms have you kept going simultaneously? How did you manage it?'** Or, **'How do you triage large numbers of telephone calls?'**"[14]

➡**From the success files:** At Women & Infants Hospital of Rhode Island, "A person must be qualified to do the job," says Karen Schoch, "but we also require the right personality. We're a hospital that puts a premium on patient care, and we want people who can deliver on the concept. Finding the right person—who has a certain blend of compassion, diplomacy, energy and confidence—is a critical ingredient in boosting patient satisfaction, reducing turnover and fueling productivity."

"For Women & Infants Hospital, molding a culture that has no uncaring doctors or cranky nurses is an obsession. In 2001, the 2,600 employee hospital, part of the Care New England Health System, embarked on a program to hire people with the right personality. They turned to behavior-based interviews and in-depth analysis of candidates. That, combined with an overall emphasis on total quality, has led to impressive results. One year later, patient satisfaction rose from the 71st percentile to the 89th percentile on a national scale, while turnover measured 8.5 percent, compared to a national average of 20 to 25 percent. At the same time, Women & Infants Hospital has seen labor disputes wither and productivity climb. 'Behavior-based hiring works,' Schoch says."[15]

➡**Reality check:** How does one evaluate the responses to both behavioral and nonbehavioral questions? The answer, say consultants Gail Heritage and Suzanne Davidson, co-founders of The Breckenridge Group, is to profile the current top performers in your practice. Interview these people. Ask them essentially the same questions you intend to ask a potential candidate. Upon completion of the interview, ask these top performers what they would consider to be an excellent response, an acceptable response, and an unacceptable response to the questions you have asked them.[16]

47 Peer Interviews

"Beginning seven or eight years ago," says Al Stubblefeld, COO of Baptist Health Care, Pensacola, Florida, "we do not hire individuals for any job in our organization unless the peers that will be working alongside that person have interviewed him or her. Peer interviewing slows down the process, and there have been multiple times when the manager is ready to hire someone when the staff says, 'No.' The outcome is that you tend to get people that fit better. When a new employee shows up, their peers have already met them. They have a vested interest in their success now."[17]

➡**Action step:** Consultant Dr. James R. Pride recommended your staff have a 20-minute meeting or 1-hour lunch (paid for by you) with each of the two or three top candidates. "The purpose of this interview," he said, "is to glean information among peers that the applicant might not reveal to you. The staff prepares work-related questions to discover the applicant's motivation and concerns, such as: **'What do you think of the interview process so far?' 'What things might be a concern for you?'** and **'What can I tell you about our practice?'** The staff's input is important," Pride said, "however, the final decision remains yours."[18]

➡**From the success files:** "Paul McKoy reports how teamwork plays a role in the hiring process at Marianjoy Rehabilitation Services in Palos Heights, Illinois, where he serves as senior physical therapist. 'After the appropriate manager conducts an initial interview with a prospective PT or other team member, we invite the candidate back for an informal team interview,' he says."

"All staff are invited to participate in the second interview. 'The team can include nurses, therapists, the receptionist, the office coordinator, even the van driver,' he notes. 'The meeting is low-key and relaxed. We'll ask questions such as why the candidates decided to enter the profession. What are they used to in terms of caseload? What is their experience working as a team member with other disciplines?' Following the interview, the team meets again to discuss their impressions.'"

"The result is a 'close-knit' team, and a low attrition rate. The process has helped us sustain our team in terms of personalities that come into our setting and that fit well with us."[19]

➡**Reality check:** If your staff is involved in the hiring process, their commitment to a new employee will be stronger. They'll be pulling for the newcomer to succeed because they shared in the hiring decision. Moreover, the team's acceptance of the new staff member helps the newcomer to quickly acquire skills necessary to function effectively as part of the team.

48 Avoid Negative Feedback

For every candidate actually hired, there will likely be several rejected, perhaps more. Some will ask why they didn't get the job.

It's always best to avoid giving negative feedback during a job interview. One reason is that you may be wrong about the person. Another is that it may create bad feelings about your practice. The objective should always be to build goodwill for your practice. You never know when a rejected candidate may later be a patient or referral source for your practice. Try to leave each job applicant with positive feelings.

It's best, therefore, not to reject a job applicant in the interview, even when you're sure you will not make a job offer. Better to advise the person that you have a number of applicants to consider and that you will be in touch once a decision has been made. This will alert the candidate that there is competition for the position and that any failure to be hired isn't necessarily due to any inadequacy, but rather due to the high level of competition. If passed over, it's best to call or write something to the effect, "We were impressed with your qualifications; however, we are unable to offer you a position at this time. We do wish you every success in your future endeavors." If an applicant persists and seeks a more detailed explanation, just say, "We liked you and we think you could have done this job; however, we had several good candidates, including you, and it was a tough decision. Unfortunately, we couldn't hire everyone."

49 Use Pre-employment Testing

Your practice is looking for a new billing coordinator. You've run an advertisement, fielded dozens of phone calls, and looked at about 30 résumés. Finally, you have five candidates you think are good, and you have scheduled interviews with them. But how will you know if they can do the job if you hire one?

The answer may be pre-employment testing.

"The current health care market is causing increased job turnover," says Mary Pat Whaley, FACMPE, administrator of Greensboro (NC) Surgical Associates. "And the legal environment makes many employers loathe to give any useful information in a reference."

"Whaley's answer," reports *Physician's Marketing & Management*: "'Set up a pre-employment testing (PET) program. We think that turnover is a result of insufficient screening,'" she explains.

"'Managers don't have human resources training and don't have the interview skills to really find the best people.'"

"Whaley started her program at the front desk. 'It is seen as an entry-level position,' she explains. 'That makes it harder to tell if someone will be good or not. You can ask in an interview how they will deal with stress or whether they can multi-task, but you have to take them on their word.'"

"'A PET scheme is better,'" she says. "'When combined with interviews, references, and applications, the test can guide you to the best hiring decision.'"

➡**Action steps:** "One powerful interview technique to use when hiring a new biller," says Pamela L. Moore, Ph.D., senior editor of *Physicians Practice*, "is to give the candidate a test. Get two or three rejections from your billing office and photocopy them. (Be sure to black out the patient's name.) Ask the candidate to walk you through the explanation of benefits (EOB). Look for familiarity with the terminology and content. Next ask the candidate how she or he would handle different EOB situations. You want to know that the candidate understands how to appeal the claim (or can submit it correctly from the get-go)."[20]

50 Offer a Test Run

"If the supervisor is interested in a candidate," says Dr. Robert J. Holzhauer, Allergy Asthma Immunology, Rochester, New York, "we offer him or her the opportunity to spend a half-day (unpaid) with one of our nurses or secretaries to see what working for AAIR may be like. The readily apparent camaraderie of our staff has often convinced candidates that our practice might be fun and an interesting place to work. On the other hand, we have had some who have decided our practice was not for them and some that, on more extended observation, were not for us."

"This process sometimes saves us from making the mistake of hiring the wrong person for a job and wasting time, money and resources training them, only to have them leave shortly thereafter."[21]

➡**Variation:** In the office of Dr. Nancy G. Torgerson, Lynnwood, Washington, job applicants are invited to observe vision therapy sessions or parent-teacher workshops conducted in her office. Current staff members then note if the applicants are well mannered, if they listen, if they interact well with patients, and if they appear comfortable doing so.

As a follow-up, Dr. Torgerson, her office manager, and her vision therapy administrator take the finalists to lunch and then make the decision.

➡**Hard learned lesson:** "You can interview somebody for an hour or two hours, and never know what you're hiring until you get them in the job," says real estate tycoon Donald Trump. "To a certain extent, it's a chance. There are many people that give great interviews and are lousy employees, and then there are people who give terrible job interviews and are fabulous employees."[22]

References

1. Ragan's Management Resources, Recruiting Ideas, *Employee Retention & Retention,* Chicago, IL, April 2000, 2.
2. Fineman SM. Hiring Service Oriented Employees. *Academy News*, American Academy of Allergy, Asthma & Immunology, April 2004.
3. Ibid.
4. Welch J, Welch S. *Winning.* New York: HarperBusiness; 2005.
5. Kennedy J. *Getting Behind the Resume: Interviewing Today's Candidates.* Englewood Cliffs, NJ: Prentice Hall; 1987.
6. Ashby FC, Pell AR. *Embracing Excellence.* Paramus, NJ: Prentice Hall Press; 2001.
7. Baum N, Henkel G. *Marketing Your Clinical Practice Ethically, Effectively, Economically*, 3rd ed. Sudbury, MA: Jones & Bartlett Publishers; 2004.
8. Ibid.
9. Brewer G. Loyalty for Hire. *Performance,* December 1995, 27.
10. Rasner SL. Hire Right. *Dental Practice Report*, October 2000, 37–44.
11. Quinn C. *Don't Hire Anyone Without Me!* Hawthorne, NJ: Career Press; 2001.
12. Ibid.
13. Freiberg K, Freiberg J. *Nuts! Southwest Airlines' Crazy Recipe for Business and Personal Success.* Austin, TX: Bard Press; 1996.
14. Weiss GG. How to Find and Keep Topnotch Clinical Staff. *Medical Economics*, March 8, 2002, 37–45.
15. Greengard S. Gimme Attitude. *Workforce,* July 2003, 56–60.
16. Heritage G, Davidson S. Recruiter Smarts. http://hr.monster.com/recruiter/recruiter_smarts7
17. Quest For Quality. *HHN Magazine*, November 17, 2005. http://www.hhnmag.com/hhnmag/hospitalconnect/search/article.jsp?dcrpath=HHNMAG/PubsNewsArticle/data/0511HHN_FEA_Dialogue&domain=HHNMAG
18. Pride JR. In Search of Your Ideal Employee. *Dental Practice Report*, May/June 1999.
19. Coyne C. Strength in Numbers: How Team Building Is Improving Care in a Variety of Practice Settings. *PT Magazine*, June 1, 2005.
20. Moore PL. Ask the Experts. *Physicians Practice*, December 15, 2005.
21. Hozhauer RJ. Recruiting and Retaining Employees. American Academy of Allergy Asthma & Immunology. http://www.aaaai.org
22. Ragan's Management Resources, *Employee Recruitment & Retention,* Chicago, IL. Sample (undated) issue, 6.

Chapter Five

HIRING

Hire People Who Fit Your Practice Culture

"**E**very organization has a set of values, and every organization has its own culture," says Dianne Michonski Durkin, author of *The Loyalty Advantage.* "It's the way management treats its staff and how people work together, speak to one another, and show their motivation (or lack of it) in their jobs and attitudes. It shows up in how customers are treated and whether they return."[1]

HCPs who recognize the critical impact culture has on performance go out of their way to select people whose knowledge, experience, abilities, and motivations reinforce their culture and ensure practice success.

In their book, *Corporate Cultures: The Rites and Rituals of Corporate Life,* Terrence E. Deal and Alan A. Kennedy write, "If employees know what their company stands for, if they know what standards they are to uphold, then they are much more likely to make decisions that will support those standards. They are also more likely to feel as if they are an important part of the organization. They are motivated because the company has meaning for them."[2]

69

When there's a good fit between the culture of a practice and its employees, people tend to be happier, harder working, more productive, *and,* as a rule, stick around longer.

This chapter explains how to make that happen.

51 Determine What Matters Most

"What matters most in this practice?" is a question I've posed to countless HCPs and staff members. What continues to surprise me is the variety of answers I often receive from people within the same practice. This lack of agreement sends mixed messages (and results in mixed behaviors) with patients. It also makes it difficult, if not impossible, to hire people who fit the practice culture.

➥**Action steps:** "Put down on paper your organization's highest priorities," advises consultant Craig R. Hickman, author of *Management Malpractice*. "Be as detailed and specific as possible to capture the true and full essence of what you think matters most in your organization."

Next, says Hickman, have your peers and employees go through the same exercise. Discuss and clarify these priorities. This discussion should be about mission, philosophies, principles, and beliefs that transcend annual objectives and strategies.

Lastly, says Hickman, "Build a commitment to the principle of doing what matters most by defining it, clearly and comprehensively."[3]

➥**Reality check:** "When what matters in your organization remains hidden, obscured, or unclear," Hickman says, "it will prevent you from building a strong organizational culture, hiring the right people, implementing focused strategies, and achieving collective results. People need to know what matters most to the organization where they work; otherwise, they become frustrated, distracted, bored, cynical, and otherwise unproductive."[4]

➥**Hard learned lesson:** The true culture of an organization is seen in the way employees behave when no supervisor is watching them. How do HCPs and managers treat employees and how do employees treat one another? How do employees treat patients?

52 Start with the Basics

Bernard Marcus, one of the co-founders of Home Depot, was interviewed about his company's corporate culture for the book, *Management*. "It starts with the basics," he says, "hiring the right people, the folks in the store who will create the shopping environment. We want extroverts, people who like other people. We look for people with pleasing personalities and people who are highly motivated and want to learn. You have to be discerning to find them. Typically, out of 8,000 applicants, we hire 200 people."[5]

Herb Kelleher, CEO of Southwest Airlines, was similarly asked about his company's corporate culture. "It starts with the hiring," he said. "We are zealous about hiring. We look for a particular type of person, regardless of which category it is. We look for attitudes that are positive and for people who can lend themselves to causes. We want folks who have a good sense of humor and people who are interested in performing as a team and take joy in team results instead of individual accomplishments."[6]

In both these examples, the top management of the companies were highly focused on the type of person best-suited to the long-term goals of their organizations. Knowing this greatly simplifies "the search."

53 Look for Job Fit and Culture Fit

Most HCPs focus on knowledge, skills, and experience when hiring new employees. However, a good skill fit does not guarantee that a person will be happy or energized about a job or organization.

"Two additional criteria are critical for hiring people who have a propensity to be engaged," says Jim Councelman, manager of leadership development at DDI, a global human resource consulting firm. "These are *job fit* and *culture fit*. Job fit describes the match between what a job offers and what a candidate desires in a position. For example, working closely with others, having daily interactions with co-workers, and working collaboratively to get things done. These people may be unhappy in a position in which they are expected to work on their own, perhaps even physically removed (in a satellite or regional office) from their co-workers."

"DDI research shows that the biggest cause of turnover," says Councelman, "isn't poor skills or abilities (11.5 percent), but a lack of job or culture fit (88.5 percent). Even the most highly skilled or experienced employees will be unhappy, let alone engaged, if there isn't a good job and culture fit."[7]

➽**Action step:** To determine if there's a good job fit, ask prospective employees such questions as: **"What types of work have you most enjoyed? What was motivating about that work? What strengths do you enjoy using the most?"** The better the fit with the job you have available, the more likely his or her talents will be engaged.

➽**From the success files:** "By hiring for skill *and* cultural fit, the interviewing process took on a new life," says Donna Cheek, vice president for clinical operations at The Outer Banks Hospital in Nags Head, North Carolina. "Most healthcare workers are accustomed to fitting in with clinical models—but when you show them that they must be part of a culture of excellence, they start to see that this team is more than what you do; it's about how we all do it together."[8]

➽**Hard learned lesson:** "You can not impose new core values on people," say James C. Collins and Jerry I. Porras in their book, *Built to Last: Successful Habits of Visionary Companies*. "Instead, find people to share your core values; attract and retain those people; and let those who do not share your core values go elsewhere."[9]

54 What Commitment Is Required?

Gulf Breeze Hospital, an acute-care facility in Gulf Breeze, Florida, earned the top spot for inpatient satisfaction in 2004—for the ninth straight year. The results come from Press Ganey Associates, the country's largest repository of patient satisfaction statistics.

The hospital's 280 staff members are trained to make three major pledges to ensure outstanding service to patients. "It all begins," says the hospital's administrator, Dick Fulford, "with a positive attitude:

> Never say, 'It's not my job.'
> Reduce and eliminate hassles.
> Provide personalized professional care."

"Fulford says that every person working at the hospital has the opportunity to make a patient's interaction exceptional. Applicants are immediately told that if they can't make this commitment, they will probably not fit in with the Gulf Breeze Hospital culture."[10]

"Disney recognizes that most of its employees will only interact with a particular customer once. The company has gone to great lengths to make sure its employees know what it wants to communicate in each of those one-time encounters: hospitality, friendliness, competence, complete knowledge, helpfulness. Disney realizes that if every encounter embodies those qualities, it will be hard for its guests not to have a good experience."[11]

55 Which Comes First?

In determining the culture of your practice, it's important to decide whether the primary focus will be on achieving a more *efficient* practice or a more *effective* one.

An efficient practice focuses on *doing things in the right way* to maximize productivity and profitability. An effective practice, on the other hand, focuses on *doing the right things* that maximize patient satisfaction and referrals. The first is an "inward" view. The second is an "outward" view.

HCPs focused on efficiency often look for ways to maximize profitability by working faster, delegating as much as possible, skimping on payroll expense, and cutting corners to save time or money. And up to a point, these are sound management strategies. Being efficient definitely has survival value in a highly competitive, cost-conscious economy such as that created by managed care and capitation.

The point of diminishing returns occurs when such cost-containment measures begin to impinge on patient care and satisfaction. For example: Does the emphasis on delegation and working faster require HCPs to take less time with patients to properly explain their findings and recommendations, and answer questions? Does skimping on payroll expenses result in being understaffed at times, or worse, having a staff that is not as knowledgeable and experienced as the job requires? Does belt-tightening require a cut-back on continuing education or state-of-the-art equipment? Alas, you can be efficient without being effective.

➡**From the success files:** "I encourage my assistants to small-talk with patients before and after, even if that means minor slowdowns in the schedule," says OBG specialist Francis A. Lombardo, Winchester, Massachusetts. "Putting a patient at ease can be every bit as important as what I do in the examining room."[12]

➡**Reality check:** "Contrary to conventional wisdom, business success is not just defined by revenue and profit growth, superior return on equity or increased shareholder value," say Thomas J. Neff and James C. Citrin, chairman and managing director, respectively, of Spencer Stuart, an executive search firm. "Rather, in our view, business success is doing the right things. When chief executives succeed in doing the right things with their companies and their businesses, the traditional measures of performance inevitably follow."[13]

➡**Hard learned lesson:** Management expert Peter Drucker said it best: "Nothing is less productive than to make more efficient what should not be done at all."[14]

56 Determine the Core Values of Your Practice

Core values represent what's truly important in your practice—the guiding principles for you and your staff, the qualities that give it a distinctive character and differentiate it from other practices.

➡**Action steps:** At your next staff meeting, ask each person to write his or her answer to these questions: **What makes our practice unique? What's important here?**

If it's the first time these subjects have been discussed, be prepared for a wide range of answers. Discuss them all and reach a consensus. It could be the most important staff meeting you've ever held.

"Visionary companies tend to have only a few core values, usually between three and six," say consultants James C. Collins and Jerry I. Porras, authors of *Built to Last: Successful Habits of Visionary Companies.* "And indeed, we should expect this, for only a few values can be truly *core*—values so fundamental and deeply held that they will change or be compromised seldom, if ever."[15]

For example, the core values at McDonald's are summarized in four letters originally conceived by founder Ray Kroc and his earliest franchisers: QSCV (quality, service, cleanliness, and value). These are the guiding principles for all of McDonald's corporate strategies and organizational practices.

➥**Reality check:** "Values drive people's behavior when they are working on your purpose and picture of the future," says prominent author, speaker, and consultant Ken Blanchard, Ph.D. "Few organizations have operational values and those that do often make one or two common mistakes. First, they have too many values—eight, ten or twelve. Our research shows that if you want values to guide people's behavior, you can't overload them with more than three or four values."[16]

"How can we be sure," ask Collins and Porras, "that the core ideologies of highly visionary organizations represent more than just a bunch of nice-sounding platitudes—words with no bite, words meant merely to pacify, manipulate or mislead? We have two answers. First, social psychology research strongly indicates that when people publicly espouse a particular point of view, they become much more likely to behave consistent with that point of view even if they did not previously hold that point of view. Second and more important, the visionary organizations don't merely declare an ideology; they take steps to make the ideology pervasive throughout the organization."[17]

➥**From the success files:** "In 1996, I sold my practice to our local hospital," recalls Dr. John L. Hudson, Denver, Colorado. "This change and general shift toward managed care put tremendous strain on the office and affected staff morale. We needed to bring meaning back into our practice in the face of these outside pressures. So we agreed to develop a mission statement and a set of core values that could guide us through these changing times."

"To accomplish this we decided to hold retreats involving all 128 staff members and physicians. We began by determining our core values. Each staff member suggested values for the group's consideration, and we listed all of them on flip-chart pages around the room. We then used nominal group process to trim the 120 suggestions to a final list of 15, ten related to patients and five related to ourselves. With these values in mind, we crafted a mission statement, again, using the nominal group process to evaluate the results. As a result, the staff has begun working together more closely." "They have bought into the power of having a mission statement and a set of core values because all staff members helped develop these documents."[18]

See Chapter 11 for a further discussion of retreats.

57 Obsession Is the Key

"There is considerable evidence," William Andres, former chairman of the Dayton-Hudson Corporation told the Harvard Business School Marketing Club, "that the very best businesses concentrate almost single-mindedly, on serving the customer. Pleasing customers," he said, "is an *obsession*. Service is an *obsession*. Quality is an *obsession*. Dependability is an *obsession*. Attention to detail is an *obsession*."[19]

His advice is dead-on for any service-driven business, healthcare included. The word *obsession* is the key. It implies not just a "lip service" promise to do these things, but rather a no-excuse, unswerving *commitment* to quality, service, dependability, and attention to detail.

For many practices, *growth* is king. For high performance healthcare practices, *excellence* is king.

➡**Hard learned lesson:** If excellence is a core value then it has to permeate the whole culture of your practice. Core values should live in the world of black and white, not shades of gray. When your core values are black and white, then everyone in your practice understands what's expected of them and you're much closer to doing what you say you're going to do 100 percent of the time.

Consider the fabled Four Seasons hotel chain, which has built a worldwide culture that puts the customer experience at the top of every employee's agenda.

"You must first decide what you stand for and then you must align every one of your systems to reinforce it," says John Young, recently retired human resources executive of Four Seasons. "You recruit for it, you select for it, you orient for it; you train for it, you reward it, you promote for it, and you terminate those who don't have it."[20]

58 Decide on the Importance of a Learning Culture

"When Sam Walton opened the first Wal-Mart in 1962, it wasn't that impressive," says Jeffrey A. Krames, author of *What the Best*

CEOs Know: 7 Exceptional Leaders and Their Lessons for Transforming Any Business. Walton knew that if his stores didn't become far better, they wouldn't last. "So his philosophy, 'Improve something every day,' wasn't just a worthy goal, but a necessity. Wal-Mart's key to improvement," Krames explains, "was to create a learning culture. By 2002, that culture had built Wal-Mart into not just the world's biggest retailer, but the world's biggest company." Among Walton's recommendations:

Hire people who love to learn. "Walton understood the importance of experience, but always looked for employees who shared his zest for business," says Krames. "If two candidates were reasonably comparable in their qualifications, he would choose the one who was hungry to learn, even if that person had had less relevant experience."[21]

By the same token, continuing education is also part of the culture of many healthcare practices. Unfortunately, this requirement comes as a surprise to many newly hired staff members who aren't prepared to give CE their time and effort—especially if it involves overnight travel.

➡**From the success files:** Nancy G. Torgerson, O.D., Lynnwood, Washington, whose practice is limited to vision therapy, looks for employees who have "enthusiasm, empathy and a love of learning."

➡**Action steps:** "Ideally, you should detail CE and associated travel expectations as part of the *hiring* process," says the *Dental Practice Advisor.* "You want staffers who make learning a personal and professional priority—and who consider CE part of their total compensation package. Be frank about your view of the responsibilities and rewards of CE, and insist on frankness in return. Explain your practice culture and ask questions such as:

- **How do your goals fit in with our practice vision?**
- **What goals have you recently pursued?**
- **What's the most valuable CE experience you've ever had?"**

"If someone doesn't show interest in these questions," says the *Dental Practice Advisor,* "or flatly states he or she doesn't care one way or the other—recognize that he or she will consider CE an *obligation*, not a benefit. At best, attendance will be half-hearted. At worst, that person will fight you or find excuses to actively avoid CE opportunities."[22]

➡**Reality check:** "Practices budget from \$500 to \$2,500 a year to cover CE for midlevel providers, according to the employment contracts from the Medical Group Management Association. Those amounts include travel and lodging expenses, and sometimes dues for professional organizations and costs for journal subscriptions. (In other contracts, paid dues and subscription costs are extra perks.) In addition, midlevels receive three to five days of paid time off for CE, unless it's factored into their overall vacation days."[23]

59 Begin the Search

To begin the search for employees who are compatible with the culture of your practice, first get a solid handle on the core values of your practice. Then when interviewing job applicants, ask questions and make observations that enable you to learn about their values, temperament, and job-related priorities.

"After the interview," says Dr. Kenneth R. James, Kent, Washington, "ask yourself whether the interviewee warrants a positive answer to these three questions:

- "Does he or she fit into our office culture?
- "Does his or her temperament suit those of the other people in our office?
- "Does he or she fit comfortably in our office environment?"[24]

If you make a mistake and hire team members who don't fit the culture of your practice, it will become readily apparent to everyone concerned—in which case, it's best to just cut your losses and move on.

➡**Reality check:** Most healthcare practices have unique cultures—in the same way that employees have job-related priorities. And these preferences are neither good nor bad; they're just different. Those differences are part of what makes some practices (and some employees) more or less attractive to one another.

60 Spell Out "The Way We Do Things Around Here"

Marvin Bower, former director of McKinsey & Company and considered the father of management consulting, has written that it's a manager's responsibility to spell out for employees "the way we do things around here" (which is an often used definition of "culture"). Bower's implied assumption is that unless you tell people what you want them to do and how you want them to do it, you have no right to expect them to infer, by some mysterious means, just what you have in mind.[25]

The following policy letter to a new office staff member illustrates Bower's principle.

Dear Chris,

Welcome aboard! We are pleased to welcome you to our healthcare team and want you to be part of our continued success. To that end, I want to take a minute to reiterate the reason for our being here. If you remember these principles, I guarantee that you will succeed at your job and reap the rewards. Remember:

- Above all, you are here to serve patients. Each of us is. The patient signs our paycheck.
- Our practice is built on medical quality and patient service. Strive for uncompromising quality in every phase of your job. Efficiency, precision, and attention to detail are all part of serving the patient.
- Every person who walks through our door—patient, postman, management consultant, sales representative—is an honored guest. Each of us is an ambassador of goodwill. We want you to astonish them with your courtesy, concern, and genuine caring for their comfort and well-being.
- Know your patients. Greet them by name and with a smile as soon as they walk through our door. Let them know you appreciate them.
- Handle any patient problems or complaints with the utmost courtesy, concern, and respect. Remember, the patient is our boss.

In short, we're all working for the same goals. If we apply these principles of patient satisfaction and professional excellence to our particular skills every day, there's no stopping us.

Again, I welcome you to our office and look forward to working with you for a long and rewarding future.

Sincerely,

Physician's Marketing (newsletter) San Francisco, CA, October 1986.

"When your staff can answer for you based on their deep belief that they know what you stand for, then they consider themselves your associate," says Dr. Irwin M. Becker, education chairman of the Pankey Institute, Key Biscayne, Florida. "They are not only taking the responsibility of their task, they take on your vision."[26]

➡**Reality check:** "Clarifying the value system and breathing life into it are the greatest contributions a leader can make," say Tom Peters and Robert Waterman in their classic management book, *In Search of Excellence.*[27]

61 It Starts at the Top

No matter what the core values of the practice are or how they are arrived at, it's the HCP who must take the lead in living those values and making the practice live up to them.

"It has to start with the doc," says Kenneth Hertz, an independent consultant with MGMA Healthcare Consulting Group. "If the doc doesn't live it and exemplify it, it will never happen. The staff tends to be a reflection of the physician culture in the practice. There's doing it and there's *really* doing it. If the doc shows up at 9 a.m. everyday when patients are scheduled at 8, why should staff think timeliness is important? What examples are you setting if you come in the door every day for 10 years and never say hello to anybody? How can you expect them to be compassionate with patients?"

"Physicians do not begin to understand the impact they can have on their staff," Hertz emphasizes. "When the physician shines his light on a staff member . . . the results are extraordinary. I have seen a staff that has gone through a long, long, long day. . . . and a doc will just walk around and say, 'I know it was a tough day. Thank you so much for all you did.' And it just lifts people up. You can literally see it. People actually straighten up."[28]

➡**Reality check:** Everything that really matters starts at the top: a commitment to excellence, kindness, courtesy, punctuality, ethics, enthusiasm, and trust. And, by the same token, employee engagement—the emotional connection that people have to their jobs and the organizations for which they work—also starts at the top.

Whether you're an HCP, a practice administrator, a manager, or a supervisor, your *personal* level of engagement will spur the engagement of others.

Think about it. Have you ever worked for someone who was truly engaged in what he or she did? How about someone who was disengaged? In each case, what was your level of effort, energy, and passion?

➡**Hard learned lesson:** "The leader's mood is for lack of a better word, catching," says Jack Welch, former chairman and CEO of General Electric. "You've seen the dynamic a hundred times. An upbeat manager who goes through the day with a positive outlook somehow ends up running a team organization filled with . . . well, upbeat people with positive outlooks. A pessimistic sourpuss somehow ends up with an unhappy tribe all his own."

"Unhappy teams," he adds, "have a tough time winning."[29]

62 Ownership Is the Key

"Major corporations are far ahead of hospitals in retaining employees," says Susan Osborne, R.N., M.S.N., M.B.A., director of inpatient services at Children's Healthcare of Atlanta, Georgia. "Southwest Airlines for example, has an outstanding track record for employee satisfaction and retention with annual turnover rate of a mere 6 percent. It is no coincidence that Southwest is also renowned for outstanding customer service and profitability in the airline industry."

"The Southwest culture includes a 'can-do' attitude and 'thinking like an owner,'" Osborne says. "Everyone pitches in to help, from the CEO to the pilots to the maintenance crew. Whatever needs to be done to get the plane off the ground and up in the air is the primary focus. The phrase, 'That's not my job,' is not in their vocabulary. Ownership is a state of mind. It is about caring, about becoming fully engaged in the active pursuit of organizational objectives."

"Owners are flexible; they bend rules to help the company," Osborne says. "They pay attention to details that others fail to notice and are willing to take action without being asked. Owners follow up on customer service issues and pick up trash that others have ignored or walked by hour after hour."[30]

63 Validate the Fit

Determining whether a job applicant is a good fit with the culture of your practice is, at best, a subjective process. The following are some ways suggested by Dr. Janice Presser, president and CEO of the Gabriel Institute, to help validate the fit:

- Do the employees deemed a good fit seem to get "on board" faster? Do they merge seamlessly into the organization's cultural mainstream and quickly learn how to work well within it?
- Do the people considered a good fit stay longer?
- Do these employees get better performance reviews?
- Are these employees good ambassadors for the practice?
- Does contact with these employees influence patients' views of the practice in a positive direction?
- Do employees considered a good fit have a greater influence on the organization's bottom line? No matter what they contribute, do they contribute more of it?

"Overall, the most important measures of employee fit," Presser says, "are the ones that make the most sense for your particular organization—the measures that have the strongest impact on whatever is most important to management."[31]

64 Hard Learned Lessons About Culture Fit

- "Although job fit is important," say Jim Harris, Ph.D. and Joan Brannick, Ph.D., co-authors of *Finding & Keeping Great Employees*, "culture fit determines whether someone is highly likely to remain with and be successful with the company. We see job fit as a minimum requirement for companies to be able to find and keep good employees. Focusing on job fit results in someone who can do the job. It does not, however, guarantee that the person wants to do the job or do it well."[32]
- Jim Brueggermann, M.D., a retired neurologist and currently a consultant based in Gordon, Wisconsin, says solid communication and a commitment to a team concept have been common characteristics of successful office cultures.

Promoting the idea that everyone's opinion is valued not only helps reduce errors, but also enhances an employee's sense of loyalty. "If there's a problem with the culture," he adds, "you have to go back to values. If people have discrepant values, you can't have a cohesive culture."[33]

- "Choosing the right physician is a more difficult and subtle task than just getting someone with an MD in the door," says Marc Greenwald, M.D., Chief Medical Officer at Fallon Clinic, a 250-physician multispecialty group practice in Worcester, Massachusetts. "The right physician is not only someone who can take good care of patients but also someone who fits in with the organization, its people, and goals. It's about your practice's culture."[34]
- "People want more than just material rewards," says Leigh Branham, author of *Keeping the People Who Keep You in Business*. "They want to believe their jobs are vital to the company's success. They don't just want 'something to do'; they want to 'do something.' What is that something that you and your associates want to do for your organization? Is the sense of meaning and purpose you create within your culture enough to attract new employees and then keep the right ones in place?"[35]

References

1. Durkin DM. *The Loyalty Advantage.* New York: AMACOM; 2005.
2. Deal TE, Kennedy AA. *Corporate Cultures: The Rites and Rituals of Corporate Life.* Reading, MA: Addison-Wesley; 1982.
3. Hickman CR. *Management Malpractice.* Avon, MA: Platinum Press; 2005.
4. Ibid.
5. Williams C. *Management,* 3rd ed. Mason, OH: South-Western College Publishing; 2005.
6. Whittlesey FE. CEO Herb Kelleher Discusses Southwest Airline's People Culture: How the Company Achieves Competitive Advantage from the Ground Up. *ACA* (American Compensation Association) *Journal,* Winter 1995, 8–24.
7. Councelman J. Driving Employee Engagement: What HR Can Do. http://www.ddiworld.com/directions/leadership_content.asp?id=387
8. Success Story: The Outer Banks Hospital Redefines Excellence in Healthcare. http://www.jacksonorganization.com/site/english
9. Collins JC, Porras JI. *Built to Last: Successful Habits of Visionary Companies.* New York: HarperCollins; 2002.

10. Sunoo BP. Results-Oriented Customer Service Training. *Workforce*, May 2001, 84–90.
11. Schlesinger L, Fromm B. *The Real Heroes of Business*. New York: Currency; 1994.
12. Lombardo FA. How to Keep Your Staff Smiling and Your Office Humming. *Medical Economics*, October 11, 1992, 179–185.
13. Citrin JM, Neff TJ. Doing the Right Things Right. *New York Times*, November 11, 1997, BU10.
14. Drucker P. *Management Tasks, Responsibilities, Practices*. New York: Harper & Row; 1973.
15. Collins JC, Porras JI. *Built to Last: Successful Habits of Visionary Companies*. New York: HarperCollins; 2002.
16. Blanchard K. How to Instill Passion in Your People. *MNWORLD*, American Management Association, Spring 2004.
17. Collins JC, Porras JI. *Built to Last: Successful Habits of Visionary Companies*. New York: HarperCollins; 2002.
18. O'Connor JP. Staff Retreats: Time for Reflection and Renewal. *Family Practice Management*, January 1998, 56–62.
19. A Customer Focus, *CPA Client Bulletin,* published by American Institute of Certified Public Accountants (AICPA), November 1984.
20. Reichheld F. *The Ultimate Question*. Boston: Harvard Business School Press; 2006.
21. Krames JA. *What the Best CEOs Know: 7 Exceptional Leaders and Their Lessons for Transforming Any Business*. New York: McGraw-Hill; 2005.
22. Advisory Publications. *Dental Practice Advisor*, October 2000, 7.
23. Lowes R. Practice Pointers: Your Staff Needs CME Too. *Medical Economics*, June 18, 2004.
24. James KR. Ask the Expert: How Can I Find the Right Employee? *Journal of the American Dental Association*, July 1999, 1101–1103.
25. Bower M. *The Will to Manage*. New York: McGraw-Hill; 1996.
26. Becker I. Building a Five-Star Practice. *California Dental Association Journal,* April 1995.
27. Peters T, Waterman Jr. RJ. *In Search of Excellence*. New York: Harper & Row; 1982.
28. Moore PL. Winning the (Office) Culture Wars. *Physicians Practice,* October 2005, 22–30.
29. Welch J, Welch S. *Winning*. New York: HarperCollins; 2005.
30. Osborne S. The Art of Rewarding and Retaining Staff—Part 1. *Nurse Leader*, June 2004, 49–51.
31. Presser J. Developing and Using a Job-Fit Standard. October 2005. http://www.shrm.org/ema/library_published/nonIC/CMS_014417.asp#TopOfPage
32. Harris J, Brannick J. *Finding & Keeping Great Employees*. New York: AMACOM; 1999.
33. Norbut M. Creating a Culture: How to Breed Success in Your Practice, July 4, 2005. http://www.ama-assn.org/amednews/2005/07/04/bisa0704.htm
34. Greenwald M. Finding Dr. "Right." *Physicians Practice*, October 2005, 34–35.
35. Branham L. *Keeping the People Who Keep You in Business*. New York: AMACOM; 2001.

Chapter Six

HIRING

Hiring Mistakes to Avoid

The cost of bad hires can far outweigh the extra costs spent on hiring the right people for your practice. In addition, people ill-suited to their jobs or your practice can wreak havoc—leading to costly errors, poor office morale, loss of patients, and daily stress for everyone. Inevitably, such employees either quit or are let go. This is bound to happen occasionally—even with the most competent of interviewers. However, *frequent staff turnover* can be extremely disruptive to the day-to-day operation of a practice.

This chapter addresses some of the most common and potentially costly mistakes of hiring.

65 Hiring Mistake #1

The #1 mistake is hiring under pressure. The bind is a familiar one: You're overworked and understaffed. The pool of applicants is small, perhaps just a handful. Out of desperation, you take the best of the batch. I call this the "buy now—pay later" approach.

"Some managers claim they don't have the time to select just the right person for the team," says Marcus Buckingham, author of *The One Thing You Need to Know*. "I have openings now, they say, and these openings must be filled. Good managers know the folly of this approach. They know that, when it comes to building the right team, time is nonnegotiable. You will spend the time. The only question is where you will spend it: on the front end, carefully selecting the right person, or on the back end, desperately trying to reform the person into who you wished he or she was in the first place."[1]

➡**Recommendation:** Don't compromise your standards for the sake of expediency. Hang in there until you can find the right person. Perhaps an employment agency can provide a temporary employee or a previous employee can be called to fill in. Employees who know each others' jobs may be able to take up the slack and allow you to keep looking.

An added thought: If the salary plus benefits you're offering are less than the going rate in your area, that might explain the small pool of applicants. A higher salary and perhaps more flexible benefits may produce more and better qualified applicants.

66 Hiring Mistake #2

The second mistake is placing too much emphasis on technical competence.

Nearly 50 percent of newly hired employees fail within 18 months because of poor interpersonal skills, according to a three-year study by Leadership IQ, a global leadership training and research company. Results were compiled after studying 5,247 hiring managers from 312 organizations. Collectively, these managers hired more than 20,000 employees during the study period.

The study found that 26 percent of new hires fail because they can't accept feedback, 23 percent because they're unable to under-stand and manage emotions, 17 percent because they lack the necessary motivation to excel, 15 percent because they have the wrong temperament for the job, and 11 percent because they lack the necessary technical skills.

"The typical interview process fixates on ensuring that new hires are technically competent," says Mark Murphy, CEO of Leadership IQ. "But hiring failures could be prevented if managers focus more on the candidate's coachability, emotional intelligence, motivation and temperament," he added.

"Technical competence remains the most popular subject of interviews because it's easy to assess," Murphy noted. "But it's a lousy predictor of whether a newly hired employee will succeed or fail. Do technical skills really matter if the employee alienates co-workers, lacks drive, and has the wrong personality for the job?"[2]

67 More Hiring Mistakes

Succumbing to the "halo effect": This refers to the tendency to be so dazzled by one quality of a candidate (e.g., computer literacy, appearance, knowledge of health insurance, friendliness) that you lose sight of the job's other requirements.

Wishful thinking: This is closely related to the halo effect. It arises because of a desperate need to hire someone and, as a result, leads you to overlook traits that under different circumstances would disqualify the job applicant. Remind yourself of the costs and aggravation involved in a bad hire.

Overselling the job: Wanting to hire a highly qualified applicant may lead to promises about job responsibilities, salary increases, vacations, and so on, that can't be kept—or if kept, would lead to a staff mutiny.

➡**Recommendation:** Don't oversell a job by promising more than you can deliver or, conversely, by downplaying the negative aspects of a job. When the facts become known, a new employee will either become demotivated or quit. Face the facts: A job *is* what it is. One solution: Rethink the position. Can the appealing aspects of the job be broadened? Can less desirable aspects be traded or possibly divided among other employees or perhaps outsourced?

➥**Hiring someone who is overqualified:** There are obvious positives to having a highly qualified person on board. Consider, however, the negatives:

- Potential turnover because the person accepting the job in a bad job market will most likely leave for a better job as soon as the market changes.
- The person will lose motivation very quickly because the job will become old.
- Others in the practice, perhaps the person's supervisor, may feel threatened by his or her presence and experience.

➥**Recommendation:** If the environment and the applicant's job-related needs are a good fit with your practice, then try to make the job more interesting and challenging by giving a highly qualified person more responsibility and/or authority fairly quickly.

68 Major Mistake: Thinking It's an Entry-Level Job

"Receptionists are the front-line and first impression at hectic internal medicine practices," says Bryan Walpert writing in the *ACP Observer* (American College of Physicians). "With the growth of managed care, receptionists' jobs have become more complex and harried. They deal with more forms, more calls for authorizations and, because managed care plans use primary care physicians as a first contact, more patients are seeking referrals."[3]

The role of receptionists has also become more important. "If internists are gatekeepers to specialists, then receptionists are the gatekeepers to the internal medicine practices," says Lynn Statz Lazzaro, a healthcare consultant with Walpert, Smullian & Blumenthal, a CPA and management consulting firm in Baltimore, Maryland.[4]

➥**Reality check:** The job of receptionist in a healthcare facility is anything but an entry-level job, as some HCPs unfortunately view it. Their responsibilities can include accurate data entry, insurance verification, appointment scheduling, telephone triage, patient flow management, and complaint resolution—in addition to their role as the official "greeter" for the practice.

➥**From the success files:** A midwest oncologist, realizing how apprehensive many of his patients are when first calling his office, decided such calls (as well as those from referring physicians) must be handled with the utmost diplomacy and skill. And, he concluded, the people most likely to have the training, experience, and personality traits needed for the job were airline flight attendants. They have the know-how to deal with emergencies of all kinds. They also have great people skills, are hard-working, are quick to learn, and are used to on-the-job teamwork.

He found the perfect candidate who, after years of international travel, was ready to settle down. Her salary compared to the standard pay for a medical receptionist is significantly higher. "But," he said, "It's the best investment I've ever made in my practice."

➥**Action step:** "Consider offering a few thousand dollars more than the average salary for your area," writes Bryan Walpert. "It will cut your after-tax income by only a few hundred dollars a month."[5]

"If that's what it takes to have a first class person representing you at the front desk, it's worth it," says C. David Carpenter, partner with PCSi Healthcare Consultants in Southern Pines, North Carolina.[6]

➥**Hard learned lessons:** "Hire the best," says management consultant Dr. Charles Blair, Charlotte, North Carolina. "Top practices always recruit the highest quality employees, even though they cost a little more. Despite the higher cost, they represent an excellent value since their productivity far exceeds that received from cheaper, but more mediocre employees."[7]

69 Misreading the Signs

Even though you may take a structured, methodical approach to interviewing job applicants, the evaluation is still, in the end, a subjective process. You can neutralize some of that subjectivity by avoiding the following:

- Being misled by your initial impression of a job applicant. This is a time when many job applicants are nervous and ill at ease. Once rapport is established, however, the discomfort usually disappears.

- Being overly impressed with maturity or experience or (conversely) overly unimpressed by youth and immaturity.
- Mistaking a quiet, reserved, or calm demeanor for a lack of motivation.
- Mistaking a person's ability to speak glibly for intelligence or competence.
- Allowing a personal bias to influence your evaluation. For example, you may judge someone harshly because he or she reminds you of someone you dislike.
- Failing to factor a person's motivation and eagerness to learn into your overall evaluation.

➡**Reality check:** First impressions of job applicants (based on emotion, bias, chemistry, personality, and all sorts of stereotypes) are largely about style. Style, or the lack of it, often has more impact on hiring than substance. We hire people whose style we like—and are often disappointed. We reject people who don't seem to have any style—and then never know what we missed. The real problem is that once we accept or reject a candidate, the evaluation process shuts down. The quicker this happens, the less new information we seek and process. We still go through the motions of asking questions, but we then either use the answers to support our first impressions or ignore them if they seem to conflict.

➡**Action step:** Heed the old adage: Hire slowly. Fire fast.

70 Making a Poor First Impression

In a study by Beatrice Kalisch, Ph.D., a professor at the University of Michigan's School of Nursing, 10 R.N.s were sent as "undercover" nurse job applicants to 122 U.S. acute care facilities with high nurse vacancy rates. These nurses were already employed as staff nurses in other hospitals. What she discovered was "an astounding number of problems" with these hospitals' hiring systems, particularly with the recruiting and interviewing processes. Even at institutions with as many as 400 vacant nursing positions, candidates struggled to get a job interview and faced unwelcoming recruiters.

Candidates' interactions with recruiters, either human resources or nurse management personnel, were central to whether or not they would choose to accept a job offer. In particular, Kalisch discovered that candidates were more likely to take a job if the recruiter displayed positive interactions. Unfortunately, many failed to do so.

Among other frustrations, applicants felt the hospitals demonstrated an off-putting culture, such as rudeness, unresponsiveness, and general lack of professionalism.

The study also revealed:

- Merely 43 percent of respondents said the recruiter seemed to be listening. Only 37 percent said the recruiter made eye contact with them, and just 36 percent said the recruiter was helpful.
- Only 59 percent of respondents said their recruiter was informed or prepared, and only 58 percent said their recruiter was friendly.
- The result: Only 29 percent of applicants said they would definitely "choose to interview with this hospital if [they] were in a real-life situation."[8]

➡**Hard learned lesson:** When it comes to nurse recruiting, first impressions are lasting impressions.

➡**From the success files:** "The Starbucks Corporation has devised all sorts of ways to add personal touches to the way it hires," says William C. Taylor, founding editor of *Fast Company.* "Whenever possible, job interviews include coffee-tasting sessions, in which Starbuck veterans discuss the various blends with applicants. A 'candidate bill of rights' emphasizes the recruiters use phone calls and handwritten notes over form response letters, set goals for how quickly applicants should hear back and encourages recruiters to send out Starbucks gift cards in nominal amounts as goodwill gestures whether or not an applicant gets a job offer."[9]

"Our aim is to treat our candidates as well as we treat our customers and to do something memorable for them," says Jason S. Warner, director of North American recruiting for Starbucks. "You can't treat people shabbily, especially in a world where there are far more open jobs than there is available talent to fill them. We strive to put the humanity back into the recruiting experience."[10]

⓻⓵ Over-Negotiating the Job Offer

Most job applicants aren't comfortable haggling about their worth. They want you to make an offer that both of you consider fair and reasonable. They don't want to feel that you are trying to hire them for the lowest possible dollar. Many say they'd rather work for someone else.

Additionally, although it's theoretically impossible in a free-market economy to hire someone at too low a salary, it happens. It happens because of job applicants' ignorance of their economic worth, because they are desperate, or because they've been oversold on the benefits of working for your practice. And what happens when they learn they've been taken advantage of? They leave. Or worse, they stay and take their resentment out in numerous ways—none of which are good for your practice.

⓻⓶ Not Being Realistic About Compensation

In many cases, a position's salary range is inadequate to attract the caliber of person required. This leads to frustrating interviews, rejected job offers, and either the hiring of a candidate without the necessary qualifications or (worse) the hiring of a qualified person at a salary lower than what he or she is worth.

What are the reasons for unrealistic salary offers?

- A departing employee was paid a below-market salary and the new salary is based on the old.
- Using cost accounting methods, salaries are based on "averages." Problems arise, however, when an ideal person for the job is not an "average" person or the position itself is not an "average" position.
- Salary guidelines are used with the objective of holding costs down.
- An attempt is made to maintain parity between this position and another position in the practice where the incumbent is underpaid because he or she has held the job for a long time.

How is the problem best solved?

➥**Action step:** Let the marketplace determine salaries. If this indicates that the practice's entire compensation program is in need of an overhaul, then that problem must be solved before the one of recruiting new employees can be addressed.

➥**Hard learned lesson:** "Don't make the mistake of paying employees less than your competitors or settling for less-qualified candidates to save a few bucks," says Bob Vidal, writing for *The Patient Centered HIV/HCV Practice*. "If your compensation package targets the lower 50 percent of the market, you would most likely require more people to do the tasks of a better-qualified individual and commit more management time or spend more dollars in staff training. Your practice will become a 'feeder' to the higher paying practices in your market— that is, you will hire and train inexperienced people, only to have them leave your practice when they gain the experience."[11]

73 Failure to Discuss Expectations

"Perhaps the greatest cause of failure of new hires," say Sam Deep and Lyle Sussman in their book, *Power Tools*, "is that people begin assignments without a complete understanding of what is expected of them. When you interview job applicants," they advise, "make sure your expectations are known in order to help prospects decide whether the position is one in which they can thrive."[12]

"Managers must clearly communicate the skills, behaviors and performance levels that employees are expected to demonstrate," says Courtney Price, Ph.D., and Alys Novak, M.B.S., co-authors of *The Medical Practice Performance Management Manual: How to Evaluate Employees,* 2nd edition. "When you communicate clear, understandable and agreeable expectations to your employees, you are creating an environment where employees can succeed. It is only in this type of environment where the organization will reach its goals, employee morale will be high, and hard work will be noticed and recognized."[13]

See Chapter 10 for a further discussion of *mutual expectations.*

74 Off-Limits Interview Questions

"Job interviews present a minefield of legal problems," states a *Memo to Managers* from the National Institute of Business Management. "One wrong question could spark a discrimination suit. That's why you should never 'wing it' during interviews. Instead, create a list of interview questions and make sure every question asks for job-related information that will help in the selection process.

"Federal and state laws prohibit discrimination on the basis of an applicant's race, color, national origin, religion, sex, age or disability. Some state laws also prohibit discrimination based on factors such as marital status or sexual orientation. If you ask a job applicant a question specifically relating to one of these characteristics, you've broken the law and are subject to being sued, as is the company."

"Every question you ask," the memo goes on to say, "should somehow relate to this central theme: *How are you qualified to perform the job for which you are applying?* Managers usually land in trouble when they ask for information that's irrelevant to a candidate's ability to do the job."[14]

75 Hard Learned Lessons About Hiring

Here are additional hiring mistakes shared by HCPs and office managers who in many cases learned about them the hard way.

- Never hire someone whose first question is, "What are the benefits?"
- Never hire someone you can't fire—such as friends and relatives.
- Don't telegraph correct responses to job applicants. This happens when you ask yes/no questions. Even a simple question such as, "Can you work overtime?" telegraphs your expected response. Body language such as nodding your head also indicates you're getting the response you want. For best results, use closed-ended questions no more than 10 percent of the time and carefully monitor your body language.
- A person with an extensive self-employment background is very likely to go back to self-employment.
- Beware of job applicants who reveal confidential information about former employers, practices, or patients. You'll be next.
- Beware of a history of "job hopping." Three jobs in five years may be too many unless the changes show a sensible pattern such as higher pay or more responsibility.

- As certain as you might be that you've found the perfect candidate, resist the temptation to hire somebody on the spot—unless you've been unable to fill the job for a long time and delay could jeopardize your chances of hiring the person. In general, though, it's always good to give yourself a day or two to make sure you're not overlooking faults that could later surface. The best approach: Let the candidate know you're interested and ask for a day or two to make the final decision.
- Don't ignore intuition. As objective as hiring needs to be, one should not ignore that "tug" inside that says "something just doesn't feel right here." Often this comes from your past experience and facts you've had to face through the years. Listen to that inner voice.

76 Failure to Do a Background Check

Another common and potentially costly mistake is the tendency to hire a new employee without first checking the details of his or her background—especially when the person truly impresses you during the interview. As a result, corners are cut, guidelines are overlooked, and unscrupulous people can sometimes slip through the cracks.

Although résumés are intended to provide factual, objective information about a job applicant's education, experience, and qualifications, too often they are sugar-coated with exaggerations, distortions, and outright lies.

➡**Reality check:** A startling 44 percent of all résumés are inaccurate, according to Eric Boden, president and CEO of HireRight, a Web-based employment-screening company based in Irvine, California. The inaccuracies could be white lies such as listing a volunteer position never held, or major whoppers such as lying about former jobs or certifications never earned. And often the people who pad their résumés are the people you'd least expect.[15]

➡**Action step:** "All employees should be subject to a standard background screening that includes a credit check; a review of motor vehicle and criminal records; reference checks; and verification of employment, education and professional licenses, and Social Security number," says Les Rosen, attorney and president of Employment Screening Resources in Novato, California. "However," Rosen adds, "it is perfectly acceptable to have different levels of screening for different positions as long as everyone is treated *fairly*."[16]

➡**Reality check #2:** "In this era of employer-related litigation, do not be surprised if employers are unwilling to be candid with you regarding your potential/their former employee," says attorney Joan M. Roediger. "If you hit a brick wall when checking references, ask the former employer 'Would you hire this employee back?' and listen carefully to the tenor of the conversation to try and discern the employer's feelings about your job candidate."[17]

If, for example, the reference confirms the applicant's clerical skills, but refuses to discuss her integrity, he may be trying to tell you something without actually saying it—on advice of his attorney.

➡**Avoid entanglements:** Although many medical practices do reference checks without permission, Ruth Lander, a practice administrator at Columbus (Ohio) Oncology, notes that special care must be taken when checking references to avoid legal entanglements. Her practice uses a release signed by job applicants that permits the practice to contact both personal references and former employers. "With the release, we can go into more depth than we could otherwise. Of course, you need to have a rock-solid release," Lander says. "Asking applicants to sign such a release serves an additional purpose. The release, in itself, is a screening mechanism for applicants. Job candidates who have past problems often choose to back off at this point," she says.[18]

➡**Hard learned lesson:** "Anyone who avoids checking employees," says Chris Mathers, vice president of KPMG Forensic, Inc. in Toronto, Canada, "does so at his or her own peril."[19]

➡**Resources**
The following guidebooks provide information on pre-employment investigations with sample forms, reference sources, and federal and state laws and agencies:

> *The Employer's Legal Handbook* by Fred S. Steingold, available from Nolo at http://www.nolo.com

25 Essential Lessons for Employee Management by Dennis L. DeMay from Facts on Demand Press at http://www.brbpub.com/books

References

1. Buckingham M. *The One Thing You Need to Know*. New York: Free Press; 2005.
2. Short Takes: Poor Interpersonal Skills Doom Many Hires. *Expansion Management*, November 2005, 2.
3. Walpert B. Tips for Finding and Keeping a Good Receptionist. *ACP Observer*, January 1998.
4. Ibid.
5. Walpert B. Problems with Patients? Fine-Tune Your Front Desk. *ACP-ASIM Observer,* March 2001.
6. Ibid.
7. Blair CW. How Top Practices Reduce Labor Costs. *Blair/McGill Advisory*, April 1998, 3–4.
8. Kalisch B. Recruiting Nurses: The Problem Is the Process. *Journal of Nursing Administration,* September 2003, 468–477.
9. Taylor WC. To Hire Sharp Employees, Recruit in Sharp Ways. *New York Times*, April 23, 2006, BU3.
10. Ibid.
11. Vidal B. The Secrets to Retaining Talent. *The Patient-Centered HIV/HCV Practice*, March 2004, 3–4.
12. Deep S, Sussman L. *Power Tools*. Reading, MA: Addison Wesley; 1998.
13. Price C, Novak A. *The Medical Practice Performance Management Manual: How to Evaluate Employees,* 2nd ed. Englewood, CO: Medical Group Management Association; 2002.
14. National Institute of Business Management. *Memo to Managers*. McLean, VA: National Institute of Business Management; March 2005.
15. Caudron S. Who Are You Really Hiring? *Workforce*, November 2002, 28–32.
16. Ibid.
17. Roediger JM. Smart Hiring for Physician Practices. *Physician's News Digest,* October 2003.
18. Beyer DJ. The Key Question of Job References. *Podiatry Management*, February 2006, 165–167.
19. Caudron S. Who Are You Really Hiring? *Workforce*, November 2002, 28–32.

Chapter Seven

HIRING

The New World
of Work

The majority of employed Americans feel deprived of time. According to Families and Work Institute's 2002 National Study of the Changing Workforce:

- 67 percent of employed parents said they don't have enough time with their children.
- 63 percent of married employees said they don't have enough time with their husbands or wives, up from 50 percent in 1992.
- In 2002, the only year in which the question was asked, 55 percent of all employees said they don't have enough time for themselves.

As a result, whole new phrases have entered our vocabularies to describe these feelings: the time crunch, the time bind, the time squeeze, the 24/7 economy, and the everytime-everyplace workplace.[1]

➡**Reality check:** One of the ways to help employees cope with these new world work/life conflicts is flexible work arrangements—the subject of this chapter.

77 The Rise of Caregiving

As previously mentioned in Chapter 3, the National Alliance for Caregiving (NAC) and AARP have reported that nearly one in four households, about 22.9 million nationally, is involved with eldercare. About 21 percent of the adult population or 44.4 million Americans provide unpaid care to an adult family member, according to the study. A rapidly graying population guarantees that the ranks of caregivers will grow. By 2011, 1 in 10 employed workers is expected to be involved in caregiving, according to data quoted in a report from the MetLife Mature Market Institute.[2]

As compelling as these statistics sound, the truth is that HCPs are just beginning to come to grips with the caregiver's role and its ability to completely transform an employee's daily routine and quality of life. Over a third of the caregivers surveyed by NAC and AARP said that on a five-point scale, where five is very stressful, caregiving rates a four or five.

The problem is most pronounced for women, who tend to be the primary caregivers for elderly or ailing relatives and who may suddenly find themselves balancing childcare, eldercare, and a demanding healthcare job simultaneously. More than 6 in 10 working caregivers said that they had to make some adjustment to their work life, according to a report entitled "Caregiving in the United States."

➡**Reality check:** In the years ahead, people are going to take care of their parents longer than their children.

➡**Action steps:** Work/life-friendly workplaces exist only if the prevailing atmosphere is one of respect for the employees. Alice Campbell, director of Work/Life Initiatives at Baxter International, says workplace support is "not about giving every employee the same thing. . . . Some have children, some have elderly parents or aunts or uncles, some have a spouse with cancer. What [the workplace] can do is help everyone recognize three key ingredients: respect, balance and flexibility. It still comes down to every manager and every peer to make it happen."[3]

78 Time Off

By a margin of almost two to one, respondents in a national survey by the Harris Poll said they'd rather have more time off than be paid more money.[4]

The average employee works almost two more hours a week than in 1982, according to the Bureau of Labor Statistics. Over the same period, the percentage of married couples who both work has risen to 47 percent from 39 percent, putting even more time pressures on families.[5]

Given these trends, something has to give, and for many employees that something is sleep. Almost half of the respondents in the Harris survey said they logged six hours of sleep or less each night.[6]

➡**Solution:** One of the emerging trends for engaging time-pressured employees is flexibility in working hours, such as time off from work—which can take many shapes and forms.

➡**From the success files:** A reasonable number of days off will not only keep employees content and loyal to your practice, but also combat burnout and increase productivity.

"Internist Jeffrey Kagan, Newington, Connecticut, recommends 10 sick days, eight paid holidays, and 5 to 15 days of vacation (depending on years of employment). Others prefer to provide a set number of days off to be used at the discretion of the employee."[7]

Deanna Perzan, office manager of NovaCare Rehabilitation in Baltimore, Maryland, says, "I like the concept of lumping all time off in one category. For example, 21 days' total leave can be used as vacation, personal time or sick time. Employees will use less sick time because they don't feel they have to use it up under a 'use it or lose it' rule."[8]

"Many of our people are raising families and have urgent needs," says W. James Stackhouse, an internist in a three-physician office in Goldsboro, North Carolina. "A son bumps his head on the school playground and they need to leave. We're flexible enough to handle that in most cases. Our office understands."[9]

See Chapter 15 for a discussion of paid time off (PTO).

79 Flexible Schedules Attract Quality Staff

The country's labor pool is increasingly made up of those who wish to work nontraditional schedules. As just described, some employees are caregivers. Some might want to get home by 3 o'clock to meet their children after school—or need time off to attend school plays, soccer games, and parent–teacher conferences. So called "morning people" might like to start at 7 a.m. And still others might just prefer and can afford to work only part time.

Flexible working hours (called flextime) mean allowing employees to work other than the standard office hours. As a rule, all employees are required to be present during the "core" or busiest hours of the practice. The core time is usually a set number of hours in the morning and afternoon; for example, from 8:30 a.m. to 11:30 a.m. and from 1:30 p.m. to 4:30 p.m. The office may be open longer than from 8:30 until 4:30, but employees may, according to their individual circumstances, choose to start work anytime between 7:30 and 8:30 and stop between 4:30 and 5:30. For example, they may arrive up to an hour before the core time and leave any time after the core hours, provided their job function is covered and they have worked an eight-hour day. The above schedule includes a mid-day flextime such as 11:30 a.m. to 1:30 p.m. that permits staggered lunch breaks.

Flextime can be utilized for a number of positions in a healthcare practice that are not time-sensitive. Filing insurance claims, collections follow-up, transcription, secretarial, bookkeeping, and accounting functions are examples. Allowing employees the flexibility to perform these tasks at different times of the day, provided the duties are satisfactorily accomplished, can help attract and retain quality staff.

Edward Norman, an internist and president of Big Thompson Medical Group PC, a 45-physician multispecialty group in Loveland, Colorado, says that nurses and other office staff work in small groups to decide how to cover hours if one employee needs extra time off.

"It works much better that way," Norman says. "As long as the employees like each other and as long as the work gets done, it's fine."

"Other practices have found success in staggering employee schedules," reports Mike Norbut in amednews.com. "If an office is open from 8 a.m. to 6 p.m., you could have some employees start at

7:30 a.m. and leave early, while others start the day at 10:30 or 11 a.m. and work until the office closes."

"Consultants also suggest rewarding employees who cover shifts for their co-workers," Norbut adds, "and working out deals with those leaving early to stay longer on days they are more available. Perhaps an employee who works six hours on Mondays can work 10 hours on Tuesdays."

"Overall, the key is to be open to finding a creative solution," says Pat O'Sullivan, president of O'Sullivan Consulting Group in Medina, Ohio. "If you show you're considerate and fair with everybody, they'll buy in."[10]

Of course, some types of practices are more suited to flextime than others. For example, solo or small practices with only a few employees have a limited degree of flexibility. Medium to large groups with more employees may find flextime more appropriate.

➡**From the success files:** "The physicians and administrators at Greenville Medical Center in Pennsylvania understand the importance of offering flexible schedules," says Theresa Defino, an editor for *Physicians Practice*. "Several physicians have job-share arrangements, as do administrative staff members. In addition, the entire 24-person billing department is on flex scheduling, an arrangement that appeals to both younger and older employees."[11]

➡**Benefits of Flextime**
- It reduces the strain on time-pressured employees and results in improved morale, greater productivity, and increased loyalty to the practice.
- It can increase the pool of qualified job applicants who otherwise might not be available. It also helps retain valuable employees because they can adjust their hours to meet personal needs instead of having to use leave or resign.
- It may enable employees to commute during nonpeak hours, making their trips less time-consuming and stressful.
- Periods of peak activity and less busy times are better managed so that more work can be done in the same number of hours.

- Employees feel more control over part of their work environment so they are more satisfied with their work. Improved satisfaction and morale result in greater productivity.
- The workplace can be improved at no cost. In some cases, overtime costs can be reduced or eliminated through improved work planning and scheduling while increasing office hours.

➡**Reality check:** Recognize that flextime isn't a perk. It's a strategic tool that takes planning and adjustment to properly set up. Thought must be given to supervisory arrangements, adequate staffing, communication, and coordination and completion of work assignments.

80 Give Flexible Schedules a Trial Period

As the new schedule is started, be sure your employees understand that within reason, individuals can determine what time they come to work, how long a lunch period they take, and what time they leave work. All of this is done with the proviso that they meet the requirements of the core practice time and a set number of hours worked during the week.

Three months should be ample time to determine whether the program is successful. During this time, don't wait for problems to occur. Clear up any minor troubles before they become full blown. Toward the end of the trial period, ask your staff to evaluate the program with written questions such as the following:

- Are you happy with the flexible work schedule?
- Do you feel it relieves the stress of getting to work on time?
- Has it permitted you to deal more easily with bus or train schedules, car pools, daycare or eldercare responsibilities, etc.?
- Have flexible hours been helpful as far as your work is concerned?
- Can the flexible work schedule be improved? If so, how?

81 Job Sharing

Healthcare practices have a number of positions, both clinical and clerical, that lend themselves to job sharing, in which two employees split the responsibilities of a single position. The key to this option is good communication between the two employees who become responsible for the total duties required, working out between themselves such details as coverage, vacation, and sickness arrangements.

Human resource managers agree that retaining skilled employees may be the major benefit of job sharing to employers. "But job sharers are also more loyal," says Carol Sladek, a work/life consultant for Hewitt Associates in Lincolnshire, Illinois. "People are very grateful for this kind of flexibility and are willing to go the extra mile," she says.[12]

Such loyalty can also translate into better coverage and productivity than one full-time employee can provide. When a job sharer is out sick or on vacation, the other partner may be able to step in. And job sharers typically schedule medical appointments and other personal business on their own time.

The most preferred arrangement is a consecutive week of work starting on Wednesday and continuing until the following Tuesday. That way, each person is at work every week and gets a nice break on weekends. There isn't the two-day lull with one person dropping everything on Friday and the other having to pick everything up on Monday. It also breaks up the holiday schedule and means that one person won't get all the Fridays off.

There are, however, other ways to split a job. Some job sharers work three days each week with an overlap on Wednesday. Others will split right down the middle, overlapping during their Wednesday lunch hour to fill each other in on what's been done and what's still pending.

Yet another variation—even though it's seldom used—has one person work mornings and the other afternoons. This schedule can have problems when one or both individuals have long commuting distances.

Regardless of how the job is split, most job sharers suggest some time of overlap, whether it be an hour or a day, to facilitate continuity.

➡**From the success files:** Job sharing is one way to create more flexibility, says Carol Gilchrist, a nurse and medical office manager in Chelmsford, Massachusetts. "One of the things we recently did to fill a position with less than desirable hours (2 to 5:30 pm, 2 to 7 pm, and Saturdays from 8 am to noon) was to find two mothers of patients in our pediatric practice who together agreed to fill those spots. They work out their schedules and let us know who is working which days. This has turned out very well for us and for them."[13]

➥**Reality check:** "Job sharers must have the same priorities, the same job standards, and be able to communicate and be committed to communicating," says Jo Pierce, senior employee-relations manager at Steelcase Inc., Grand Rapids, Michigan. "You must have a partner who is compatible. If you don't have the same urgency to work, job sharing won't work."[14]

82 Compressed Workweek

Compressed workweeks allow employees to condense their hours into fewer days by working more hours per day; for example, either four days per week or nine days over a two-week period. For example:

Compressed workweek = Employee works four 10-hour days						
Weekly Schedule	Mon	Tues	Wed	Thurs	Fri	Total Hrs
Regular	8 hrs	8 hrs.	8 hrs	8 hrs	8 hrs	40 hrs
Compressed	10 hrs	10 hrs	10 hrs	10 hrs	0 hrs	40 hrs

Compressed workweeks are appropriate in situations in which employees do not need to keep pace with incoming work on a daily basis or where there are several employees to do the same job.

Advantages include:

- Employees have blocks of time off work.
- Employees can arrange schedules to accommodate family needs.
- Employees have longer periods of time away from work with no reduction in pay.
- There is less commuting time; hours scheduled can avoid peak traffic times.
- The employer can control overtime and optimize staffing levels.
- Departments can provide expanded hours of service.
- The use of equipment and technology is maximized.

→**Reality check:** The potential downside of a compressed workweek is the possibility that long work days will fatigue employees, cause stress, and cause a decline in productivity.

83 Telecommuting

Telecommuting continues to grow in popularity as a tool for attracting and keeping a workforce that wants flexibility. "It's a great answer to reduce commutes and address employees' needs to care for their families," say Courtney Price, Ph.D. and Alys Novak, M.B.A., co-authors of *The Medical Practice Performance Manual: How to Evaluate Employees,* 2nd edition.

"It also addresses social concerns such as congested highways and pollution. For some organizations, telecommuting broadens their pool of job applicants because it removes geographic boundaries of employees capable of performing quality work from a distance. Other organizations have found that telecommuting also reduces stress in the workplace and that employee productivity is up along with the quality of their work.

"Winston-Salem, North Carolina-based Novant Health offers job-sharing and telecommuting for jobs that allow it, like medical coding, transcription and billing. The hospital's family-friendly benefits are important to employee retention."[15]

→**Resource**
The Medical Group Management Association's book, *Tracking Hot HR Trends*, offers a policy guideline and issues to consider before offering telecommuting or telework options to employees.

84 Reality Check About Flexible Work Arrangements

"In a 2005 study titled 'Making Flexibility Work: What Managers Have Learned About Implementing Reduced-Load Work,' professors at Michigan State University in East Lansing found that productivity and team effectiveness soared at companies that responded creatively to the demand for flexibility."

"'Just because an employee works long hours doesn't necessarily mean that he or she is productive,' said Ellen Ernst Kossek, a professor of labor and industrial relations at the university and one of the authors of the study. 'Sometimes a flexible work schedule or slightly fewer hours can do wonders for an employee's effectiveness and desire to get involved.'"[16]

The kinds of flexible work arrangements discussed in this chapter send an important message to employees—that the organizations for which they work know they have lives outside work and want to make their lives easier so they'll have less stress and more energy when they are at work.

Fortune's annual list of the "100 Best Companies to Work For in America," for example, includes the following breakdown of flexible work arrangements:

Benefit	Number Offering
Flexible schedules	70
Job sharing	72
Telecommuting	87
Compressed workweek	89
Reduced summer hours	45

The healthcare professions have many compensations that may well override the appeal of these flexible work arrangements. Nevertheless, you are depending on a job applicant's priorities, competing with organizations like these in the war for talent.

References

1. Galinsky E, Bond JT, Hill EJ. A Status Report on Workplace Flexibility: Who Has It? Who Wants It? What Difference Does It Make? http://familiesandwork. org/3w/research/status.html
2. Aschkenasy J. Eldercare Grows Up. *Financial Planning,* September 2005, 125–128.
3. Warner F. People Who Need People. *Working Mother,* August/September 2002, 27–28.
4. McClain DL. Forget the Raise, Give Me Some Time Off. *New York Times,* July 12, 2000, G-1.
5. Ibid.

6. Ibid.
7. Krohn T. Hiring and Keeping Good Clerical Staff. *Medical Economics*, January 11, 2002, 51.
8. Ibid.
9. Walpert B. Tips for Finding and Keeping a Good Receptionist. *ACP Observer*, January 1998.
10. Norbut M. Meet Flex-Hour Requests with Consistency. http://www.ama-assn.org/amednews/2003/08/25/bica0825.htm
11. Defino T. Hiring Young. *Physicians Practice,* March 2006, 85–88.
12. Hirschman C. Share and Share Alike. *HR Magazine*, September 2005, 52–57.
13. Krohn T. Hiring and Keeping Good Clerical Staff. *Medical Economics*, January 11, 2002, 51.
14. Verespej MA. The New Workweek. *Industry Week*, November 6, 1999, 11–21.
15. Price C, Novak A. *The Medical Practice Performance Manual: How to Evaluate Employees,* 2nd ed. Englewood, CO: Medical Group Management Association; 2002.
16. Villano M. Nine to Five, and Then Some. *New York Times*, April 16, 2006, BU8.

Section Two

"Management is getting people to do what needs to be done. Leadership is getting people to want to do what needs to be done. Managers push. Leaders pull. Managers command. Leaders communicate."

—Warren Bennis, distinguished professor of business administration at the University of Southern California's Marshall School of Business

Chapter Eight

MANAGING

Hard Learned Lessons About Motivation

The law of individual differences states that no two people are alike. They have different needs, different skills, different attitudes, and different motivational triggers. There's no one management style that works across the board. No pat answers. What works with one employee may have a negative effect on another.

HCPs who are aware of these varied needs will better understand the seemingly contradictory behavior of a newly hired, bright, energetic, ambitious person who loses interest in his or her work and perhaps quits—even though he or she is well paid.

➟**Hard learned lesson:** The more you can identify and address the *job-related needs* of your employees, the more prone they'll be to engage in what psychologists call motivated behavior—the subject of this chapter.

85 Management Style Sets the Stage

In his classic book, *The Human Side of Enterprise,* Douglas McGregor described how managers view employees according to different concepts of human nature, which he labeled Theory X and Theory Y.

McGregor said that managers who subscribe to Theory X assume that work is inherently distasteful and the average person is lazy, unambitious, avoids responsibility, and is primarily motivated by money. In sharp contrast, managers who subscribe to Theory Y assume that people basically enjoy their work, exhibit creativity, want responsibility, and seek recognition and self-fulfillment as much as money.

Think about how you act toward your employees. How you treat them. How you talk about them. Where are you on the Theory X–Theory Y continuum? It's important to know because we treat others according to our beliefs about human nature.

Theory X managers, for example, believe that the typical employee avoids responsibility and must be coerced or bribed to achieve organizational goals. They tell employees what to do, how to do it, closely supervise them, and in other ways communicate a lack of trust. (The installation of time clocks is an example.) Employees often react negatively to such actions which, in turn, convinces managers that their original assumptions were correct.

Theory Y managers, with entirely different assumptions, make decisions by consensus whenever possible. This helps employees feel "ownership" of what they do and how they do it. They empower employees to have more authority and responsibility. They encourage creativity and teamwork and give recognition for work done well. The result? Employees react positively to being treated with respect and receiving the support they need to do a good job. Again, it's a case of assumptions becoming fact.

"The set of assumptions that McGregor labeled as Theory X and Theory Y are extremes on a continuum," say Anne Bruce and James S. Pepitone, co-authors of *Motivating Employees.* "There are probably no managers who are a pure X or Y. But this approach to management beliefs," they say, "should help you understand your natural management instincts. It might also help you appreciate when your attitudes might adjust to a specific situation, within a particular environment, in a given culture, or with certain employees."

"So it's not a question of whether you're a Theory X manager or a Theory Y manager," say Bruce and Pepitone. "Each type has to get the job done working with and through people. The key to success is determining which management style is most consistent with bringing out the highest levels of motivation in your employees."[1]

86 Five Myths About Motivation

➥**Myth #1:** There is a "secret button" to push to get people to do what you'd like them to do.

➥**Reality check:** In truth, motivating others is a *process* that's more like farming than manufacturing, with some factors you can control and others over which you have no control.

➥**Myth #2:** If you can *say* or *do* the right thing, you can motivate others.

That's true . . . up to a point, especially for the short term.

Praise, recognition, and money, for example, can be very motivational but the effect doesn't last long.

Threatening people with dismissal (the "shape-up-or-ship-out" type of reprimand) may jumpstart some people's motivational batteries—but in most cases is also short-lived. Others (depending on the demand for their job skills) may select the second option—and just leave (the "take this job and shove it" type departure).

➥**Reality check:** "The door to change is opened from the inside," goes an old saying. People can choose to be motivated, but we can't make them choose.

➥**Hard learned lesson:** All motivation is *self*-motivation. The challenge is to create the kind of climate that will allow such motivation to flourish. Or as Bob Townsend, former CEO of Avis, so aptly put it: "Create the kind of climate that pays people to bring their brains to work."[2]

➥**Myth #3:** Employees' motivational needs are the same as yours— or in the same order of importance.

➥**Reality check:** Unlikely. No two people have the same job-related needs, in the same order of importance, with the same standards of satisfaction. Employees have varying degrees of experience, energy levels, and interest in the jobs they're performing.

A single parent with two school-age children, for example, may have very different job-related needs than a person from a two wage-earner household with grown children.

➥**Myth #4:** Money is a universal motivator.

➥**Reality check:** Unfortunately, money has less motivational and staying power than many HCPs believe.

A 2005 Gallup poll of 3,023 adults employed full or part time were asked: "If you won 10 million dollars in the lottery, would you continue to work, or would you stop working?"

Sixty-one percent said, "Yes," they would continue working.[3]

Still skeptical?

If starting tomorrow, you gave everyone on your staff a $1,000 raise, how much harder would they work—and for how long?

➥**Myth #5:** Hire the right people to begin with (highly motivated, self-starters, for example) and you'll be home free.

Many employees begin a job with high-level motivation to do a good job, learn all they can, and be promoted.

➥**Reality check:** In all too many cases (and especially in an environment that fails to address employees' job-related needs) they tend to lose that initial self-motivation and become *demotivated* and only marginally productive.

➥**Hard learned lesson:** "It's not my job to motivate players," said Lou Holtz, legendary football coach at Notre Dame. "They bring extraordinary motivation to our programs. It's my job not to demotivate them."

87 The Hierarchy of Needs

As emphasized in the previous secret, all motivation is *self-motivation*. But where does self-motivation originate?

Psychologist Abraham Maslow, Ph.D. attempted to answer this question by studying the needs that motivate human behavior. He arranged these into what he called a Hierarchy of Needs, according to their perceived importance.

He suggested that the needs that first motivate us are *physical needs* such as food, shelter, physical comfort, and other fairly basic necessities.

➥**On-the-job application:** Adequate salary, pleasant working conditions, vacations.

Once a person's physical needs are relatively gratified (few if any needs are 100 percent gratified), their impact on behavior diminishes. A new set of higher-level needs then emerges, which Maslow called *safety needs*. These include the enduring satisfaction of lower level needs and the avoidance of risk.

➥**On-the-job application** Feeling safe at work, fringe benefits, healthcare insurance benefits, retirement and pension plans, job security. Safety needs are also seen in a preference for the "familiar"—which explains why some people resist "change" in what they do or how they do it—and the uncertainty that goes with it. They wonder: Will I fail? And if I do, will I lose my job?

Money as a motivator is most effective at levels 1 and 2. However, once employees believe the salaries and benefits they receive are fair and reasonable—and consistent with the type of work they do—then continued attempts to motivate them to higher levels of performance based on money alone will be less than successful.

If both the physical and safety needs are fairly well met, the third level of needs emerges for what Maslow called *love* and a *sense of belonging*.

➥**On-the-job application** Opportunities for interaction with co-workers, staff meetings, team projects. A person with high social needs who is forced to basically work alone will very likely be unhappy.

*Esteem need*s emerge at the next level; these are divided into two subsidiary sets: (1) the need to experience self-worth, competence, and achievement; and (2) the need for appreciation, recognition, and respect from others.

➥**On-the-job application** Salary increases or promotion based on performance, on-the-job training, more responsibility and authority, being asked for one's opinion or advice, and most importantly, appreciation of work performed and recognition from others within the organization.

Because of their importance, the entire next chapter is devoted to the many highly meaningful ways that praise and recognition can be given to employees.

Money may also motivate at this level—not so much for what it can buy, but for the *pride* it brings. At this point, money is an ego satisfier because it is the means by which most organizations express their evaluation of a person's performance.

The uppermost level in Maslow's hierarchy is the *need for self-actualization* (a term first coined by Kurt Goldstein in his book, *The Organism*). This term refers to the need for self-fulfillment, job mastery, personal growth, and the realization of a person's potential. As Maslow wrote, "A musician must make music, an artist must paint, a poet must write if he is to be ultimately at peace with himself. What a man *can* be, he *must* be."[4] ("Man or woman" would of course have been more correct.)

➡**On-the-job application** Doing work that is challenging and meaningful, job enrichment, continuing education programs.

➡**Reality check:** "As a basic foundation for understanding motivation," says James F. Evered, author of *Shirt-Sleeves Management*, "it's imperative that we establish two premises basically agreed upon by most behaviorists: All behavior is needs-oriented and all behavior is caused."

What this means, Evered says, is everything we do, no matter how rational or irrational it may seem, is to satisfy some basic need we feel at the moment. The need causes behavior. Therefore, an unsatisfied need is a motivator; it causes behavior. A satisfied need is *not* a motivator. It has no effect on behavior.[5]

88 The Motivation Inventory

At the management seminars I conduct, I'm often asked, "How do I get my employees to do what I want them to do?"

It's the wrong question.

The real question is, "How do I get my employees *to want to do*, what I want them to do?"

The answer to that question is: by first identifying their job-related needs.

To start the process of identifying your employees' job-related needs, place an X next to the *five job-related needs* below that you believe are most important in motivating the *one employee* in your office you would most like to motivate. In all likelihood, this will require a guess on your part.

➡**Note:** These job-related needs, patterned after Maslow's hierarchy, are listed in ascending order, starting with basic needs and ending with higher level, self-actualization needs.

1. Assurance of regular employment
2. Satisfactory working conditions
3. Feeling safe at work
4. Good pay
5. Health insurance and other fringe benefits
6. Maintenance of adequate living standards for my family
7. Adequate vacation arrangements and holidays
8. A low stress environment
9. A written job description so I know what's expected of me
10. The right equipment to do my job well
11. A good performance review so I know how I'm doing
12. Being told that I'm doing a good job
13. Getting along well with co-workers
14. Involvement in decisions affecting my work
15. Participation in management activities
16. Feeling my job is important
17. Respect for me as a person and/or a professional at my job
18. Have more autonomy on the job
19. Have more job responsibilities
20. Interesting work
21. Opportunities to do work that is challenging
22. Chance for self-development and improvement

Others _____

Seminar audiences typically struggle with this Motivation Inventory simply because it's difficult for them to know their employees' job-related needs—unless they've discussed the subject with them.

➡**Reality check:** In order to put employees' motivation in high gear (and keep it there) you must first identify their job-related needs and then make their jobs so satisfying, they will want, *really want*, to do their very best.

89 Learn What Motivates Your Employees

"Many managers fail to take the time to find out what is satisfying and dissatisfying to each employee," says consultant Thad Green, Ph.D., author of *Motivation Management.* "When motivating employees, many managers make the mistake of believing and acting as though everyone is motivated in the same way. But motivations differ. For example, some employees are motivated by challenging work, while others find it intimidating. Some prefer the certainty of a fixed routine; others thrive on task variety."

"Managers also cannot assume," says Green, "that each individual employee will be satisfied if the three 'big outcomes'—money, advancement and job security—are fulfilled. Other outcomes such as praise, recognition, openness or honesty, may be more motivating to some employees."

"The solution to the problem," Green says, "is simple: Ask your employees what outcomes motivate them. Employees will gladly tell you what they want from you. Another interesting point is that when the work itself is satisfying, employees tend to be very forgiving when there is a shortfall in rewards. Why? Because employees are getting something that is highly prized by most people in today's work environment: enjoyment from their work."[6]

➡**Hard learned lesson:** "The Golden Rule—do unto others as you would have them do unto you—means that you treat others exactly the same way you would like to be treated," say Claire Raines and Laura Ewing in their book, *The Art of Connecting.* "It works best," they add, "when we're the same. But the Golden Rule can cause a disconnect when the other person is different."

"It is far better," they argue, "to treat people they way they like to be treated."[7]

➡**Reality check:** If you can help people connect what's important to them with what's important to the organization, you can make a positive impact on their job satisfaction, commitment, and contribution.

90 Identify Job-Related Needs

"The need to identify employees' critical motivators is important, because simply put, most managers are terrible at motivating their employees," says John Sullivan, Ph.D., professor of management at San Francisco (California) State University. "When managers don't know what motivates an individual, they mistakenly assume that all workers want the same thing, or they make random guesses about what motivates an individual. Both are serious errors."[8]

There are several ways to learn such motivational needs:

1. Ideally, the initial job interview will uncover an applicant's job-related needs. The underlying purpose of many of the interview questions listed in Chapter 4 is to help you ascertain if you have the right person for the right job in your office (e.g., What about your last job did you like most? Least?).

2. Consider asking current employees similar questions to identify their job-related needs. In this case, put them in writing. Give them time to think about their answers, perhaps discuss them with someone else. Explain also, that if they'd like to do so, you'll schedule a one-on-one conference to discuss the results. Such questions might include:

   • **What part of your job do you like best—and why?**
   • **Are there additional things you would like to be doing?**
   • **What, if anything, frustrates you about your job?**
   • **What is there about your job (if anything) that you would like changed to help you get more of what you want from your work?**

3. "Ask your employees what is important to them and why they work for you when they have so many other opportunities," says Roger Herman, author of *Keeping Good People.* "Listen carefully to what they say, and then give them more of what they want. Then use those same factors to recruit, recognizing that the people you want will have similar desires to those who have chosen to be part of your team."[9]

4. The Motivation Inventory, although not intended for this purpose, can be used to identify employees' job-related needs.

5. Performance reviews (discussed in Chapter 12) are a more formal, in-depth way to learn employees' job-related needs.

Having identified employees' job-related needs, the next step is to help them get more of what they want from their work.

Here are some examples based on the Motivation Inventory.

91 Satisfactory Working Conditions

This was #2 in the Motivation Inventory.

Louis Harris did a survey of office workers regarding their work environment. Not surprisingly, the factor considered most important was "good lighting." Number two was "comfortable seating"—again not surprising considering that back ailments affect 60 percent to 80 percent of the population and are the #2 cause of absenteeism. (The #1 cause is the common cold.)

What *is* surprising is how often employees complain about uncomfortable chairs in which they have to sit all day!

➡**Reality check:** Uncomfortable chairs contribute to more frequent stretch breaks, employee errors, and lower job satisfaction—*especially if employees complain about the problem and nothing is done.*

When a government department in New Jersey installed ergonomically correct workstations in their new offices, computer-related health complaints fell by 40 percent and doctor visits dropped by 25 percent in less than a year.

A study from Cornell University found that the 356 employees reported relief in all the places that hurt after a day of hunching over a keyboard: shoulders and neck, wrists and hands, and backs. What made the difference? Chairs with adjustable armrests, backs, and seats; tilting keyboard holders; and mouse platforms. The workers also took regular breaks and stretched.[10]

92 The Need to Feel Safe

This was #3 in the Motivation Inventory and represents an increasing concern among today's employees.

"In only two years, the number of employees who say feeling safe at work is a priority to their job satisfaction, has jumped 28 percent. According to the Society for Human Resource Management (SHRM) and the financial network of the CNN News Group (CNNfn) 2004 Job Satisfaction Survey, 62 percent of employees report feeling safe at work is 'very important' compared with 36 percent in 2002."

"Terrorist warnings in the U.S.A. have put employees' concerns for safety at the forefront," says Susan R. Meisinger, president and CEO of SHRM. "Employers need to be keyed into what's important to employees in order to implement practices that will keep valuable employees satisfied and productive in the workplace. It's a priority for all employers to do all they can do to create and maintain a safe workplace."[11]

➡**Action steps:** Speaking of bio-terrorism, Bernd Wollschlager, a family physician in North Miami Beach, Florida, advises that "Every primary care office should have decontamination kits and protective gear. Nothing fancy; just plastic covers, sealable plastic bags, masks, gloves, shoe covers, and bleach. Make sure enough potable water is available. Buy those now," he says. "Don't wait until everyone else needs supplies. When things start happening, you have to act fast."[12]

➡**Reality check:** "Bomb threats, violent incidents, fires, explosions and natural disasters can take lives and disrupt or destroy businesses," says Suzanne Taylor of the SHRM Workplace Health and Safety Committee. "Yet most executives take an 'it can't happen here' approach to emergency preparedness, and even repeated calamities often find them unprepared. The chance is good that a business, organization or institution will experience some type of crisis. The existence of a plan can save lives and assets and make the difference between survival and failure. The high cost of being unprepared is a convincing argument for disaster planning."[13]

➡**Hard learned lesson:** "HR's efforts in showing that safety receives major attention, not only day after day but also in disaster preparedness planning can help improve employee job satisfaction overall," says Jennifer Schramm, manager of the Workplace Trends and Forecasting Program at SHRM.[14]

93 A Low Stress Environment

This was #8 in the Motivation Inventory and is also becoming of increasing importance in today's new world of work, as described in Chapter 2.

➡**Reality check:** A study by the Families and Work Institute asked 1,003 employed adults (18 or older) how *often* or *very often* during the past three months they "felt overworked" (26 percent did) or "felt overwhelmed by how much work they had to do" (27 percent did). The percentages increased substantially when the question was whether these feelings were *sometimes* felt (54 percent and 55 percent, respectively).

What impact do such feelings have on employees? The study indicates the more overworked employees feel, the more likely they are to make mistakes at work, feel angry toward their employers for expecting them to do so much, resent co-workers who don't work as hard as they do, and look for a new job—in addition to the toll these feelings take on their health and home life. What wasn't mentioned was that overworked employees, who are angry and resentful, are unlikely to be friendly and attentive to patients.

The study found 89 percent of overworked employees agree:

- "My job requires I work very fast" or "very hard" or
- "I never seem to have enough time to get everything done on my job."

In addition, 56 percent said they often or very often experienced one or both of the following problems:

- I have to work on too many tasks at the same time.
- I am interrupted during the workday, making it difficult to get my work done.

The study also shows that employees who have poorer quality jobs—less autonomy, fewer learning opportunities, less job security—feel more overworked. The same is true for those who have less supportive workplaces—inadequate materials and the equipment to do a good job.

➥**Action steps:** Many of the workplace characteristics associated with the feeling of being overworked are within the power of employers to change. However, some employers will dismiss this study, believing that pushing employees to do more and do it faster is the only way to remain competitive or reduce overhead. Others will conclude that they can get the same or greater effort out of employees by providing more work schedule flexibility or redesigning work to reduce unnecessary demands.

The study concludes: "Our findings strongly suggest that every employee reaches a point when increasing work demands become too much—a point at which personal and family relations, personal health, and the quality of work itself are seriously threatened. Today's 24/7 economy appears to be pushing many employees to and beyond this point."[15]

94 The Right Equipment

This was #10 on the Motivation Inventory—and based on our surveys, often a source of employee complaints such as: "office equipment that's not where you need it and/or available when you need it."

"Charlotte Kohler, president of Kohler HealthCare Consulting outside Baltimore, Maryland, has seen practices that require two front desk employees to share a computer. Or receptionists who must walk two offices down the hall to make copies of insurance cards or use a fax machine. She has found that when practices are reluctant to invest in equipment, it ends up costing them, because front-line staff can't function effectively."[16]

Another equipment-related source of complaints: office or medical equipment that is out-of-date, frequently requires repair, or needs to be replaced.

The inference in each of these cases is, "You and your work are not important enough to remedy the situation."

➡**Action step:** "Modern technology can ease many communication problems," says practice management consultant/speaker Elizabeth Woodcock. "Purchase an electronic medical record system," she suggests. "Place computer monitors in exam rooms and workstations. Give your staff two-way radios, text pagers, or personal digital assistants. Introduce email or instant messaging. Develop a robust intranet or shared drive in which to place staff memos, the practice's calendar, and contact information for vendors. Agree on a means to communicate, and use that channel to enhance face-to-face discussions."[17]

➡**From the success files:** "The 759 nurses at Hamot Medical Center, Erie, Pennsylvania," as reported by modernhealthcare.com, "were undergoing more and more stress and fatigue from doing more for their patients in less time."

"At the urging of Veronica Maras, senior vice president and chief nursing officer, the 309 bed hospital invested $3 million in an effort to make it easier for nurses to do their job well. The money paid for new bedside technology, including an automated medication-administration system and wireless computers. The medication-administration check requires bar codes for medication, nurses and patients, ensuring that nurses will make fewer errors. With a simple scan, nurses learn if the medication matches the patient and the physician's order.

"Nurses also benefited from wireless technology, as they were able to bring their laptop computers into the patients' rooms so they could perform other functions, such as admissions work, while keeping an eye on patients. For nurses who are not computer-savvy," Maras adds, "the hospital developed a team of computer system mentors that works with nurses to help them feel comfortable with the new technology.

"In part a result of the investment, nurse vacancy rates at the hospital have remained steady from 5 percent to 7 percent, lower than the national average of 13 percent."[18]

95 The Need for Camaraderie

This was #13 in the Motivation Inventory.

"When we ask in a 'write-on' question in our employee surveys," says David Sirota, Ph.D., author of *The Enthusiastic Employee*, "what respondents like most about their organizations, *the most frequent and consistent comment concerns the people they work with* [sic].

"The quality of interaction in organizations," Sirota says, "is greatly affected not just by friendliness and mutuality of interests but also by co-workers' competence and cooperation. People want to work on a team in which members not only enjoy each other's company but are also productive. That type of environment is not just a nicety—it satisfies very strong needs. And in that environment, a friendly slacker is an oxymoron: being unhelpful to co-workers is, by definition, unfriendly."[19]

➡**Action steps:** "Although employees derive pleasure from socializing with others, such as during breaks," says Sirota, "*their greatest satisfaction comes from interacting as a team on the job in the service of common performance goals*" [sic]. That is a tremendous source of morale for employees. . . . In effect, through teamwork and simple and repeated social interaction, a work *community* is established: people enjoy each other's company and have a shared commitment to each other and pride in the group's achievement."

Managers are well advised, says Sirota, to enhance opportunities for face-to-face interaction among employees and to avoid practices, organizational structures, and physical environments that discourage interaction.[20]

➥**Reality check:** For many employees, the social life at work is extremely important. For some, it is their only social life.

96 The Need to Have a Say in Decisions Affecting One's Work

This was #14 in the Motivation Inventory.

Children's Medical Center of Dallas, Texas, has discovered "that offering employees greater involvement in the decision-making process generates allegiance among high-potential workers. For example, the nursing department encourages independent work teams to try to get decision-making closer to the people who actually deliver the care.

"They're encouraging what Shirley Lopez, VP of HR for the medical center calls 'independent practice.' It's an attitude that encourages autonomy and creates an environment in which the nurses who care for the children use their expertise. In doing so, each nurse's contributions are appreciated."[21]

➥**Reality check:** Sharing decision-making power demonstrates respect for employees and their expertise and increases the likelihood of better decisions. It also helps your employees develop a sense of ownership of their jobs which, in turn, makes their work more motivating and satisfying.

Equally important: When employees feel they have some say in the decisions that vitally affect their work, they're more highly motivated to perform with distinction than if they feel they're merely being told what to do.

➥**Action steps:** "Ask for your team members' opinions on materials, delivery systems, and equipment selection," says Dr. Lori Trost,

Columbia, Illinois. "After all, they are the ones who will be using them. Their input is invaluable."[22]

Begin such a discussion by saying, **"I'd like your opinion (advice, thoughts) on this . . . ."** You'll have the person's full attention. Guaranteed.

Team meetings are another way to tap into your staff's creativity and on-the-job smarts. Because of its importance, Chapter 11 is devoted to this one topic.

➡**Hard learned lesson:** "At Mary Kay Cosmetics," said Mary Kay Ash, "we want our people's ideas. We encourage them and openly solicit them. Their participation is vital to our growth and health. The more that people are permitted to participate in a new project, the more they'll support it. Conversely, the more they are excluded, the more they will resist it."[23]

See Chapter 10 for a discussion of participative management.

97 The Need for Autonomy

This was #18 in the Motivation Inventory.

"Research has demonstrated that hospitals providing nurses with professional autonomy and control over nursing practice not only have better retention rates for nursing staff but also have better outcomes for patients."[24]

"Giving autonomy requires that managers let go," say Beverly Kaye and Sharon Jordan-Evans, writing in *Fast Company*, "and trust their talented employees to manage and continuously improve their work—without micromanagement."[25]

➡**Action step:** Find out what employees need to do their jobs to the best of their ability—and then provide it. When people feel they have little or no control over their work, they become demotivated and feel negative about the organization. The question to ask is:

What do you need to feel more in control of your work?

"The ultimate form of recognition for many employees," says author/speaker Bob Nelson, Ph.D., "is to be given increased autonomy and authority to get their job done, whether it's the ability to spend or allocate resources, make decisions or manage others. Greater autonomy and authority says in effect, 'I trust you to act in the best interests of the company, to do so independently and without approval of myself or others.'"[26]

➡**From the success files:** "As surgeons, we're accustomed to being in control when performing procedures," says ophthalmologist Ella G. Faktorovich, owner and director of Pacific Vision Institute, San Francisco, California. "I found that when I applied this style of managing to administration, the practice stopped growing. The staff became passive and frustrated, and I had to supervise them even more. This of course, distracted me from clinical care."

"I've since adopted a 'hands-off' management style and allowed my employees to take charge of their areas of expertise," Faktorovich says. "I no longer micromanage. I now encourage my staff to solve problems on their own without consulting me. This means allowing them to make mistakes and learning how to correct them on their own. Consequently, the staff became more responsible, more enthusiastic and more creative, and our practice has grown tremendously.

"I think very few material rewards can match the sense that competency and power instill in our staff."[27]

➡**Action step:** Ask more questions. Provide fewer answers.

When people come to you with questions, consider asking them:

> **What do you think should be done?**
> **What's worked in the past when this situation has arisen?**
> **What choices do you think we have?**

According to Tom Peters, author of *Liberation Management*, 75 percent of all questions can be best answered by the person who's asking.

➡**Hard learned lessons:**
- The people doing a job know more about it than anyone else.
- Motivation tends to increase as people are given an opportunity to participate in decisions affecting their work.
- Empowered employees do a better job and take more pride in their work than "do as you're told" employees.
- "Nothing creates more self respect among employees than being included in the process of making decisions."[28]

98 The "D" Word

Rather than give their employees greater autonomy and authority, many HCPs continue to perform operational tasks that could be done at lower cost (if not better) by qualified trained staff members. Which brings us to the "D" word: delegation.

Some HCPs justify their failure to delegate by saying, "If I want it done right, I have to do it myself" or "It's easier (or faster) to do it myself." Unfortunately, this line of reasoning becomes a self-fulfilling prophecy. Staff members can't learn to do what HCPs insist on doing themselves. So HCPs keep on doing what they've always done.

There's a lot to be gained if you're willing to allow qualified staff members to tackle new responsibilities (#19 in the Motivation Inventory).

"It's been our experience," says Dr. Chris E. Vance, Everett, Washington, "that the more medical assistants do for the doctor, the more time is available for diagnosing, triaging and interacting with patients so they receive the best possible care."[29]

➥**Action steps:** "Identify the tasks you don't need to do, and find the right person to assign the task to," says Judy Capko, principal of Capko & Co., a healthcare consulting firm based in Thousand Oaks, California. "A good rule of thumb? If a staff member can do a task 80 percent as well as you can, delegate it. In addition to saving your own time, delegating is an expression of confidence in your staff. It strengthens the skills and is a source of job enrichment and fulfillment that helps improve teamwork."[30]

➥**Hard learned lesson:** Delegation of authority does not mean abdication of your responsibilities.

Let's use as an example the purchase of new office equipment. Rather than handle the entire transaction yourself, empower the employee who uses the equipment on a daily basis to recommend (or buy outright) what's needed.

There are, of course, degrees of empowerment. Decide which is most appropriate based on the nature of the task and the abilities of the employee. For example, you can tell an employee any one of the following:

- Investigate the situation. Report back to me. I'll decide.
- Investigate. Make recommendations. I'll decide.

- Investigate. Decide. Let me have final approval.
- Take action. Let me know what you did.
- Whatever you do is OK with me.

Empowerment to make such recommendations or decisions is extremely satisfying to people with a job-related need for autonomy and who seek more on-the-job responsibility and authority. In fact, many would consider it insulting *not* to be consulted in such matters.

A complaint I often hear from disgruntled employees: "I'm treated as if I don't have a brain in my head."

➡**Reality check:** As beneficial as delegation can be, it's not for everyone. Some HCPs prefer not to let go of the reins and some employees don't want the responsibility of taking them.

The following are among the reasons that employees have expressed at focus groups to explain why they shun responsibility:

- They're unsure how much authority they have.
- They don't have enough direction to handle the jobs that are sometimes delegated to them.
- They fail to see what's in it for them.
- They haven't been gradually prepared to accept increasing levels of responsibility.
- They think the tasks that are delegated to them are inappropriate for their job description or temperament.
- They feel overworked already.
- They've made mistakes in the past that have angered their supervisors.
- They really don't want responsibility, leadership, or risk. The fact is: They'd rather be told what to do.

99 The Need for Interesting Work

This was #20 in the Motivation Inventory.

When asked, "What makes a job satisfying?" 30,000 readers of *Working Woman* magazine ranked "interesting and challenging work" number one.[31]

➡**Reality check:** It's been said that 75 percent of jobs can be learned in 3 years. For some people, doing the same thing every day is fine. For others, it results in boredom.

One of the best ways to make work more interesting is to give people with this need a chance to grow on the job; tackle tasks that require what industrial psychologists call s-t-r-e-t-c-h. The principle involved: *The competence of most people is increased when given a challenge.* It's the same principle as playing a sport with someone who's a *little* better at it than you. It could be ping pong, dancing, or Scrabble. It's motivational. Makes you perform better. That's s-t-r-e-t-c-h. And because you play better, you also have a *sense of achievement.*

➥**Action steps:** Among the ways to make a job more interesting, consider the following:

- *Cross-training:* Gives employees an opportunity to try different jobs in the office. Provides a change-of-pace. Avoids burn out. Helps everyone better understand the demands of each other's jobs. Promotes teamwork. (See Chapter 16.)
- *Continuing education programs:* Enable employees to learn new clinical, laboratory, and office-related skills. (See Chapter 16.)
- *Job enrichment:* Involves increased autonomy, authority, and/or responsibilities.

(100) The Desire for On-the-Job Training

Staff training is most appealing to people who have such job-related needs as: #19, more job responsibilities; #20, interesting work; #21, opportunities to do work that is challenging; and #22, chance for self-development and improvement—as listed in the Motivation Inventory. For many, it's the key to job satisfaction.

Among the topics you might consider for in-service training: OSHA and HIPAA review, clinical assisting, office computers/practice management software systems, electronic health record (EHR) system, communication with patients, CPR and other patient emergency procedures, insurance filing and coding, and explaining financial policies to patients.

➥**From the success files:** "In our offices, we train, train and retrain," says Dr. Hal Ornstein, Howell, New Jersey. "With the dynamic nature of medicine and the insurance industry, our staff is trained in several ways to stay on top. At first, we were afraid of the extra cost associated with training a new employee. We've since learned that investing in training new employees delivers an awesome return."[32]

Because of its importance, Chapter 16 focuses on training and skills development.

101 Learn from O.P.M.

One of the easiest, lowest cost, and most practical ways to learn about management is from O.P.M.: *other people's mistakes.* In fact, the many hard learned lessons throughout this book are the direct result of just such experiences.

In a recent study of 1,400 leaders conducted by The Ken Blanchard Companies, a training company based in Escondido, California, managers cited their biggest mistakes when working with others. Paying close attention to these mistakes may be helpful in your efforts to manage and motivate your employees.

The top two mistakes managers cited have to do with communication, or lack thereof. "Eighty-two percent cited failing to provide adequate feedback, praise or redirection as a top management mistake, while 81 percent cited failing to listen to or involve others."

"Some managers don't listen intently; they're not present in their conversations, they interrupt, and they give advice when they should be asking questions," says Scott Blanchard, director of client services at The Ken Blanchard Companies.

"Seventy-six percent of managers say failing to use a leadership style that is appropriate to the person, task, or situation (leading to over-or-under-supervision) is the next most common mistake."

"Some managers are leaving beginners to their own devices, which leaves the beginners confused," Blanchard adds. "And on the flip side, they are over-managing people who are really good at their jobs." All of this leads to a demotivated staff.

➡**Reality check:** These are mistakes that may well cost HCPs not only top performers but also bottom-line results. "Most organizations don't realize there is a link between leadership and profits," Blanchard says. "Managers must have a constant check on how useful their conversations and relationships with employees are. If there are ineffective relationships or dynamics, they should take care to address these issues to improve them. Hope," he adds, "is not a strategy."

Other common management mistakes noted by the Blanchard survey include failing to set clear goals and objectives, and failure to train and develop employees, cited by 76 percent and 59 percent of managers respectively.

➥**Hard learned lesson:** "Overwhelming research shows that employee passion really drives an organization's success or failure," Blanchard says. "So ultimately, good leadership is critical to an organization's success."[33]

Succeeding chapters address the remedies for each of these management mistakes starting with the importance of feedback—which Ken Blanchard himself, has labeled, "The Breakfast of Champions."

102 Beware of These Assumptions

- Treating all employees the same regardless of differences. Treating everyone the same communicates the message, "I don't care enough about you to find out what makes you unique." To remove this block, you must identify and understand the differences among individuals.
- Assuming you know others' expectations and needs without discussing them.
- Believing employees should respond the way you would respond in the same situation. Most of us can't help projecting our own attitudes and priorities on others.
- Seeing employees as they once were and not recognizing changes or improvements. Locking employees into a past perception ignores the fact that people change, often in major ways. People acquire new knowledge and skills, learn from experience, and shift their priorities. To see employees as they are today, track their progress (or perhaps backsliding) with a keen radar.
- "When executives assume without asking, that they understand the expectations and needs of their employees, they risk making poor decisions about such important factors as working environment, delegation, employee recognition, and communication methods," say Craig R. Hickman and Michael A. Silva, co-authors of *Creating Excellence: Managing Corporate Culture, Strategy, and Change in the New Age.* "To overcome this," they say,

"you must listen carefully when employees discuss their expectations and needs."[34]

(103) More Hard Learned Lessons About Motivation

- Trying to motivate others without understanding their job-related, motivational needs is like trying to start a stalled car by kicking it.
- Whenever possible, implement changes in office policies and procedures by *consensus*. People tend to be more supportive of decisions in which they have some input. *And*, they're more interested in seeing a successful outcome than they are for decisions made by others and passed along to them to implement.
- "A vital factor in morale," said David Ogilvy, who built one of the largest advertising agencies in the world, "is the posture of the boss. If he or she is miserable, it will filter down through the ranks, and make the whole office miserable. You must always be contagiously cheerful."[35]
- Distinguish between employees who aren't doing their jobs because they can't, and those who aren't doing their jobs because they won't. If a person's life depended on it, could he or she get the job done? If the answer is yes, the problem is motivational. If the answer is no, the problem is the employee's ability.
- "People who work in a fulfilling work environment where they feel both valued and respected, are more productive and loyal," says Tom Chappell, co-founder and president of personal-care product manufacturer Tom's of Maine.[36]
- "People start work with the right ideas," says John Mole, author of *Management Mole: Lessons from Office Life*. "They are eager to do well, work hard, learn new skills, make a good impression, get promoted, and do something meaningful. Managers," he continues, "spend a lot of time wondering what they can do to make the organization more efficient and the people in it, more productive. They might be better off thinking of what they can *stop doing* that keeps people from working as hard as they can."[37]

- "Unfortunately, most doctors attempt to motivate their employees simply by giving them higher pay and/or benefits," says the *Blair/McGill Advisory*. "Even if your practice offers above average salary, an excellent benefits package and vacations, these are employee *retainers*, not employee *motivators*."[38]
- "Very few people will stay in a job just for the paycheck," says Jack Welch, former CEO of General Electric and one of the most effective CEOs of all time. "They also need to feel that they matter and that what they do for eight hours a day means something. You can fulfill those needs with open appreciation, a sense of fun, an exciting shared goal, and individual attention to the challenge of each job. It's a tall order for any boss, but the returns are incalculable."[39]

References

1. Bruce A, Pepitone JS. *Motivating Employees*. New York: McGraw-Hill; 1999.
2. Townsend R. *Up the Organization: How to Stop the Corporation from Stifling People and Strangling Profits*. Greenwich, CT: Fawcett Publications; 1970.
3. $10 Million Question: To Work or Not to Work? September 2005. http://poll.gallup.com/content/default.aspx?ci=1720&pg=3
4. Maslow AH. *Motivation and Personality*. New York: Harper & Row; 1954.
5. Evered JF. *Shirt-Sleeves Management*. New York: AMACOM; 1981.
6. Green T. Create an Environment That Promotes Confidence, Trust and Satisfaction to Motivate Employees. *Managing Smart*, Winter 2001.
7. Raines C, Ewing L. *The Art of Connecting*. New York: AMACOM; 2006.
8. Sullivan J. Personalizing Motivation. *Workforce Management*, March 27, 2006, 56.
9. Cole C. How to Build IT Loyalty. *Workforce*, July 2001, 53
10. Rudakewych M, Valent-Weitz L, Hedge A. Effects of an Ergonomic Intervention on Musculoskeletal Discomfort Among Office Workers. *Proceedings of the Human Factors and Ergonomics Society 45th Annual Meeting*, Vol. 1, 791–795, 2001.
11. Cohn S. Employees More Concerned with Feeling Safe at Work. http://www.shrm.org/press_published/CMS_008301.asp
12. Pennachio DL. Guarding Against Biological Agents. *Medical Economics*, October 25, 2002.
13. Taylor S. Disasters and Emergency Preparedness. SHRM White Paper. http://www.shrum.org/hrresources/whitepapers_published/CMS_000146.asp
14. Schramm J. Disaster Readiness. *HR Magazine*, November 2005, 168.
15. Galinsky E, Kim SS, Bond JT. Feeling Overworked: When Work Becomes Too Much. *Families and Work Institute*, 2001.

16. Walpert B. Problems with Patients? Fine-Tune Your Front Desk. *ACP-ASIM Observer*, March 2001.
17. Woodcock E. *Physician Practice Pearls*, March 16, 2006.
18. Workforce Report 2004: One Answer: Productivity. http://www.modernhealthcare. com/page.cms?pageId=866
19. Sirota D, Mischkind LA, Meltzer MI. *The Enthusiastic Employee.* Upper Saddle River, NJ: Pearson Education, Inc.; 2005.
20. Ibid.
21. Solomon CM. The Loyalty Factor. *Personnel Journal*, September 1992, 52–62.
22. Trost L. Building Your Dream Team. *Woman Dentist Journal*, March/April 2003, 62–66.
23. Krauss P. *The Book of Management Wisdom: Classic Writings by Legendary Managers.* New York: John Wiley & Sons, Inc.; 2000.
24. Kay, M. A Brave New World. *American Journal of Nursing*, March 2005, 81–83.
25. Kaye B, Evans SJ. Give Employees the Space They Need. *Fast Company.* http://www.fastcompany.com/resources/talent/bksje/041006.html
26. Bob Nelson's Tip of the Week. September 4, 2002. maillist@nelson-motivation.com
27. Faktorovich EG. Putting Faith in Staff. *Ophthalmology Management*, September 2001.
28. Bardwick JM. *The Plateauing Trap.* New York: AMACOM; 1986.
29. Guiliana JV, Vance CE, Schiraldi-Deck FG, Mozena JD, Ornstein H, Cernak CR. Roundtable: Staff Management. *Podiatry Management*, January 2001, 93–106.
30. Capko J. Put Time on Your Side. *Physicians Practice,* February 2005.
31. Ciabattari J. The Biggest Mistake Top Managers Make. *Working Woman*, October 1996, 47–55.
32. Guiliana JV, Vance CE, Schiraldi-Deck FG, Mozena JD, Ornstein H, Cernak CR. Roundtable: Staff Management. *Podiatry Management*, January 2001, 93–106.
33. Galea C. Learning from Mistakes. *Sales & Marketing Management*, July/August, 2006, 13.
34. Hickman C. *Creating Excellence: Managing Corporate Culture, Strategy, and Change in the New Age.* New York: New American Library; 1984.
35. Ogilvy D. *Blood, Brains & Beer.* New York: Atheneum; 1978.
36. Finnigan A. Benefits Under Fire. *Working Woman*, July/August 2001, 54, 56, 58, 78.
37. Mole J. *Management Mole: Lessons from Office Life.* London, UK: Bantam Press; 1989.
38. *Blair/McGill Advisory,* April 2002, 3.
39. Welch J, Welch S. Ideas! The Welch Way. *BusinessWeek,* March 27, 2006, 122.

Chapter Nine

MANAGING

The Power of Positive Reinforcement

B F. Skinner is the psychologist generally credited with discovering the power of positive reinforcement, a behavior modification technique that can greatly improve employee performance and productivity.

In some of his early experiments, Skinner found that any random act of a pigeon would be repeated if it was immediately reinforced with value (a kernel of corn). Thus, if he wanted a pigeon to peck a disc the size of a quarter, he would reinforce the pigeon with corn if the pigeon just happened to peck near the disc. If it pecked the disc itself, it would get several kernels. After a short time, the pigeon would peck the disc and keep on pecking it any number of times.

Skinner discovered that people, too, would repeat behavior that was immediately reinforced with value. They didn't even have to know they were being reinforced. The value could be psychological reinforcement such as praise, recognition, or appreciation.

Other psychologists have used such reinforcers as a smile, a head nod, the words "fine," "good," and even a "hmmm" to get subjects to be more communicative; express more personal opinions; and ask more questions, and all without the subject realizing what was happening.

There are countless ways to harness the power of positive reinforcement to encourage employees to repeat desirable behavior. For example, tell them:

"Thank you for always being so _____ (cheerful, punctual, helpful). We really appreciate that."

"Mrs. Johnson told me how sensitive and caring you were following the bad news she received last Wednesday. Thank you for your thoughtfulness."

"Congratulations on a terrific job! I'm proud to have you on our team."

The words you use are less important than the fact that you're acknowledging someone's efforts in a way that has motivational value.

➡**Principle involved:** Behavior that's reinforced tends to be repeated. Behavior that's ignored tends to be extinguished.

This chapter includes many practical applications of this important principle.

104 The Importance of Praise

In an Internet survey conducted by best-selling author Bob Nelson, Ph.D., 87.9 percent of 762 respondents ranked "being personally thanked for doing good work" as either "extremely important" or "very important." In addition, 60.8 percent of the respondents did the same for "being praised for good work in front of others."[1]

Finding something nice to say about others may seem trivial, but it satisfies a universal hunger. Unfortunately, people who feel appreciation often fail to express it.

Many healthcare office personnel whom I've interviewed feel most thwarted and frustrated about their work because of a lack of appreciation. Included are those who do above-average work, but receive no special recognition or appreciation. Many have said, "The only time I get any feedback about my work is when I make a mistake." And they believe their efforts to do a good job are not even *noticed*, let alone appreciated.

Some HCPs mistakenly assume their employees' need for appreciation can be *internally* met. ("She knows she does a good job" or "My employees know I value them—I don't have to tell them.") Even if that were true, a verbal pat on the back or a written note of thanks for a "job well done" provides the kind of psychological satisfaction for which there is absolutely no substitute.

When President Reagan wrote "Very Good" on the draft of a speech written by Peggy Noonan, she cut the words out, taped them to her blouse, and wore them all day.[2]

➡️**Hard learned lesson:** Good work that goes unnoticed and unappreciated tends to deteriorate, almost without exception.

➡️**From the success files:** "We implemented thank you notes in our organization and the impact has been beyond imagination," says Phil Bagby, CEO, Ozarks Medical Center, West Plains, Missouri. "The release of energy is felt as one walks the hallways. I get a thrill watching people do a great job who are excited about coming to work. This is new. And great."[3]

➡️**Action step:** Systematically start to thank your staff members when they do good work, whether it's one-on-one in person, in the hallway, at a staff meeting, by voicemail, through a written thank-you note, by email, or at the end of each day at work.

I guarantee it'll make their day. And by expressing appreciation, you may start a chain reaction. Praise begets praise. People will like you more for saying kind things, and you'll feel good for having said them.

"A lot of physicians don't stop during their busy days," says allergist Robyn Levy, Atlanta, Georgia. "Without meaning to be rude, they can be egocentric because the work revolves around them. But they need to stop and say things like, 'I really appreciate your filing all those charts. You did a great job.' It takes two seconds to say it."

"Nancy Merry, executive director of Medical Employment Directory of Springfield Inc., a healthcare recruiting firm in Springfield, Missouri, adds, 'As the medical community realizes quality staff is becoming more scarce, their efforts are starting to be acknowledged. If physicians don't acknowledge them, they are going to lose people and those practices are going to be floundering.'"[4]

➡**Reality check:** "The number one reason that physical therapists leave jobs is that they don't feel valued," concludes a Bernard Hodes survey conducted in partnership with Advance Magazines. "Thirty percent of PTs left their last jobs for that reason."[5]

105 Ask for Patient Feedback

While doing an in-service training program at a major hospital, I visited the ICU and noticed a lone patient's handwritten letter taped to the wall. It was a heartfelt note of thanks to all the nurses in the ICU—for their kindness, care, and attention received during the person's recent stay. The note was almost a year old.

When I stopped to read the note, I was told it was the first and only note they had received in several years.

➡**Reality check:** As grateful and appreciative as countless patients are for the services they receive, very few ever take the time to write a note of thanks.

➡**Action step:** In the office of periodontists Richard Roth, J. J. Boscarino, and Kevin Loshak, Westbury, New York, a patient survey included the following question:

> **Are there any of our staff members who should have special acknowledgment?**
>
> **Who?** _____
>
> **Why?** _____

One might say this is "fishing" for compliments. It does, however, generate feedback that might otherwise never be expressed. It results in recognition and reinforcement for those who have earned it. And as a bonus, it lets everyone on staff know the kinds of things that patients notice and appreciate.

106 The Feedback Gap

In the course of conducting seminars, I've asked more than 2,500 doctors to consider the following statement: *I let my employees know when they're doing a good job* and then rate themselves on a scale of 1 to 5 (1 = never; 5 = always). Their average response, 4.4.

So far, so good.

I've also asked *staff members* to consider the statement: *The doctor lets me know when I'm doing a good job*, using the same rating scale. The average response? Only 1.7.

The difference between the amount of positive feedback doctors *say* they give their employees and the amount employees say they *get* is what I call the Feedback Gap. And often, it's the underlying cause of employee resentment, diminished productivity, and turnover.

➡**Reality check:** "At a time when employees are being asked to do more than ever before, the resources and support for helping them are at all time lows," says Bob Nelson, Ph.D. and author of *1001 Ways to Reward Employees,* 2nd edition. "What used to be common courtesies have been overcome by speed and technology in today's businesses. Managers tend to be too busy and too removed from their employees to notice when they have done exceptional work—and to thank them for it. Because of technology, interfacing with one's computer terminal has replaced personal interaction between manager and employee."[6]

107 Letters to Home

At my seminars, one of the questions I've asked audiences is, How many of you have ever received a thank you letter from your boss . . . at your home? Invariably only a handful of people have ever received such a letter (which is in keeping with the previously stated point that very few people ever take the time to write a note of thanks).

When asked if they have kept these letters, the answer is invariably, "Yes"—with some admitting their letters were received long ago, but still treasured.

➡**Reality check:** Being acknowledged at home about your day-to-day work in a way that can be shared with one's family and friends is a morale builder—second to none. Part of the power of praise comes from the knowledge that someone noticed your efforts and took the time to write such a thoughtful note.

➡**From the success files:** The following is a year-end letter received by Wanda Clough, a receptionist in the office of Dr. Thomas H. Risbrudt, San Clemente, California:

Dear Wanda,

Introverts don't always communicate like they should. They hold a lot of things inside and many, many things go unsaid. A sentimental introvert like me is even worse. He gets choked up when he gives compliments, and because getting choked up isn't "macho," even compliments sometimes are left unsaid.

So, I'm using an introverted approach with this note to let you know how much I really appreciate you and the job you're doing for me. It staggers me when I think of all your duties and responsibilities; the stress of our tight budget; making collections; shouldering crank calls and screening out others; being the queen of the appointment book; the mounds of insurance forms; correspondence; the post-op calls; and appointment confirmations; and all the many, many things that you do in the line of duty which are above and beyond.

All this I get and as a bonus, a cheerful, professional attitude. I count myself very lucky to have you in my employ, Wanda—and at this special thankful time of year, I just want to express my warmest, personal thanks for a job well done.

Dr. Tom

108 Letters to Family Members

Employees who start work at an extremely early hour—or work late— or put in overtime hours—are, in many cases, depriving their families of time with them. Here are a few examples of how that kind of sacrifice can be acknowledged.

- Write a letter to the employee's family expressing your appreciation for extra hours the employee has given to the job, and explaining specifically what he or she has done and what it means to you and the practice.
- A certificate for dinner for two (at a choice of Toronto, Canada's top restaurants) is presented by the Toronto office of IBM of Canada to an employee by his or her manager for putting out extra effort on a special task—especially when

it involved extra hours that had an impact on his or her personal or family life.

- A few years ago, while I was conducting a weekend seminar in California for the accounting firm Ernst & Young, my wife Martha (at home in New York) received a lovely gift package of fruit and cheese from the firm. It was timed to arrive during the weekend of the seminar—and with it was a note of thanks for sharing me with the group.

109 Letters to Volunteers

"It's true that most employees do not feel appreciated," says best-selling author Bob Nelson, "but the group of employees I've found to be the most unappreciated are volunteers. Of course, they're not there because of the money, but more times than not they still get taken for granted."[7]

"Several years ago as director of a local state hospital," wrote Dr. Walt Menninger, former president and CEO of the Menninger Clinic, "I was aware of the enormous number of hours of time spent by volunteers working in the hospital. They came to arrange social activities for patients, escort patients on shopping trips, work in the shops, help the staff with tasks of filing, and do so many other things. All too often the regular staff tended to take their efforts for granted."

"I knew these people weren't volunteering just to get somebody's thanks," Menninger wrote. "They did it because it made them feel good to be of service and to give time and concern to others who needed it. They did appreciate the annual ceremony of recognition for their hours which was held each spring. But I thought Thanksgiving would be a good time to thank them again, and sent each one a note to again say thank you. And the positive reactions which I received were striking, in large part because the additional thanks were unexpected."[8]

➥**Reality check:** How often do you give praise? More to the point, how often have you failed to do so in situations where praise was truly deserved?

110 Hard Learned Lessons About Appreciation

- *Appreciation* results in short-term motivation. *Achievement* leads to long-term motivation.
- "Silent gratitude isn't very much use to anyone," —Robert Louis Stevenson.
- "Money is a powerful incentive—it will help get people to do what you want—but money does nothing to stoke a person's internal fire," say Roger Dow and Susan Cook, co-authors of *Turned On.* "Enduring motivation comes from inside, and heartfelt recognition gets it going. When you give sincere praise, you connect with people emotionally—they work harder because they want to, not because you pay them to."[9]
- "One of the keys to Atlanta allergist Robyn Levy's success as a solo practitioner," writes Karen Gatzke in *Physicians Practice*, "is thanking her staff of 15 every day. It takes no effort to say, 'Thanks for your hard work' or 'I couldn't have done it without you today.' 'I really do mean it,' she says, adding, 'and when a patient compliments the staff, I'm sure to pass it on.'"[10]
- "Outstanding leaders," said Sam Walton, founder of Wal-Mart, "go out of their way to boost the self-esteem of their personnel. If people believe in themselves, it's amazing what they can accomplish."[11]
- Southwest Airlines earns its loyal customers by putting its employees first, according to Kathy Pettit, director of customers. "When employees feel happy, rewarded, recognized and ennobled by their work, they're more inclined to serve their customers well. Ennobled," Pettit explains, "is feeling appreciated that what they do has value. We thank our employees all the time for their contributions and their hard work."[12]
- Some people would rather have *praise* than a *raise.*

111 The Power of Recognition

In a research study of 1,500 employees in a variety of work settings, Dr. Gerald Graham, professor of management at Wichita State University in

Wichita, Kansas, found that personalized, instant recognition from managers was the most powerful motivator of the 65 potential incentives he evaluated. Second was a letter of praise for good performance written by the manager.[13]

"When Baptist Health Care employees, Pensacola, Florida, are surveyed about what they most want in their jobs, recognition for a job well done always ranks the highest."[14]

➡**Reality check:** Lack of recognition and praise is the number one reason employees leave an organization, noted MeChelle Callen, SPHR, director of human resource development at Wishard Health Services in Indianapolis, Indiana, at the 2005 Society for Human Resource Management (SHRM) Conference on "Why Money Doesn't Buy Happiness— or Employee Loyalty."[15]

Callen cited SHRM's *Survey of Human Resource Trends,* which found that 70 percent of employees listed "lack of appreciation" as one of the top reasons they would leave their job.

112 Create an A.B.C.D. Award

An A.B.C.D. (Above and Beyond the Call of Duty) Award is given for exceptional service.

In their book, *Managing Knock Your Socks Off Service*, Chip R. Bell and Ron Zemke tell the story of a patient at St. Luke's Medical Center in Milwaukee, Wisconsin, who lost an inexpensive but favorite pair of slippers during his stay. Housekeeping, after learning of the man's complaint, concluded that someone had mistakenly thrown out the slippers and was quick to offer a heartfelt apology. Not good enough. Offers to pay for the patient's slippers were also not satisfactory. The patient wanted *those* slippers.

A young, part-time housekeeper who knew of the situation decided to do what he could. Acting on his own, he got a detailed description of the slippers from the patient, went to a store, and using his own money purchased a replacement pair of identical slippers. The patient was surprised. And elated. And the young part-time housekeeper? He received St. Luke's first ever award for a most meritorious act. It's called the Golden Slipper Award.[16]

ⓘⓘⓑ Individualization Is the Key

"People differ in what they want to be applauded and appreciated for, depending on what personal qualities and talents they're most proud of," says Marc Talbin, CEO of a high-tech staffing consulting company in Sunnyvale, California. "My experience in managing people is that everyone is different," he adds. "Some want to be recognized for the quality of their work, some for the quantity of their work. Some people want to be recognized for their cheerful attitude and their ability to spread their cheerful attitude. Some like to be recognized individually; others want to be recognized in groups. No one has ever said, 'Just recognize me for anything I do well.'"

To identify which parts of individual employees' egos need scratching, Talbin takes an unconventional approach: he *asks* them.[17]

➡**Reality check:** A report at an Academy of Management meeting showed that individuals differed significantly in their responses to these two statements:

- "Even though I may think I have done a good job, I feel a lot more confident of it after someone else tells me so."
- "As long as I think I have done something well, I am not too concerned about how other people think I have done."

In other words, people differ dramatically in their need for and responsiveness to external feedback.

➡**Tested tip:** One clue to a job applicant's need for appreciation is his or her answer to the question: **In your last job, did you receive the recognition and appreciation you felt you deserved?**

A good follow-up question is: **What was the best recognition you've ever had?**

ⓘⓘⓓ Good Intentions May Miss the Mark

With the very best of intentions, many HCPs have made a "ritual" about an annual holiday party or year-end gifts. In many cases, they have missed the mark.

➡**Reality check:** "University of Michigan Hospitals and Health Centers, Ann Arbor, had held summer picnics as far back as people could remember. "When we began questioning managers about their recognition practices, they all pointed to that day as if to say, 'Well, we *did* the picnic,' says Denise White, chairwoman, employee recognition programs."

"White was hired about five years ago to question assumptions, so her next task was to ask employees what they thought of the picnic. 'The data was fairly compelling,' she jokes. 'They hated it. They said they didn't feel appreciated by a once-a-year blowout picnic.'"

What UMHHC considered to be one of its major recognition events was actually a flop. Not long after her arrival, White embarked on a comprehensive employee recognition program. "Where before, UMHHC's strategy put patients and families first, now employees are considered important customers as well. There is a newsletter applauding employee efforts, a Web site, a TV station, and numerous recognition programs and ceremonies. Included in the vision statement is not only that UMHHC be 'the first place people want to come when they need healthcare,' but also 'the place where people prefer to work.' With each new wave of surveys, it's clear that customer service is up, and workers feel more motivated."[18]

➥**Action step:** The consensus of HCPs and practice managers I've queried about annual parties, dinners, picnics, or gifts is: "Ask employees what they want and listen to them."

115 Hard Learned Lessons About Recognition

- "Recognition really matters—to people, performance and your organization," says consultant Wendy Leebov, Ed.D. "It says, 'I see you. You make a difference. You matter to me and the organization.'"[19]
- Prove the significance of your employees. Make sure everyone on your staff feels famous for something. You want them to always have a reason to come to work.
- A key to effective recognition is recognizing the person immediately following his or her efforts. Delayed mention of it is similar to a belated birthday card. It is perceived as an afterthought and loses its value. Make time for recognition.
- One of the guidelines for employee recognition at The Jackson Organization, Columbia, Maryland—a full-service

market research firm that offers a combination of customized research and healthcare expertise—is: "Have a system where *any* employee can recognize *anyone*. No matter what their position is (or the position of the person they wish to recognize), let them go right ahead. With this approach, it's up to each and every employee to drive the recognition program. Our philosophy is direct and proactive. Supervisors and managers—don't wait for your employees to do it. Employees—don't wait for your supervisors to do it."[20]

- In order for recognition to be effective, it must be *earned*. Many HCPs think it is a good idea to recognize employees who are struggling in hopes of motivating them to improve. Their intentions are good, but the results are detrimental. Doing so reinforces the wrong behaviors, condones poor performance, and may discourage the high-performing employees. Instead, conduct a performance review to determine the root cause of the issues and encourage such employees. Once they have improved to a higher level, then recognize their achievements.

- A Harris poll among a nationwide cross-section of 695 adults revealed that: "Among those who work who get a lot of recognition and appreciation, fully 68 percent are very satisfied with their jobs; only 13 percent of those whose work receives little or no recognition are very satisfied."[21]

- Employees will occasionally slip. We all have bad days. Applaud their successes rather than criticize their failures.

116 Make "Heroes" of Your Staff

According to management consultant and author Rosabeth Moss Kanter, "Saying thank you in public and perhaps giving a tangible gift along with it, has multiple functions beyond simple courtesy. To the employee, it signifies someone has noticed and cares. What is the point," she says, "of going all out to do something special if no one notices and it does not seem to make one whit of difference? To the rest of the organization, recognition creates role models—*heroes*—and communicates the standard: these are the kinds of things that constitute good performance around here."[22]

➡**From the success files:** After reading a chapter titled "All the Good Things" in *Chicken Soup for the Soul* by Jack Canfield and Mark Victor Hansen, the staff of Dr. Marty Becker in Boise, Idaho, passed around a form with every employee's name. "Everyone wrote something nice about each employee," Becker says. "The doctors then laminated a list of individual comments for each employee."

"Then we invited employees to the first Annual Employee Appreciation dinner," he recalls. "Doctors and managers prepared and served the meal. After dinner, the doctors read each list and everyone tried to guess the person being described. Employees laughed and cried. No longer a cog in the wheel, these heroes were awakened to their worth and career possibilities. That night," he adds, "we ignited long-term motivation."[23]

⑪⑦ Express Pride in Your Staff

- Have a staff directory with names, earned credentials, and job titles. It will "personalize" your practice.
- "Start a 'Wall of Fame,'" suggests *Practice Marketing & Management.* "Highlight outstanding accomplishments and employees in a place where staff and patients can see it. The employee's name and photograph are hung on the wall along with a brief description of why that person is being honored. It not only boosts morale, but it helps your patients know your staff better."[24]
- To express pride in their staffs, many HCPs include photos and write-ups of their employees on their practice Web sites. North Suburban Dental Associates in Skokie, Illinois, is an example whose Web site, www.nsdadentists.com, features individual color photos of more than 30 staff members and comments in their own words about their families, careers, jobs, or the practice itself. An appealing "family feeling" comes through. Many of the employees have been with the practice for well over a decade, some two decades, and one even three.

➡**Additional benefit:** Since launching their Web site, North Suburban Dental Associates has found that this staff longevity has also proved to be an important element to people who visit the site before showing up at the office. "We have found," says Dr. Barry Freydberg, "that staff longevity has been a major confidence-builder in new patients we haven't yet met. We didn't know this would be an influence on new patients but it has. Our credibility gets a boost based on staff longevity."[25]

➡**Hard learned lesson:** "Health care is really about valuable human beings caring for vulnerable human beings," says Wendy Leebov, Ed.D., author of *Service Excellence: The Customer Relations Strategy for Health Care.* "It is the work of the soul. Health care employees have always deserved to be admired and supported in their caring work. It is our job," she says, "to create caring communities that help them flourish. They will feel gratified in their lives. Our patients will benefit by receiving the care and service they deserve. And your organization will be able to maintain a more experienced, harmonious and stable team."[26]

➡**Reality check:** "Building pride is hardly a new idea," writes John A. Byrne in *Fast Company.* "The most effective leaders have always known that the best work is inspired not by economics alone, but also by emotions, and they have engaged employees as allies, creating a sense of accomplishment, camaraderie, and emotional attachment that helps achieve big goals. Pride building," he says, "is at the core of many high-performing organizations, ranging from the U.S. Marines to Southwest Airlines."[27]

(118) Winter Holiday Surprise

At last year's year-end holiday party, Dr. Chris Kammer, president and owner of the Center for Cosmetic Dentistry in Madison, Wisconsin, had a surprise for his staff of 25. "When the employees finished eating, he asked them to wait a few minutes. Then two stretch limousines driven by chauffeurs in Santa outfits pulled up to the curb outside the office. The staff was invited to climb into the limos and drink Champagne, eat bonbons and sing along to a holiday CD that Dr. Kammer himself had burned."

"The employees were whisked to a local mall, where he presented each of them with a $100 bill and gave them an hour to spend it all. Whatever money they didn't spend in that time, they had to return."

"While the main reward was still money, Dr. Kammer said he believed that the experience surrounding it would be more fondly remembered than the cash of years past."

"The money alone was drab," he said. "This is something they're never going to forget."[28]

119 Don't Neglect the "Little Things"

- Those "good mornings" at the start of the day really do matter. Don't forget them.
- Those "good nights" at the end of the day combined with a "thank you" matter even more.
- For years, patients have been told to see "the girl at the front desk." It's no surprise that some employees feel like second-class workplace citizens.
- When an employee has a private matter to discuss with you, telling your receptionist to "hold all calls" sends a very different message than taking numerous calls (other than medical emergencies) during your conversation.

➡**From the success files:** A medical assistant with whom I was speaking at a recent seminar told me about a job offer she received from another practice. It offered her more money but she turned it down.

I asked her why.

"I can't leave this office," she said. "The doctor is thoughtful in ways I'll never forget. For example, when my husband and I recently vacationed in Bermuda, we found on our arrival, a tremendous bouquet of flowers in our room from him and his wife. He had remembered that this was where we had honeymooned."

Over the years, I've heard countless, similar stories. They reinforce my conviction in the importance of the "little things"—not as a *substitute* for salary and benefits, but as an important *supplement*.

120 Discretionary Effort

Why do some employees pitch in and help each other when needed or go out of their way to be friendly and accommodating to patients, while other staff members do only what's required of them and no more?

The answer has to do with *discretionary effort.*

Discretionary effort is the difference between the *minimum* a person is required to do to keep one's job and avoid reprimands and the *extra effort* a person is capable of making on the job, above and beyond the job description.

"Work is contractual; effort is personal," say Bill Catlette and Richard Hadden, co-authors of *Contented Cows Give Better Milk*.

So what makes the difference? they ask. Why do some people give a 110 percent effort to a job while others give only 60 or 70 percent?

"Some of this," say Catlette and Hadden, "is institutional. Some organizations seem to have more people playing their 'A' game more of the time than most of their competitors. Another large part of the equation," they add, "simply has to do with how we're wired. Call it what you like—character, commitment, work ethic. Some of us are simply more devoted to giving our all than others, regardless of the presence or absence of outside motivators. Everyone has an 'A' game and a 'C' game. But for some folks, 'A' just seems to be the default condition."[29]

➡**Action steps:** Among Catlette and Hadden's recommendations:

- Hire people with a proven record of going the extra mile. Look for it in their résumés and listen for it in interviews. Watch for signs of self-initiated development efforts like taking courses outside of work, taking on unpopular assignments, and volunteering in the community.
- Make an extra effort to build, maintain, and protect trust between people and the people with whom you work. We'll do an awful lot for those we trust and precious little for those we don't.
- Don't take advantage of those who customarily give their all. Everyone has a limit, say Catlette and Hadden. The fastest route to an "A" player's "C" game is to take their extra efforts for granted.
- "When people do, indeed go above and beyond the call of duty, let them know you appreciate it. Really appreciate it. Thank them genuinely. Reward them. Acknowledge their work as truly special and let them know you know the difference between doing the minimum required and playing one's 'A' game."[30]

How does one tap into and nurture the discretionary effort of employees? The next chapter addresses that question.

References

1. Nelson B. What Do Employees Want? Employee Recognition Practices Inventory. www.nelson-motivation.com
2. Nelson B. *1001 Ways to Reward Employees,* 2nd ed. New York: Workman Publishing Company; 2005.
3. Stavrenos L, Crouch L. Maximizing the Power of Thank You Notes. www.studergroup.com
4. Gatzke K. A Satisfied Staff Pays Off. *Physicians Practice,* July/August 2002.
5. Raphael T. Health Professionals Share Their Candid (and Mixed) Feelings About the Field, August 9, 2005. http://www.workforce.com/section/00/article/24/13/49.html
6. Nelson B. *1001 Ways to Reward Employees,* 2nd ed. New York: Workman Publishing; 2005.
7. Ibid.
8. Menninger W. Thank You—The Magic Words, *Universal Press Syndicate,* November 27, 1975. INSIGHTS by Dr. Walt Menninger. © 1975 Universal Press Syndicate.
9. Dow R, Cook S. *Turned On.* New York: HarperCollins; 1996.
10. Gatzke K. A Satisfied Staff Pays Off. *Physicians Practice,* July/August 2002.
11. Bergdahl M. *What I Learned from Sam Walton: How to Compete and Thrive in a Wal-Mart World.* New York: John Wiley & Sons, 2004.
12. The HSM Group. Loyalty Lessons. *The Loyalty Line.* http://www.hsmgroup.com
13. Nelson B. Dump the Cash, Load on the Praise. *Personnel Journal,* July 1996, 65–70.
14. Baptist Leadership Institute. Reward and Recognition. http://www.baptistleadershipinstitute.com/Articles/Articles.aspx?ContentID=100002
15. Callen M. *Why Money Doesn't Buy Happiness or Employee Loyalty,* 2005 Society for Human Resource Management (SHRM) Conference, Indianapolis, Indiana, July 31, 2005.
16. Bell CR, Zemke R. *Managing Knock Your Socks Off Service.* New York: AMACOM; 1992.
17. Buchanan L. Managing One-to-One. *Inc.,* October 2001, 83–89.
18. Atkinson W. Inside Job. *Corporate Meetings & Incentives,* November 2005, 19–21.
19. Leebov W. How Do You Say Thanks. *HHN Magazine,* August 30, 2005.
20. Around the Office, March 2006, http://www.jacksonorganization.com
21. The Harris Poll #74, Three Factors Appear to Have Big Impact on Job Satisfaction, December 20, 2000. http://www.harrisinteractive.com/harris_poll/index.asp?PID=208
22. Nelson B. Celebrating Employee Achievements. *Potentials in Marketing,* June 1995, 10.
23. Becker M. Celebrate Everyday Heroes. *Veterinary Economics,* June 1997, 30–35.
24. When You Can't Afford to Give Raises. *Practice Marketing & Management,* June 1998, 78.

25. Spaeth D. Winning Web Sites. *Dental Practice Report*, January/February 2002, 36–40.
26. Leebov W. Less Turnover, Better Care. *HHN Magazine*, October 18, 2005.
27. Byrne JA. How to Lead Now. *Fast Company*, August 2003, 62.
28. Ligos M. Those Year-End Bonuses Aren't Always Green. *New York Times*, December 28, 2003, BU8.
29. Catlette B, Hadden R. *Fresh Milk*, January 2005. http://www.contentedcows.com
30. Ibid.

Chapter Ten

MANAGING

From "Satisfied" to "Engaged"

Y ou sense it the moment you walk in the front door of an office where people are engaged. The most noticeable characteristic is the level of energy and emotional commitment that employees exhibit. Even the casual observer can feel the difference when walking the halls. People move faster, interact with more visible animation, communicate with more palpable emotion and enthusiasm, listen more intently, and respond more vigorously—and really enjoy themselves in the process. Moreover this energy seems to persist throughout the day, day after day. Some call it fun. Others describe it as challenging and stimulating. To outside observers, it can appear exhausting as well.

How does it happen?

121 The "Showing Up" Mindset

Comedian/filmmaker Woody Allen observed that 80 percent of success is showing up. Presumably he was joking, but countless HCPs have confided that many of their employees seem to have taken this advice to heart. They walk through the door each morning, go through the motions of work, collect their pay, and at the end of the day, care little about whether or not the practice is successful—so long as it continues to provide for their employment.

The prevalence of this "showing up" mindset is what separates the top performers from their less-valued co-workers. It doesn't stop there, however. It also separates the practices that are able to sustain practice growth from those that struggle. Those practices that sustain success have employees who aren't just in jobs, but also are *into their jobs*. They are, in a word, *engaged.*

Engaged employees put more discretionary effort into their work. They have greater psychological commitment to their work, go above and beyond their basic job descriptions, and want to play a key role in fulfilling the mission of their organizations. A radiology technologist who sees a patient shivering as she climbs onto the X-ray table and places a blanket on the table to keep the patient warm provides just one example of the caring attitude and willingness to take extra steps that are characteristic of engaged healthcare employees.

In contrast, those employees who aren't engaged tend to do, at most, only what's required to get by. These differences have a tremendous impact on productivity, patient satisfaction, patient loyalty, and ultimately, profitability and practice growth.

122 The Engagement Gap

Jack Welch, former CEO of General Electric, once said, "Any company trying to compete . . . must figure out a way to engage the mind of every employee."[1]

In a massive, in-depth study of employee engagement, The Gallup Organization correlated performance data from over 2,500 business units and opinion data from over 105,000 employees. Its findings indicated that between 50 and 60 percent of employees are not doing their best work. On top of that, in those organizations Gallup studied, 15 to 20 percent of employees were what Gallup called "actively disengaged," meaning they're just showing up and going through the motions, and might quit at any moment. The study concluded that 75 to 80 percent of these employees were achieving much less and feeling far less enthusiastic about their work than they could be.

In their book about this study, *Follow This Path,* Gallup executives Curt Coffman and Gabriel Gonzalez-Molina, Ph.D. say this state of affairs is more costly than one might think. "It costs the U.S. economy up to $300 billion dollars a year in lost productivity—undoubtedly an underestimate because it does not account for absence, illness, and other problems that result when workers are disengaged from their work."[2]

To the extent it exists in your practice, this chapter focuses on ways to narrow that engagement gap.

123 How Engaged Is Your Healthcare Team?

In its study of employee engagement, The Gallup Organization wanted to identify the issues about which the most engaged employees felt most strongly about.

After extensive analysis (including a combination of focus groups, factor analysis, regression analysis, concurrent validity studies, and follow-up interviews) the following 12 questions were used to measure the core elements needed to attract, focus, and keep the most talented employees. The research is documented in the book, *First Break All the Rules,* written by Marcus Buckingham and Curt Coffman.

The employees (who represented a cross section of 12 distinct industries) were asked to respond to each of the 12 questions on a scale of 1 to 5, 1 meaning "strongly agree" and 5 meaning "strongly disagree."

1. Do I know what is expected of me?
2. Do I have the materials and equipment I need to do my work right?
3. At work, do I have the opportunity to do what I do best every day?
4. In the last seven days, have I received recognition or praise for good work?
5. Does my supervisor, or someone at work, seem to care about me as a person?
6. Is there someone at work who encourages my development?
7. At work, do my opinions seem to count?

8. Does the mission/purpose of my company make me feel like my work is important?
9. Are my co-workers committed to doing quality work?
10. Do I have a best friend at work?
11. In the last six months, have I talked with someone about my progress?
12. At work, have I had opportunities to learn and grow?

What the authors found was that "those employees who responded more positively to the twelve questions also worked in business units with higher levels of productivity, profit, retention and customer satisfaction. This demonstrated for the first time, the link between employee opinion and business unit performance, across many different companies."[3]

You may be wondering why there were no questions dealing with pay, benefits, or advancement. "There were initially," say Buckingham and Coffman, "but they disappeared during the analysis. This doesn't mean they're unimportant. It simply means they are equally important to every employee, good, bad or mediocre. Yes, if you are paying 20 percent below the market average, you may have difficulty attracting people. But bringing your pay and benefit package up to market levels, while a sensible first step, will not take you very far. These kinds of issues are like tickets to the ballpark—they can get you into the game, but they can't help you win."[4]

➥**Action step:** By *guessing* how your employees would answer these questions (or better yet, actually *learning* first-hand) you can estimate the degree to which your employees are engaged—and perhaps identify what is needed to improve their mindset.

Each of these issues is addressed throughout this book—starting with expectations, the subject of the first question in the previous list.

124 Agree on Mutual Expectations

It's an old story. A new employee discovers, perhaps on the first day, or in the first week, or maybe not until months later, that the job is not what he or she expected, and quits. When this happens, the recruiting process must begin again, followed by training, lost productivity, and expenses that might have been avoided.

Truth be told, recently hired employees often have unrealistic expectations about their jobs, as do HCPs and office managers about the people they hire. These one-sided, unspoken expectations often lead to disappointment and resentment on both sides. They're based on the presumption that both sides will cooperate with a plan that has never actually been discussed between them.

➡**Reality check:** "Research reveals that less than 50 percent of employees claim that they know what is expected of them at work," says Marcus Buckingham, author of *The One Thing You Need to Know . . . About Great Managing, Great Leading, and Sustained Individual Success.* "Apparently, while all managers know that setting clear expectations is paramount, most struggle to execute."[5]

➡**Action step:** "In the interview process, you have to let people know exactly what you expect of them, and find out what they expect of you," says Harvey McKay, author of *Swim with the Sharks Without Being Eaten Alive.* "Find out what their goals and dreams are, where they want to be in five years, and be honest about whether or not you can give them what they want."[6]

125 The Psychological Contract

In his classic article, "The Psychological Contract: Managing the Joining-Up Process," John Paul Kotter defined the psychological contract as "an implicit contract between an individual and the organization which specifies what each expects to give and receive from each other in the relationship."[7]

As shown below, matches and mismatches can occur based on the four sets of expectations in this hidden contract.

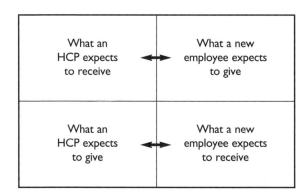

The psychological contract: two parties, four sets of expectations[8]

➥**Reality check:** When HCPs and newly hired employees have entirely different agendas and worse, never discuss these agendas, invariably one or both parties are surprised when things don't turn out as expected.

For example, new employees may be resentful when, *after* being hired, they first learn about:

- The long hours they're expected to work
- The volume of paperwork (or patients) they're expected to handle
- The routine and repetitive aspects of their job
- Tasks they never expected (or want) to perform (about which nothing was said at the time they were hired)
- How closely their work is supervised and micromanaged
- The lack of input they're allowed in decisions made about their job responsibilities
- The slow progress of increased compensation

By the same token, HCPs may be equally disappointed when recently hired employees:

- Complain about staying late so the last patients of the day can be seen
- Spend too much time socializing with co-workers and/or patients
- Fail to take an interest in continuing education and professional growth
- Won't conform to the organization's culture
- Are unable (or unwilling) to work effectively in teams
- Have unrealistic expectations about salary increases, bonuses, and promotion

The failure to have up-front discussions about such matters is understandable. An HCP who is anxious to hire an employee doesn't want to scare off a good candidate by making excessive demands about the future. Likewise, a job applicant doesn't want to jeopardize a good career opportunity by doing the same. However, without discussing such expectations at the start, it is unlikely that everyone will end up "on the same page." Disappointment for one or both parties is inevitable.

Kotter's research confirmed what most of us would expect—that the greater the matching of mutual expectations, the greater the probability of employee engagement, job satisfaction, and productivity.

➡**Action steps:**

- Ask prospective employees about their job-related expectations. Often, in listening to their answers, it becomes obvious that they would not fit the job or the culture of the practice.
- "A detailed and accurate job description is crucial for recruiting and hiring personnel," says Robert J. Holzhauer, M.D., M.B.A., Rochester, New York. "It is impossible for even an inexperienced nurse or clerical worker to know how well they will fit into a job situation without an idea of what will be expected of him or her."[9]
- Initiate a frank and open discussion of job-related responsibilities, performance expectations, working conditions, rules and policies, practice culture, management style, or other topics where surprises need to be minimized. Emphasize the positives but don't gloss over potential negatives that, when later encountered after hiring, may cause a new employee to abruptly quit or disengage.

➡**Reality check:** If you do lose a prospective employee by divulging the truth about the job or workplace, then you probably would have lost him or her anyway within the first few months on the job. By discussing the truth up front, and allowing prospective employees to opt out, you've actually saved the cost of having to replace and retrain.

126 Energize the Job

"Energizing a job means structuring ways for employees to get the growth, challenge, and renewal they seek without leaving their current jobs," say Beverly Kaye and Sharon Jordan-Evans, co-authors of *Love 'Em or Lose 'Em: Getting Good People to Stay.*

"Changing what your employees do (content) and how they do it (process) is the key," say Kaye and Jordan-Evans. "Energizing allows employees to take on different tasks and responsibilities or to accomplish them in ways that promote personal autonomy and creativity. An energized job promotes setting and achieving personal and group goals;

allows employees to see their contributions to an end product or goal; challenges employees to expand their knowledge and capabilities; and gives employees room to initiate, create and implement new ideas."

"How do you energize the job? Try asking your employees questions like these:

- **Do you know how your job is important to the organization?**
- **What skills do you use on the job? What talents do you have that you don't use?**
- **What about your job do you find challenging? Rewarding?**
- **In what areas would you like increased responsibility for your current tasks?**
- **What would you like to be doing in the next three to five years?**
- **In what ways would you like your job changed?"**

➡**Reality check:** "These are important issues that don't all have to be resolved in just one conversation," say Kaye and Jordan-Evans. "Don't feel as if you're required to have all the answers—or be the "problem solver. To (re)energize the job, these discussions should be collaborative."[10]

➡**Hard learned lesson:** High-quality jobs—jobs that offer autonomy, learning opportunities, meaning, and a chance to get ahead— energize employees and win their commitment. Supportive workplaces help employees be more effective workers, people, and parents. Employers who can provide these better quality jobs and supportive workplaces have a clear competitive edge.

127 Job Sculpting

Job sculpting involves using what we know about employees to customize jobs—building on their particular strengths, making their work schedules do-able and their lives manageable, says Wendy Leebov, Ed.D., co-author of *The Indispensable Health Care Manager: Success Strategies for a Changing Environment.* "The age of generic solutions to people management," she adds, "is gone."

"Some organizations," Leebov says, "are making individual work arrangements with caregivers. For instance, recruitment and retention 'swat teams' work with one patient care unit at a time to address issues that different individuals within that unit identify as interfering with their job satisfaction. Some negotiate for conference attendance and additional learning opportunities instead of certain other benefits. Some negotiate for tuition support for their children instead of themselves. Some negotiate for physical help for all patient lifting, so they can work despite back problems. While it is complicated to do job sculpting to this degree, and it requires human resource guidance to stay within the law," says Leebov, "imagine the talent and energy it unleashes for patient care and service."[11]

➥**Action steps:** Leverage people's intrinsic motivation. Go beyond the traditional management practice of simply observing what employees do well and what they do, if anything, that needs improvement. Look, instead, for when they are operating at peak performance, radiating energy and showing total engagement. Then provide more of these optimal performance opportunities, if possible, in their daily routine.

Gallup research indicates that only 20 percent of employees feel that their strengths are in play every day. In the book based on this research, *Now Discover Your Strengths*, authors Marcus Buckingham and Donald O'Clifton interpret this alarming statistic to mean, "most organizations operate at [only] 20 percent capacity." They further suggest that to spur high-margin growth and increase organizational value, organizations need only focus inward to find the wealth of unrealized capacity that resides in every single employee.[12]

HCPs and practice managers who help their employees discover and operationalize their intrinsic motivators by identifying their personal talents and interests create an environment in which peak performance flourishes, job satisfaction soars, and practice growth occurs—all at no cost.

➥**Reality check:** In some cases, job sculpting may simply mean adding another assignment to existing responsibilities. In other cases, it may require moving that employee to a new position altogether.

128 Job Challenge

Providing employees with adequate job challenges is another key tool for keeping them engaged. One way to think about job challenge is to consider the gap between employees' current abilities and the demands of the tasks they are to accomplish. Too little challenge leads to boredom, and too much challenge leads to job stress.

➡**Action step:** "Help your employees stretch their skills. It will help make their jobs more interesting," says Buffalo, New York, internist Allyn M. Norman. "People like to work to their maximum level." Of course when you hire staff, you have to look for individuals who want to be challenged, he adds.

The way to get staff functioning at the upper range of their capacity, says Norman, is to give each staffer a little more responsibility than what he or she can handle. "Sometimes you have to push a little. If someone is at the border, you may have to spend a little more time training her, so next time she can do it herself."[13]

➡**Reality check:** "When you're considering whether to increase the responsibilities of a particular staffer, make sure you know what the state regulations are," cautions Linda Turner, operations coordinator for internist Charles S. Burger in Bangor, Maine. "Be careful not to ask your employees to take on something that falls outside the lawful scope of duty for their discipline," she stresses.[14]

➡**Hard learned lesson:** *Achievement* leads to motivation (not the other way around). You see it in the "high fives" that athletes trade after scoring a touchdown or hitting a homerun. You see it in the expression of someone on a diet who discovers after weeks of self-discipline that he's lost 5 pounds.

And you'll see it in the faces of your employees when they succeed at tasks that at first seemed challenging.

The point is: If you want to motivate employees, don't lecture them. Don't threaten them with dismissal if they don't improve. Instead, provide *s-t-r-e-t-c-h* and opportunities for growth.

➡**Reality check:** Along with stretch must go a willingness to accept some mistakes. Without risk there is no growth.

➥**Action step:** Ask employees what specific knowledge and skills they'd like to learn. Then design a program that incorporates the needs of individuals as well as the practice itself.

129 Participative Management

Another way to close the engagement gap is to give employees a voice in the decisions that affect them—often called "participative management."

HCPs who use participative decision making do not simply count the votes of their employees and then do whatever the majority wants. But they do consult with their employees before making a decision that affects them—partly to enlarge their information base, but also to tap into people's *self*-motivation.

➥**Hard learned lesson:** Most people will work harder to carry out a decision that they have helped to influence than they will work to carry out a decision that is imposed on them.

Skillful leaders understand the power of involving people in solving problems. When individuals and groups realize they truly have influence and authority to make a plan and execute it to reach the goal, engagement goes into high gear.

I've seen it happen at countless staff meetings that I've been allowed to attend as an outsider. The leader asks such questions as: "Why do you think this problem exists? What do you think we should do about it?" The brainstorming begins. As the group works together to solve the problem, their first joint decision ignites a spark. When they are then empowered to make decisions that lead to positive outcomes, it sets the team on fire.

➥**From the success files:** At ThedaCare's family practice group in Appleton, Wisconsin, "change isn't imposed from the top down; rather ideas are solicited from those staff members most familiar with particular aspects of the practice. Physicians and staff meet on a weekly basis to talk about what's working, what's not, and what fixes to make," says practice administrator Anne VanEpern. "Even staff members who have the day off, come in for the meeting."

"Everyone is involved in the decision-making," she says. "As a result, staff members realize that the day-to-day operation is ours to design. They know the doctors and administrators aren't creating policies behind closed doors, because decisions are made out in the open." VanEpern admits, however, "that it took time to convince the staffers that they could play a meaningful role."[15]

➥**Reality check:** "It's mostly a matter of dignity," says Saul W. Gellerman, Ph.D., author of *Motivation in the Real World.* "One of the best ways to recognize someone's abilities is to ask for his or her opinion. And one of the most effective ways to demonstrate contempt for someone, even if you don't intend to, is to act as if he or she has no opinions worth asking for. Participation," he adds, "is a good way to make sure that those who have to implement a decision will feel reasonably good about it."[16]

130 The Trust Factor

"Trusted leaders get many rewards: engaged employees, retention of top talent, positive work culture, and—most important—results," say Robert W. Rogers and Sheryl Riddle, president and senior vice president, respectively, of Development Dimensions International (DDI).[17]

"At the Great Place to Work® Institute we have been studying trust for many years," says Amy Lyman, founder and CEO. "Trust is found in three characteristics of workplace relationships. First, trust grows out of the ability to perceive others (management in particular) as credible—that what they say is true, that their actions are consistent with their words, and that they will be ethical in their business practices."

"Trust also depends," she says, "on how much employees experience respect—through support provided for professional growth, the inclusion of employees' ideas in decision-making, and through care, both within the workplace and in life outside work."

"Finally," Lyman says, "trust also grows out of a sense that one will be treated fairly by others—that regardless of position or personal characteristics, one can expect a certain level of fair and equitable treatment by people within the organization in terms of pay and benefits, career development opportunities, and the just resolution of problems or concerns."[18]

➥**Reality check:** Trust in organizational strategies and top management is the most critical component in creating commitment toward a common goal. Achieving that trust, however, can be difficult. "Maybe the boss can force a person to show up for work, especially in trying times," says management consultant/author Tom Peters, "but one cannot by definition, force a person to contribute his or her passion, and imagination on a regular basis."[19]

131 The Keys to Employee Trust

"The keys to developing employee trust," says The Jackson Organization, a healthcare market research firm in Columbia, Maryland, "are proactive and responsive management and communication. One way to reduce barriers between managers and staff at all levels is through better communication and the overall understanding among employees that management truly wants to hear their opinions and receive their input. When this is achieved, employees feel valued, and managers often receive invaluable feedback. To begin building a strong open-door policy, managers should ask themselves the following questions:"

> **"Am I easy to find?** By being where the action is, you'll learn what your physicians and employees need. You'll hear their concerns. Best of all, they'll understand your concerns with greater clarity.
>
> **Do I actively encourage criticism?** Think of criticism as an early warning system. But it must be solicited often enough that people take the requests seriously. This can occur at regular staff meetings, at one-on-one meetings, or each time a new project or idea is unveiled.
>
> **Am I quiet when they talk?** Managers must refrain from defending themselves when receiving criticism. If they are defensive each time someone criticizes them, co-workers will be hesitant to approach them.
>
> **Do I show them I'm listening**? When receiving criticism or suggestions for improvement, managers should paraphrase what was said. In this way, employees will know they were heard correctly, and managers will be sure that they know exactly what the speaker meant.
>
> **Do I say "thank you" when people criticize me?** Certainly, this feels awkward, but it demonstrates that the

manager really wants to hear other people's thoughts and suggestions."[20]

➥**From the success files:** "I build trust by being consistent in the kinds of values and ideas I hold, coupled with openness to other people's points of view," says Lillian R. Gorman, vice president of HR for Edison International. "I try to develop a style that lets other people participate meaningfully and bring their best thinking to the table. I need to allow others to prove me wrong and help me change course when my assumptions are questionable. I gain access to better ideas and more trust and cooperation if I listen well and keep an open mind. When you've been in human resources for a long time and dealt with similar employee, management and organizational problems over and over again, you tend to reach conclusions more quickly than you might have earlier in your career. The patience factor is critical to adding value. If somebody brings me a problem they've been laboring over, I might see the answer in a second. If I see a quick solution and convey a sense that it's simple, then immediately I have negated their concerns and in effect am saying, 'Why couldn't you see this?' It's better to really honor people and help them evaluate options to get to the conclusion, rather than just saying, 'Look, I've seen this 30 times before. This one's easy, just go and do this.'"[21]

132 Empower Employees

Simply put, empowerment means giving employees at all levels—the knowledge, confidence, and authority to make important decisions. Management offers guidance and leadership but issues few orders. Doing so sends a strong message that says, "I think you're trustworthy." This tells people you have faith in their abilities and you believe they've got what it takes to do the job. It's a confidence-builder second to none.

Management consultant Tom Peters claims that "trust is the issue of the decade."[22] "If employees feel you don't trust them to do their jobs correctly and well, they'll be reluctant to do much without your approval," say Anne Bruce and James S. Pepitone, co-authors of *Motivating Employees*. "On the other hand, when they feel trusted that you believe they'll do the right things well, they'll naturally want to do things well and be deserving of your trust."[23]

"As a physician," says urologist Neil Baum, co-author of *Take Charge of Your Medical Practice—Before Someone Else Does It for You,* "I am most effective when eyeball to eyeball with a patient—not enmeshed in office operations. Operational responsibilities are best left to my staff and I make every effort to empower my staff to make all non-medical decisions. If staff members come to me with questions or problems, I ask them what ideas or solutions they would suggest for those problems before I give my opinion. I want to encourage my staff to think on their own and to make every effort to solve the problems themselves. When employees know that you trust them to make decisions and that office procedures are in their hands, they work harder to accomplish what is expected of them to reach the practice goals and objectives."[24]

➡**From the success files:** "Our people feel empowered," says Jose Kottoor, P.T., M.S., director of physical therapy/occupational therapy in the Department of Physical Medicine and Rehabilitation (PMR) of the University of Michigan Health System (UMHC). "I can throw ideas out to them, and say, 'You make the decision.' A recent case in point was the need to combine PT/OT outpatient support staff to ensure 11-hour coverage in the outpatient area. The supervisors began discussing moving people, and we soon saw it wasn't working. We decided to ask the staff themselves—the ones who would be most affected by this change. We set the parameters—that we need this many people working these hours—and asked them to develop a schedule. After a few days, they came back with a schedule that was appropriate for everyone."[25]

Another type of empowerment is in play at Gulf Breeze Hospital in Gulf Breeze, Florida, where any employee can open the hospital gift shop and spend up to $250 to replace a patient's lost belongings or to buy flowers for a patient with a complaint.[26]

And still another: "When the stress of the practice turns the most cheerful of us into the most crabby, we treat the condition fast," says Pam Glick, hospital manager at Banfield, The Pet Hospital of Gurnee, Illinois. "Every team member is empowered, without repercussion, to alert any other team member—including doctors—that it's difficult to be around him or her at a given point. If that doesn't correct the situation (and it usually does) then the rest of the team determines the punishment for the unchecked crabby behavior."[27]

➡**Nordstrom's one rule:** The retail giant Nordstrom knows a lot about giving its employees space and empowering them to make decisions and manage their own work. In fact, managers credit their corporate culture for one of the highest retention rates in the retail industry. The primary rule, stated in Nordstrom's employee handbook, is this: Use your good judgment at all times.[28]

➡**Reality check:** Empowerment can be very challenging for people who are or who have become comfortable *not* being empowered, says management consultant James R. Lucas, author of *Fatal Illusions.* "Some people don't want to take or have responsibility, and they're uncomfortable with expectations in any form. They resist taking responsibility, leadership or risk. They'd rather be told what to do."[29]

➡**Action steps:** "The best way to empower team members is gradually and systematically," says Aubrey Daniels, author of *Bringing Out the Best in People.* "You can't say to people, 'Okay, after all these years of reporting to your boss, getting everything approved, and working within limited boundaries, you are free! You're on your own! Start taking responsibility and making decisions!' Responsibilities for self-management and decision making should bet turned over to employees on an as-ready basis and the responsibilities given initially should be limited in scope."[30]

133 Issues That Matter in the War for Talent

At the seminars I conduct throughout the country, many HCPs have a hard time accepting that so-called soft issues really matter to employees. Yet the "war for talent" is making it harder for them to ignore these issues.

In a recent study of 3,000 workers, 56 percent of employees said their companies failed to show concern for them, 45 percent said the companies failed to treat them fairly, and 41 percent said their employers failed to trust them. Partly as a result, only 24 percent of employees said they were "truly loyal" to their employers and plan to stay for at least two years.[31]

Another study on motivation has found that "softer, fuzzier" considerations that focus on the individual—not concrete factors such as salary or incentives—are what *really* matter to employees. These findings come from a research study of more than 1,500 workers by Blessing/White Inc., a Princeton, New Jersey–based career development and management firm. The study says that employees will go the extra mile in their jobs if they feel responsible for the results of their work, have a sense of worth in their jobs, believe their jobs make good use of their skills, and receive recognition for their contributions.[32]

References

1. The Gallup Path to Business Performance. http://consulting.gallup.com/content/?ci=1531
2. Coffman C, Molina GG. *Follow This Path*. New York: Warner Books; 2002.
3. Buckingham M, Coffman C. *First, Break All the Rules*. New York: Simon & Schuster; 2004.
4. Ibid.
5. Buckingham M. *The One Thing You Need to Know . . . About Great Managing, Great Leading, and Sustained Individual Success.* New York: Free Press; 2005.
6. Brewer G. Loyalty for Hire. *Performance*, December 1995, 27.
7. Kotter JP. The Psychological Contract: Managing the Joining-Up Process. *California Management Review,* Spring 1973, 91–99.
8. Branham L. *The 7 Hidden Reasons Employees Leave*. New York: AMACOM; 2005. Used with permission.
9. Holzhauer RJ. Secrets for Recruiting and Retaining Employees. *Academy News*, August 2004.
10. Kaye B, Jordan-Evans S. *Love 'Em or Lose 'Em: Getting Good People to Stay*. San Francisco: Berrett-Koehler; 2005.
11. Leebov W. Less Turnover, Better Patient Care, *HHN Magazine* online. October 18, 2005. http://www.hhnmag.com/hhnmag/hospitalconnect/search/article.jsp?dcrpath=HHNMAG/PubsNewsArticle/data/backup/051018HHN_Online_Leebov&domain=HHNMAG
12. Buckingham M, O'Clifton D. *Now Discover Your Strengths*. New York: Free Press; 2001.
13. Grandinetti D. Make the Most of Your Staff. *Medical Economics*, April 24, 2000.
14. Ibid.
15. Ibid.
16. Gellerman SW. *Motivation in the Real World*. New York: Dutton; 1992.
17. Rogers RW, Riddle S. *Monograph: Trust in the Workplace*. Pittsburgh, PA: Development Dimensions International, Inc.; 2003.
18. Lyman A. Building Trust in the Workplace. *Strategic HR Review*, November/December 2003.
19. Peters T. Peters on Excellence. *Washington Business Journal*, 1993, 51.
20. Building Trust Towards Top Leadership and Management. *Random Samples,* January 2006. http://www.jacksonorganization,com/site/english/KnowledgeNetwork/ EmployeeDiscoveries/BuildingTrust

21. Koch J. The Leading Edge/Leaving a Legacy of Trust. *Workforce,* November 1998, 27–30.
22. Bruce A, Pepitone JS. *Motivating Employees.* New York: McGraw-Hill; 1999.
23. Ibid.
24. Baum N, Zablocki E. *Take Charge of Your Medical Practice—Before Someone Else Does It for You.* Gaithersburg, MD: Aspen Publishers; 1996.
25. Coyne C. Strength in Numbers: How Team Building Is Improving Care in a Variety of Practice Settings. *PT Magazine*, June 1, 2005.
26. Sunoo BP. Results-Oriented Customer Service Training. *Workforce*, May 2001, 84–90.
27. Empower Your Team to Improve Attitudes. *Veterinary Economics*, February 2004, 14.
28. Kaye B, Evans SJ. Give Employees the Space They Need. http://www.fastcompany.com/resources/talent/bksje/041006.html
29. Lucas JR. *Fatal Illusions.* New York: AMACOM; 1997.
30. Daniels A. *Bringing Out the Best in People,* 2nd ed. New York: McGraw-Hill; 1999.
31. Stafford D. Employers Lose Hold of Workers. *Kansas City Star,* February 3, 1998.
32. Amster R. How Employees Feel: The Biggest Motivator? Update. *Corporate Meetings & Incentives*, March 1997, 15.

Chapter Eleven

MANAGING

Team Meetings: A Catalyst for Practice Improvement

Dr. Rensis Likert of the University of Michigan's Research Center has found that high-performance organizations are invariably characterized by feelings of group pride. His studies indicate that a decisive factor in such cases is the degree to which people:

- Meet and interact with one another.
- Identify with one another.
- Seek to achieve organizational goals through collaborative efforts.[1]

Championship teams of all types do each of those things. The scientists, astronauts, and ground crews at NASA do them, as do people in high performance healthcare practices.

One activity that incorporates each of the elements identified by Rikert is *team meetings*—the subject of this chapter.

134 Listen to Everyone

Wal-Mart has appeared on the *Fortune* most admired companies list 10 times during the past 20 years for good reason, says consultant Craig R. Hickman, author of *Management Malpractice*. "With 1,500,000 employees and $300 billion in revenue, this massive discount retailer manages to share ideas of every kind at every level in its organization. At weekly meetings, the employees, called associates or partners, are encouraged to share their ideas openly and with passion. Every idea is taken in to consideration. Every day in the stores, associates are encouraged to look for ways to improve the operation. At Wal-Mart, it really works."

The following is one of the rules Sam Walton followed to help fuel the sharing of ideas, information, and knowledge throughout the organization:

"Rule 7: Listen to everyone in your company. And figure out ways to get them talking. The folks in the front lines—the ones who actually talk to the customer—are the only ones who really know what's going on out there. You'd better find out what they know. This is really what total quality is all about. To push responsibility down in your organization, and to force good ideas to bubble up within it, you must listen to what your associates are trying to tell you."[2]

➥**From the success files:** Dr. Rudolf W. Cisco, Gainesville, Georgia, makes it a point to listen intently to his staff's input. He works hard at cultivating a "safe to say" environment in the office, where employees are not afraid to be open and honest at all times. "I have found that 99 percent of the time," he says, "that my employees are right on target when they bring a problem to my attention. Patients often provide candid feedback to my staff, which means my employees know more about the 'real issues' than I do. It may be hard to hear, but it would be foolish for me not to take heed of what they say."[3]

➥**Hard learned lesson:** "You can't forget to ask the people on the front lines for their opinions," says Stephen Deas, executive director at Georgia Neurological Surgery (GNS) in Athens, Georgia. "They're the ones who can see where there might be ways to get from A to B much more quickly. Saving money and getting patients in and out quicker—these are goals employees can suggest as well as help you reach. Everyone has to be involved to make it a cohesive environment."[4]

135 The Benefits of Staff Involvement

Baptist Health Care, which includes five hospitals, a nursing home, and a network of mental health services, is the largest nongovernmental employer in northwest Florida. One of its entities, Baptist Hospital Inc., received the nation's highest business honor, the Malcolm Baldrige National Quality Award, presented by President Bush in 2004.

"Our success," said Alfred G. Stubblefield, president/CEO of Baptist Health Care in Pensacola, Florida, "isn't tied to employee benefits or compensation. It's tied to our culture."

"Stubblefield advocates total involvement from his staff, so he solicits their ideas for delivering better services and reducing costs," writes Ellen Lanser May, senior editor of *Healthcare Executive.* "'If our employees know a better route to get us where we want to be, we want them to tell us,' says Stubblefield. 'When you show your employees that you care about and respect what they have to say, you'll find that instead of watching your employees trudge into work every day, you'll see their morale go through the roof.' Stubblefield is not exaggerating. A Baptist R.N. reported to the *Fortune* magazine survey (for its annual list of the "100 Best Companies to Work For") that many nurses actually hum while they work."

➡**Reality check:** "Not only does the emphasis Baptist places on engaging its staff create a pleasant environment," May says, "but it has also had a significant impact on the organization's financial outcomes. Since 1998, Baptist has implemented more than 25,000 staff suggestions—for a savings or enhanced revenue of $20 million. 'That means that more than 25,000 times, our staff members have felt how important they are here,' Stubblefield says."[5]

136 "No-Holds Barred" Team Meeting

One of the most important uses of team meetings is to obtain feedback about the practice—feedback that would be difficult, if not impossible, to obtain in any other way. The reason? Staff members frequently hear patients' comments about the practice but may not share such information. One reason they don't is because the HCPs with whom they work never ask.

To obtain this highly valuable information, distribute a list of questions to your staff well in advance of a scheduled staff meeting. It will give them time to think about their answers, perhaps discuss them with their co-workers. Explain that it's a no-holds barred meeting and what you're looking for is their candid responses.

Sample questions might include:

- **How would you describe the practice to an outsider?**
- **What compliments about the practice do you hear most often?**
- **What complaints do you hear?**
- **Is there anything patients have been consistently asking for that we should consider doing?**
- **Where, when, and why do misunderstandings with patients most frequently occur? What are your recommendations?**
- **What changes will improve patient satisfaction?**
- **What is it about the practice that gives you the greatest pride?**

Staff members tend to be more objective about a practice than HCPs are. They also view patients from a different perspective and see and hear things that HCPs don't. Listen to their ideas and insights. They may open your eyes to opportunities for improved patient satisfaction and practice growth.

➥**Tested tip:** Use what's called *encourager phrases* to keep employees talking to you about their thoughts and ideas. Examples: **"Keep talking, that sounds good . . . ", "That would be interesting to try . . . ", "Let's see how we can make that work . . . . "**

If you use encourager phrases often enough, you'll find yourself becoming a better listener and a more effective meeting leader.

137 Early Morning "Huddles"

An early morning huddle refers to a mini-team meeting, typically 5 to 10 minutes in length, held at the start of the business day. Among its purposes:

- To review the highlights of the previous day, including what went particularly well and any compliments heard about staff members, the HCP(s), the service, or the practice in general. This discussion starts the day on a positive, upbeat note.

- "Anticipate, anticipate, anticipate," says consultant Elizabeth Woodcock, M.B.A. "Was your 10:30 a.m. patient admitted to the hospital last night? Is your 9:30 a.m. a chronic no-shower? Does the mother of your 11:30 a.m. always bring the child's disruptive siblings? Did the CT interpretation for your 1:15 p.m. arrive? If not, can you see the patient without it? Make sure," Woodcock says, "that your scheduler is at the huddle every day so that she can make any necessary adjustments. Although you can't eliminate the chaos that's inherent in a medical practice, you most certainly can reduce it."[6]
- To learn if anyone needs help with anything on the day's schedule. Doing so acknowledges that a busy day is coming up, proactively deals with problems, and creates a collaborative atmosphere.

Among the benefits of early morning huddles:

- Eliminates "surprises" (the avoidable ones anyway)
- Greatly improves office efficiency and patient relations
- Fosters teamwork

HCPs and staff members who have early morning huddles are invariably enthusiastic about them. Once the habit is developed, the day seems strangely empty without one.

➥**From the success files:** "'A Morning Report meeting has been the daily ritual at the Shepard Eye Center in Santa Maria, California for more than 18 years,' says Peggy Schenck, R.N., administrator of the practice. The Report is a gathering of all employees and Dennis Shepard, M.D. The meeting begins promptly at 8 a.m. (no tardiness allowed) and lasts only 15 minutes. The meeting is led by a staff moderator, usually Ms. Schenck. It follows a regular agenda that includes schedules, new procedures or changes to existing ones, announcements of coming events, problem solving and employee recognition. Patient condition reports are often included."

The payoff? At the Shepard Eye Center, the staff members answer that question themselves: "We know what to expect each day." "It is our news report." "When a problem occurs, we can all hear the same information about it and present ideas to solve it." "The Morning report is an energizer. It gets us all going in the right direction."[7]

(138) Brainstorming Sessions

Looking for ways to improve the efficiency of your practice/organization? Reduce operating costs? Boost patient satisfaction? Improve relations with referring physicians? A brainstorming session with your staff may provide some answers.

This method for developing ideas was originated by Alex F. Osborn, founder of the world famous Batten, Barton, Durtsine, and Osborn Advertising Agency. He called it "brainstorming." Today, it is used by government, business, and professional organizations of all kinds to pool the creative talents of their members.

The basic principle of brainstorming is that no one person can have all the ideas, but one person's ideas can spark a chain reaction. A problem is presented and a group of experienced people collectively use their ingenuity and imaginations to find solutions.

In his classic text on the subject, *Applied Imagination,* Alex Osborn states four ground rules for success:

- Criticism is ruled out. Adverse judgment must be withheld until later.
- Free-wheeling is welcomed. The wilder the idea the better. It's easier to tame down than to think up.
- Quantity is wanted. The greater the number of ideas, the more likelihood of useful ideas.
- Combination and improvement are sought. In addition to contributing ideas of their own, participants should suggest how the ideas of others can be turned into better ideas, or how two or more ideas can be joined into still another idea.[8]

➥**Reality check:** The worst possible position to be in when it comes to ideas is to have too few of them. That's why the primary rule of brainstorming is to amass quantity, not force quality. Unfortunately, many people forget this rule, ask for ideas, stifle the conversation by judging each idea as soon as it's mentioned, and then wonder why their people just don't brainstorm well. If you want to get ideas to improve your practice in some way, you need to generate lots of ideas and consider them all—even the ones that are too costly, too time-consuming, or too outrageous.

Creativity is messy. The best ideas never appear fully formed and practical. They are often hidden inside an idea that is impractical and silly. These best ideas need to be coaxed, nurtured, and defended. Creating an environment that encourages creative thinking isn't always easy, but it's usually fun.

➡**Action steps:** Brainstorming is most effective with groups of 8 to 12 people and should be conducted in a relaxed environment. If participants are at ease and feel free to joke around, they'll stretch their minds further and produce more creative ideas.

A brainstorming session requires a facilitator, whose role is to get the proceedings started and steered in the right direction. As the group joins in, he or she should encourage participation, see that everyone gets heard, and maintain the tempo and enthusiasm.

A scribe is also needed to keep track of the ideas using a whiteboard or flip chart that is visible to everyone.

A time limit of 25 to 30 minutes is recommended, although more or less time may be needed depending on the size of the group and the flow of ideas.

The most important element of a brainstorming session is the spirit in which it is conducted. For best results, it should be relaxed, permissive, friendly, and uninhibited. Laughing is encouraged. Criticism is not.

The hardest thing to accept until you have tried it is the complete suspension of critical judgment and negativity of any kind. The group can think creatively or it can think critically. If the group tries to do both at once, the inhibiting effect will stifle the flow of new ideas. Avoid at all costs what I call Idea Killers, such as "We tried that once before . . . " "That won't work in this practice . . . ."

When the time is up, discuss the criteria for judging which ideas best solve the problem or achieve the goal stated at the beginning of the session. These might include cost, legal issues, or time or space constraints. Then reach a consensus about which idea(s) will be implemented.

In addition to generating many usable ideas, brainstorming encourages people to build on each other's ideas in a positive way.

One idea acts a springboard for others and creative thinking is stimulated. Psychologists have also found that the mere presence of a group stimulates and releases spontaneity in an individual that he or she would not express otherwise.

➡**From the success files:** At the Oakwood Hills Animal Hospital in Eau Claire, Wisconsin, staff members set goals during brainstorming sessions (held without the doctors) by answering two key questions: "How can we improve our hospital for clients and patients?" and "How can we make our work more enjoyable and productive?"

"Last year the group designated 25 ideas as critical," says Dr. Robert Bohnacek. "Staff members had great suggestions and we've implemented 22 of the 25 this year. Brainstorming sessions" he says, "empower employees to guide their futures and help us create a cohesive team."[9]

➡**Important action step:** Whenever possible, implement changes in office policies and procedures by *consensus*. It's worth repeating: People tend to be more supportive of decisions in which they've had some input.

(139) "How We Can Do It Better" Meeting

Creating a high performance practice is not a set formula. It's a mindset. And that mindset must lead to constant innovation and change. It may be awkward at first, but eventually it will become a way of life in your practice.

Ask yourself: Do you embrace change? Do your staff members know you desire ongoing improvements? Is this something you think about and communicate to them?

If change is overdue in your practice, consider holding what Dr. Gene M. Kangley and his staff in Pompano Beach, Florida, call a "How We Can Do It Better" meeting.

First, Kangley asks everyone in the office to submit a list of practice-related matters that need change and/or improvement. Two weeks before the meeting, a compiled list is circulated. I saw one with 13 items. Among them: security measures needed in the office and general building area, remodeling of the bathroom, medical emergency procedures, protocol for a new patient emergency visit, out-of-office public relations, and appointment scheduling.

The meetings are held quarterly on a Friday from noon to 2:00 p.m. with a catered lunch. Follow-up meetings are held each Monday from 8:30 to 9:00 a.m. to monitor the progress of the agreed-upon changes and to review the week's schedule. It's a team approach to make change an *ongoing* process.

➡**Reality check:** "When issues come up that affect your employees working together," says Stephen E. Anderson, past president of the Private Practice section of the American Physical Therapy Association, "you have a choice in trying to solve the problem. You can dictate what the solution will be and more than likely your ingenious solution will fail, or you can gather a few of the employees who are in control of the circumstances and ask them to work it out."

"Call a meeting and introduce the issue at hand," Anderson says. "As the manager, you can leave or sit quietly, but what you are asking them to do is to take responsibility, work together, and find a solution. Listening to the concerns of the participants and asking them to reach a solution by consensus brings them into the process, and now they own not only the problem, but the outcome. This empowers people to believe they have a say in what goes on, and if you've hired well and have self-motivated people, you can trust them to handle it. Most of the time, all you have to do is organize and coach them to carry out what they know is the right thing to do."[10]

(140) "What Can We Do by Next Tuesday?"

Most improvement efforts fail because so much time is spent analyzing the problem and/or the possible solutions, that nothing ever changes. The solution? Begin small-scale tests right away.

"Improvement teams should ask, 'What changes can we make *by next Tuesday?*'" say Joanne Lynn, M.D., Janice Lynch Schuster, and Andrea Kabcenell, R.N., M.P.H., authors of *Improving Care for the End of Life: A Sourcebook for Health Care Managers and Clinicians.* "By running small scale tests 'by next Tuesday,' teams can break the inertia that keeps many improvement teams from getting off the ground."

"In general," the authors say, "make the strongest change that the team can do quickly, on the smallest sample that will be informative. Even an ambitious and innovative change can be tested first on a small scale—for example, with only one or two physicians, with the next five patients, or for the next three days."

"If a change works on a small scale and is improved with successive tests, it can then be implemented with assurance on a larger scale."[11]

141 "Go for Broke" Meetings

To give managers the information they need to provide the right kind of support to the people reporting to them, Smith & Hawken, a marketer of quality garden tools and equipment, stages an affair known as "Go for Broke." It allows each employee to list everything that is broken in his or her department or elsewhere in the company. "By 'everything'" says Paul Hawken, author of *Growing a Business,* "I mean just that, including relationships between employees. It is a companywide inventory of what needs to be noticed, changed, improved, or checked out, and it lasts the entire month of September (traditionally a period of slow sales). We give out awards for the longest Go for Broke report, the most original, the most humorous, and the most thoughtful. Everybody joins in."

"We have had three Go for Brokes," says Hawken, "and I have never seen or heard of any process that so thoroughly improves a company. These have made Smith & Hawken a better place for all of us to spend our waking hours. It would never have happened however, if we had tried to manage people rather than work with them."[12]

142 Staff Retreats

Want fresh ideas for improving your practice? Take your staff away from it all for a while.

"Some staffs pause annually or even twice a year to review policies and procedures, evaluate systems and processes, and rethink resource allocation. The focus is on continually increasing your quality of care and your practice's efficiency," says consultant J. P. O'Connor, M.A., president of O'Connor Consultation, Facilitation, and Training based in Burbank, California.[13]

Retreats vary in length from a half-day to several days and are held anywhere from local restaurants to exotic locations.

"To minimize time away from family for our 18 staff members and physicians," says Dr. John L. Hudson, Denver, Colorado, "we didn't choose a weekend but met twice during the week, closing the office at 3 p.m. and working until 9 p.m. We served dinner and paid the staff to attend."[14]

➥**Action step:** "Just about anything that goes on in your office is fair game for discussion and improvement," says O'Connor, "from patient relations to office management, record keeping and personnel issues. The point is to get people's views about your strengths and weaknesses on the table so you can plan how to do a better job. Clearly, the discussions must be frank and free-flowing, and even sensitive issues must be brought into the open."

"Ask the staff to imagine that the practice will be profiled in a journal," suggests O'Connor. "Have the staff outline the points they hope the article would make about the practice (such as the quality of the medical staff, the office's efficiency, and the staff's focus on 'customer service'). Then discuss how this ideal compares with reality, and brainstorm how you might move closer to that ideal."[15]

➥**From the success files:** Every year, the office of Drs. Albert Ousborne Jr., Thomas Keller, and Patrick Ousborne in Towson, Maryland, plans a two-day retreat in December and a one-day retreat in June. "To me," says Dr. Albert Ousborne, "it's a time to relax, review, update, organize, plan, and share input with the entire team. This is a chance to put it all together, bond with your group and have fun."

Among other activities, says Ousborne, "We address the past. We cover the history of our group for newcomers and review last year's happenings in detail. Your history brings with it your traditions and heritage. Passing along this information highlights your roots and promotes your organization's culture."[16]

Claire Crittenden, a professional facilitator and founder of Integrative Performance Technologies in Rochester, New York, offers these additional reasons to hold a retreat:

- To explore new territory
- To begin the change process for enhanced culture, procedures, attitudes, behavior, or services
- To profit from group dynamics and creativity
- To resolve a problem
- To establish a higher level of relating to one another
- To enhance or create a collective vision or mission

- To facilitate decisions
- To explore "what if" scenarios[17]

➡**Reality check:** Don't overload the agenda, say consultants Mary Tomlinson, Orlando, Florida, and John Dreyer, Los Angeles, California. "Too often, the plan is to evaluate last year's performance, have each department give a status report, develop next year's plan, set out the 10 year vision, do team building exercises before lunch, and play golf in the afternoon. With this approach, participants will either have sky-high expectations that can't possibly be met or will snicker about how management thinks it can stuff 20 pounds of potatoes into a five pound bag. Discussions end up being short-circuited."

The solution, say Tomlinson and Dreyer, is to reduce unrealistic expectations. Subjects worthy of business retreats are generally large and difficult and require more than a cursory discussion. Choose one to three objectives that can be thoroughly discussed in the time allotted. Allow ample time for determining the next steps and establishing an action timeline. Real discussion that achieves genuine results communicates that participants' opinions really do matter and the organization is willing to commit the time necessary to attain its objectives.[18]

➡**Hard learned lesson:** "Retreats are expensive," says Dr. Jim Bacon, Somerset, New Jersey, "both in real costs and in the hidden cost of lost practice income during the retreat. However, we have been able to use them successfully to discuss important changes in the ways we practice, to motivate staff and to enhance the bond that makes us a team. And each has been followed by a surge in practice income easily capable of covering the costs."[19]

143 Hard Learned Lessons About Team Meetings

If your team meetings have become a waste of time; if the participants sit in stony silence with their arms folded, contributing little if anything to the discussion and waiting for the meeting to end, give the following tips a try. They may revive the meetings by making them livelier, more interactive, productive, and fun.

- Ask your staff what they consider the best time for a meeting and pay them if it's not during regular office hours. (Asking staff members to stay late or come in early is not conducive to getting their best thinking.) If lunch time is selected, make it your treat. You'll see the difference this one change will make in people's attitudes.

- Give advance notice of both the date and the agenda of staff meetings rather than catching people off-guard and unprepared. Encourage staff members to add appropriate topics of their own.

- Rotate the leadership of the meeting among everyone in the practice—on a volunteer basis. Make it a leadership *opportunity* not an *obligation.*

- Stick to the agenda. If a real give-and-take discussion is the goal, the meeting leader should make short statements, not speeches. Pass over minor points. Encourage participation. Avoid negativity. At staff meetings held by Dr. Jan Wolf, Kenosha, Wisconsin, participants used "clickers" to signal someone who was being unnecessarily negative, long-winded, or otherwise out-of-order. It kept the discussion positive and on-target.

- Avoid interruptions. Have your answering service pick up all calls.

- It's worth repeating. Do not allow staff meetings to become *gripe sessions.*

- Don't argue with participants. Discuss, yes—argue, never.[20]

- Set a time limit and stick to it. If necessary, schedule another staff meeting. It's better to quit on a high note than to have people looking at their watches, waiting for the meeting to end.

- If you're the leader, spend more time *listening*—than talking. "If you're called upon to solve a problem, prompt staff members to propose a solution to you first," says Dr. Richard Green, director of business systems development at the Pankey Institute, Key Biscayne, Florida. "Then, if it is acceptable, let them do it their way."

- Hold some meetings without the doctor(s). They often inhibit the proceedings. "Allowing staff to hold their own meetings helps maintain employee satisfaction," says allergist Robyn Levy, Atlanta, Georgia. "They like it when I don't attend. It gives them a sense of autonomy."[21]

➥**Tested tip:** Two questions I've used as a guest facilitator at staff meetings held without doctors present are: **What helps you do your jobs?** and **What hinders you in your jobs?** Both of these resulted in long, lively discussions.

- Have everyone bring to a meeting at least one idea to improve office décor or appointment scheduling or collections.
- Have everyone bring to a meeting at least one idea to save time or money or needed office space.
- Award prizes for the best such ideas.
- Make it a practice, at least initially, to call on people who appear interested and attentive, to help get the discussion under way—rather than those who avoid eye contact and indicate little interest in participating.
- "Don't allow monopolizers and ego-trippers to take over," says Charles R. McConnell, author of *The Effective Health Care Supervisor.* "Although certain talkative people may have significant contributions to make, their constant presence center stage serves to narrow the discussion and discourage marginally vocal contributors from opening up at all."[22]
- "When employees and colleagues are making suggestions and coming up with great ideas," says Marshall Goldsmith, executive coach and *Fast Company* columnist, "don't squash their thoughts by always having the last word, by always trying to make the idea or point better. The problem with doing this," Goldsmith says, "is that while the leaders' thoughts may improve the idea by five percent, they reduce the employee's commitment to executing it by 30 percent—because they've taken away the person's ownership of the idea."[23]
- Periodically hold staff meetings at which everyone *stands.* You'll be surprised how much can be accomplished in so little time.
- Invite outside speakers such as allied healthcare professionals, management consultants, or perhaps patients themselves to address the group.

- For a change of pace, show a videotape for in-service training or inspiration.
- Focus on a positive approach. There's a world of difference between "How can we work better as team?" and "Why is there so much friction and backstabbing in our office?"
- Serve refreshments. Food is fun.
- Always conclude meetings with one or more *decisions.* Don't leave everyone wondering, What did we decide? Where do we go next? Make sure a plan of action is spelled out along with a schedule of implementation.
- Close staff meetings with an idea from the office of Dr. Jim Lanier, Jacksonville, Florida: "Each staff member compliments another who has helped make his or her job easier during the past month. This includes the doctors, office manager and all staff positions."[24]
- Schedule staff meetings as often as they are needed and continue to be productive. Once a month is a common practice. Often, shorter meetings are scheduled every two weeks or even weekly.

➡**From the success files:** At the office of cardiologist M. P. Ravindra Nathan, Brooksville, Florida, Wednesdays are "employee appreciation day." "My wife who acts as practice manager and office coordinator, orders a pizza lunch with various side dishes," Nathan says. "These get-togethers allow the staff to talk about problems that may have surfaced, including differences of opinion about what task is whose job. Airing these differences helps us put down minor skirmishes before they become major clashes. Mostly, though, these sessions are friendly, and everyone looks forward to them even though, with many of the staff on a diet, there's been less pizza lately."[25]

➡**Reality check:** What goes on in team meetings tends to be a reflection of the organization's culture. For example, if the culture does not tolerate mistakes, participants will be reluctant to admit to a mistake in an open meeting. In fact, the things that cause poor meetings—problems in communication, handling conflict, critique, and feedback—are the same factors that can cause the day-to-day operation of a practice to go sour.

References

1. Likert R. *New Patterns of Management.* New York: McGraw-Hill; 1961.
2. Hickman CR. *Management Malpractice.* Avon, MA: Platinum Press; 2005.
3. Simmons K. Seven Deadly Management Mistakes to Avoid. *Podiatry Management,* February 2006, 81–84.
4. Stokes LR. A Job Well Done. *Physicians Practice,* May/June 2002.
5. May EL. Are People Your Priority? *Healthcare Executive,* July/August 2004.
6. Woodcock E. How to Improve Flow. *Physicians Practice Pearls,* June 16, 2005.
7. Wunder H. Share a Morning Cup of Communication. *Review of Ophthalmology,* February 14, 2003.
8. Osborn, A. *Applied Imagination.* New York: Charles Scribner; 1953.
9. Grubb DJ. A Hospital That's Like Home. *Veterinary Economics,* September 1999, 72–76.
10. Anderson SE. Community Creation. *Rehab Economics,* March 2003, 46–47.
11. Lynn J, Schuster JL, Kabcenell A. *Improving Care for the End of Life: A Sourcebook for Health Care Managers and Clinicians.* New York: Oxford University Press; 2000.
12. Hawken P. *Growing a Business.* New York: Simon & Schuster; 1988.
13. O'Connor JP. Staff Retreats: Time for Reflection and Renewal. *Family Practice Management,* January 1998, 56–62.
14. Ibid.
15. Ibid.
16. Ousborne Jr. AL, Revisiting Retreats. *Dental Economics,* June 2005, 32.
17. Crittenden C. Timeline for a Retreat. *Corporate Meetings & Incentives,* May 2006, 25–29.
18. Tomlinson M, Dreyer J. The 7 Deadly Sins of Business Retreats and How to Avoid Them. *Corporate Meetings and Incentives,* May 2004, 56–58.
19. Bacon J. Staff Motivation. *VHMA Newsletter,* May/June 1995, 14–15.
20. McConnell CR. *The Effective Health Care Supervisor,* 5th ed. Sudbury, MA: Jones & Bartlett Publishers; 2003.
21. Gatzke, K. A Satisfied Staff Pays Off. *Physicians Practice,* July/August 2002.
22. McConnell CR. *The Effective Health Care Supervisor,* 5th ed. Sudbury, MA: Jones & Bartlett Publishers; 2003.
23. Goldsmith M. Adding Value—But at What Cost? *Fast Company,* August 2003.
24. Christensen B. Staff Training + Delegation + Teamwork = Success. *Optometric Management,* March 2000, 104–105.
25. Nathan MPR. How I Learned to Be a Better Boss. *Medical Economics,* August 7, 2000.

Chapter Twelve

MANAGING

Performance Management

"Performance Management," as defined by the University Human Resource Services at Indiana University, "is a philosophy which values and encourages employee development through a style of management which provides frequent feedback and fosters teamwork. It involves clarifying the job duties, defining performance standards, and documenting, evaluating and discussing performance with each employee."[1]

Jack Welch, co-author with his wife, Suzy Welch, of the book *Winning*, condenses the action steps needed for performance management into down-to-earth terms:

- You have to evaluate—making sure the right people are in the right jobs, supporting and advancing those who are, and moving out those who are not.
- You have to coach—guiding, critiquing, and helping people improve their performance in every way.
- And finally you have to build self-confidence—pouring out encouragement, caring, and recognition.[2]

This chapter will delve into these issues. Let's start with the one question every employee wants answered.

144 "How'm I Doing?"

Studies show that a high percentage of employees are in the dark about how well they're doing on the job or how they can do better—simply because they've never been told and have no way of knowing.

When asked, HCPs and office managers list numerous reasons for this failure to provide feedback:

- A dislike of having to criticize an employee's work and perhaps having to argue about it
- A reluctance to review an employee's performance because of a concern that he or she will ask for a raise
- A lack of time for such discussions

One result is that exceptional employees are unaware of their strengths and may or may not be consistent in what they do or how they do it. Those who feel their efforts are unnoticed and unappreciated may become demotivated or worse, start looking for another job.

Another consequence of failing to tell people how they're doing on the job is that marginal employees tend to become complacent—and may assume that silence means approval (i.e., "If the doctor didn't like the way I do things, she would tell me.").

➥**Reality check:** It has been estimated that approximately 50 percent of the nonperformance problems in business occur because of lack of feedback, and about 50 percent of what appear to be motivational problems in business are actually feedback problems.[3]

145 Close the Communication Gap

One solution to this communication gap is the *performance review*. It's been defined as a two-way dialogue between employer and employee about the latter's past, present, and future job performance. It includes a discussion of such matters as

- Recognition of good work
- Clarification of job responsibilities, priorities, and performance goals

- The employee's strengths
- Weaknesses of which the employee may have been unaware
- Personal growth issues
- Problems of which the employer may have been unaware
- Questions that might normally never come up in the daily routine

Such discussions let people know how their performance on the job compares with your expectations. This helps employees identify their strengths, develop their talents, and enjoy their work.

➡**Reality check:** Salary raises should not be discussed during performance reviews for two reasons: One is that many people tend to become defensive and refuse to admit even the possibility that their work has been less than satisfactory—if they think it's going to affect their salary. Another reason not to talk raises during performance reviews is that when an employee is waiting to hear "how much" and "when," comments about his or her work and how it might be improved have a tendency to go in one ear and out the other.

➡**Hard learned lessons:**
- Performance reviews help to keep everyone focused on doing the right things, in the right way, at the right time to achieve organizational goals.
- Performance reviews reduce employee turnover, which often occurs when problems aren't addressed early.
- Evaluations also offer important legal protection should a disgruntled employee file a wrongful termination lawsuit.

146 Avoid Confrontations and Surprises

"Many managers avoid performance reviews because they fear confrontation," says Ronald M. Katz, president of Penguin Human Resource Consulting in New Rochelle, New York. "They see it as an 'us versus them' event."

"If the performance review is the only time managers talk with staff about how they are doing," Katz says, "and especially if employees feel that this one meeting has a tremendous impact on their salary increases, the meeting takes on enormous proportions. With all the tension in the room, how can it be a successful interchange? Ongoing communication throughout the year is the key to reducing the fear and anxiety associated with this meeting for both participants."

"When asked what they want out of the performance review meeting," Katz says, "both managers and staff most often respond, 'No surprises.' Continuous assessment and feedback is the key to ensuring that there are none, which of course also lessens the likelihood of a confrontation. Surprises beget confrontations. Communication prevents them."[4]

➥**Action step:** Schedule periodic performance reviews in advance and give employees a list of those topics and/or questions (such as those that follow) that are most appropriate for their situation. It will give them time to think about the issues that concern them.

147 The Critical Document with Which to Start

The critical document needed for a performance review is a job description detailing the duties and responsibilities of each employee. Job descriptions divide the work among employees, make sure someone is responsible for each task, prevent duplication of responsibility, identify a chain of command, facilitate cross-training, and provide a quick way to let temporary employees know their exact duties. In addition, written job descriptions provide guidelines for both hiring and firing.

"Some doctors and office managers prefer not to develop job descriptions, fearing they'll discourage teamwork and give employees the opportunity to say, 'It's not my job,'" says healthcare business consultant Michael J. Wiley, with Healthcare Management and Consulting Services in Bayshore, New York. "You can prevent this," he says, "by coming up with descriptions that list primary and secondary tasks. For example, a receptionist's main job should include greeting patients, answering the phone, and booking appointments. Her secondary responsibilities might include backing up the checkout clerk and assisting the billing clerk and office manager."[5]

➥Resources for Job Descriptions

The Medical Group Management Association's (MGMA) *Job Description Manual for Medical Practices* by Courtney Price, Ph.D., and Alys Novak, M.B.A., contains hundreds of job descriptions that you can customize for your practice: http://www.mgma.com

The *Performance-Based Job Descriptions for Healthcare* manual and initial CD-ROM (updated quarterly) contains 15- to 18-page descriptions of countless jobs that are both age/population-specific and performance-based. Available from HCPro's Healthcare Marketplace: http://www.hcmarketplace.com/prod-2645.html

➡**Action steps:** Review current job descriptions. You may have different ideas about the exact nature of each job than your employees do. For that reason, it's best to review each person's job description to see if it needs revision. Then ask such questions as

- **Do we agree on what tasks your job entails?**
- **Do we agree on how the tasks are to be accomplished—and in what order?**
- **Which do you think are the most important elements of your job? Do we agree on these?**
- **Do we agree on the standards of performance by which your work will be evaluated?**

This last question refers to how well the employee is expected to achieve each of the primary responsibilities in the job description. It sets the par for the course (much like golf) so the employee knows at all times how he or she is progressing toward expectations. Among the parameters by which performance standards can be expressed are frequency, accuracy, timeliness, and allowable margins of error for a given task.

➡**Reality check:** Job descriptions need to be periodically reviewed for accuracy. If more than two years have elapsed or if more than two people have held the same position since a job description was written, it's probably obsolete. In addition, practices expand, merge, downsize, affiliate, specialize, and generally change. As they do, the tasks necessary for success may also change.

➡**Tested tip:** Just before performance reviews are scheduled, send out a current job description to the employee who is scheduled for review. Get the employee's input on any job changes so the manager and employee can discuss this input during the performance evaluation.

➡**Hard learned lesson:** Jobs change faster than do people.

(148) Use an Evaluation Form

Another critical document needed for a performance review is an evaluation form that lists the abilities, traits, or characteristics deemed important to success on the job.

Performance evaluation forms come in all varieties, including rating scales, checklists, fill-in-the-blanks, and free-form essays. "The form you use should focus only on the essential job performance areas," says practice management consultant Judy Capko, whose company, Capko & Co., is based in Thousand Oaks, California. "Limiting these areas of focus makes the assessment more meaningful and relevant and allows you and the employee to address the issues that matter most. For most staff positions, these include job knowledge and skills, quality of work, quantity of work, work habits and attitude. In each area," Capko says, "the appraiser should have a range of descriptors from which to choose (e.g., far below requirements, below requirements, meets requirements, exceeds requirements, far exceeds requirements). Depending on how specific the descriptors are, it's often important that the appraiser also have space on the form to provide the reasoning behind his or her rating."[6]

➥**From the success files:** Physical therapist Susan Davis, owner of Marlboro Physical Therapy in Morganville, New Jersey, says her company uses written evaluation forms for various positions, including physical therapists (PTs), physical therapy assistants, aides, and office staff. "All evaluations have sections regarding traits you want in any employee, like attendance, professionalism, and customer service skills," she says. "PTs are also evaluated on their problem-solving skills, and aides are assessed on how well they work with PTs and patients. We evaluate everyone on knowledge or clinical conditions that pertain to their jobs. We compare their performance with their job description as well as last year's evaluation and the goals we set for them."[7]

➥**Resource**

Performance Appraisal Source Book by Mike Deblieux, published by the Society for Human Resource Management. A wide range of sample performance appraisal forms are available in hard copy and electronic format, as PDFs and easy-to-use RTFs, on the included CD-ROM: http://www.shrm.org

149 Hard Learned Lessons About Job Evaluations

- Base evaluations on job performance rather than personality traits.
- On the other hand, many HCPs have expressed the belief that an employee's rapport with patients is the most important item on an evaluation form. In their view, the potential impact of the employee/patient relationship on the practice exceeds in importance the impact of any other trait or attitude of the staff member, particularly if it's a negative one.
- Ask employees what traits *they* think should be evaluated. Their answers may include some that you may have overlooked or underestimated.
- "Avoid forms that use numerical rating systems alone," says Robert B. Maddux, author of *Effective Performance Appraisals.* "They tend to create confrontation because people don't like having their skills boiled down to numbers. Most employees want to be measured against descriptive standards."[8]
- Use the same form from year to year so that your standards remain consistent.
- Many HCPs have employees fill out identical evaluation forms about themselves prior to the review. When the evaluations differ substantially, there are usually performance problems. This technique offers a way to uncover and discuss them.
- Approach performance reviews in a positive manner. Explain that, "The purpose of this meeting is to review how you've been doing and to help you succeed in the future."
- If an employee takes exception to one or two of the rating factors, emphasize the importance of the employee's overall rating and try to downplay the individual components. This will keep you from getting bogged down in an extended debate over every single element on the evaluation form.
- "When there is choice between knowing the unvarnished truth or not, people would rather know—than be in the dark" say Bruce Bodaken, chairman and chief executive of

Blue Shield of California and Robert Fritz, a founder of the consulting firm Innovation Associates, co-authors of *The Managerial Moment of Truth.*[9]

150 Ask Before You Tell

Instead of *telling* employees what you think of their work, *ask* them (individually) to tell you what they think they have done well and what they would like to do better. Many will criticize themselves more readily than they will accept criticism from you. In fact, they may judge themselves more harshly than you would. The following questions may help facilitate the discussion:

- **What do you think are your greatest strengths?**
- **In which areas do you feel less competent?**
- **Do you feel you are becoming more competent as time goes by? If so, in what ways?**
- **What, if anything, do you need to do your job better?**

Management expert Peter Drucker said, "The greatest boost to productivity would be for managers to ask, **'What do we do in this organization that helps you do the job you're being paid for—and what do we do—that hampers you?'**"

If employees feel completely safe in answering the second part of that question, you may get an earful. Whatever you do, don't belittle what may seem like a trivial complaint. As the next secret indicates, listen.

151 Listen Intelligently, Understandingly, and Skillfully

The importance of listening has been discussed in the chapter pertaining to the interviewing of job applicants (Chapter 4). It's equally important during performance reviews.

The psychologist Carl Rogers has said, "The biggest block to personal communication is one person's inability to listen intelligently, understandingly and skillfully to another person."[10]

This is especially important to remember during performance reviews. Listening to employees talk about themselves is the surest way to get to know them as individuals, their values, attitudes, and aspirations. It also tells them that you have a genuine interest in their job satisfaction and future development. As a result, they become more willing to discuss the things on their minds that may be affecting their work.

This willingness to patiently listen to an employee may produce some rather startling reactions such as, "This is the first time since I started working here that anyone has ever asked my views on things."

In many cases, I suspect that what impresses and pleases employees most is the mere fact that such a conversation takes place—even though nothing profound was said. For an employee who feels unnoticed and unappreciated, a performance review represents more than the opening of a door. It represents the opening of a mind that previously seemed closed.

➥**Reality check:** If, while explaining a problem he or she is experiencing on the job, an employee senses that you're either not listening or not interested, he or she may become guarded and uncommunicative. It might be a remark on your part such as, "I really don't know what we can do about that," or "Too bad, but we all go through that." Regardless of your intentions, the dialogue in all likelihood will come to an abrupt stop.

➥**Action steps:** The remedy is simple. Get the message across—unequivocally—that you're interested in what your employee is saying. In the above case, a more appropriate response might be, **"At this point, I can't think of a solution—but I know where we might look for help . . . "** or **"I think I know how you're feeling. I can remember a similar experience . . . ."**

➥**Hard learned lesson:** When people feel understood, they tend to become less defensive. The more accurately you can judge feelings and the more calmly you can accept them, the better will be your chance of helping employees tell you what is most important to them.

152 Avoid Unfair Comparisons

It's a complaint I hear more often than I should from newly hired employees: "I'm sick and tired of hearing how wonderful my predecessor was. That's all I ever hear!"

Comparisons of this type predispose people not to listen—even when a criticism is justified; in time, they completely demoralize and demotivate a new employee. What's overlooked in these situations is that it's impossible to *replace* an individual. All that can be done is to put another person in the job.

A new employee will have a different personality, a different perspective, a different approach. In time, the person may become as valuable to the organization as his or her predecessor, perhaps more so. To make that happen, consider the following suggestions:

- Separate the *job* from the *person* who previously did the job. When training a new employee, stress the way you'd like things done, or the way you've found works best in your practice or with your patients. Omit references to "the way Mary did it." It adds nothing but pressure for the newcomer to measure up.

- Make sure other employees who held the newcomer's predecessor in high esteem understand that it's a new start for everyone. They may be accustomed to the old way of doing things. Changes may lead to grumbling, "That's the way *Mary* did it." Make it clear the new employee has his or her own strengths and should be judged on individual merit and future progress.

- Be flexible. Most jobs change in little ways over time. When a new employee comes on board, try to tailor the job to his or her talents, interests, and goals, even if it requires some changes in the job description.

- Be patient. It's tough for anyone to follow in the footsteps of a "legend." Give a new employee time to grow into the job and succeed in his or her own way. If you do, you may eventually find yourself with another "irreplaceable employee."

153 Focus on Strengths

When conducting performance reviews, don't dwell on an employee's shortcomings. There's no faster way to put people off than to criticize them—even under the guise of "performance evaluation."

Instead, talk to their strengths. When you address employees' strengths, it generates positive energy within the practice. It builds people up and empowers them to do more of what is best for the practice.

➥**Action steps:** Start by observing people's everyday behavior in broad categories, and then get more specific.

How attentive to detail is the person? Is he or she especially good with children? Older people? How proficient is the person with time management? Accounts receivable? CPT codes?

Is the person cheerful, friendly, caring, creative, diplomatic, willing to help others, kind, enthusiastic, hard-working, a good listener, funny, intelligent, interesting, open-minded, well-organized, patient, upbeat, punctual, polite, sensitive, self-starting, thoughtful, unselfish, versatile?

These are only a few positive characteristics you or an office manager can reflect back to a team member at a performance review—or anytime for that matter. The HCP or office manager who addresses his or her people's strengths only at performance reviews is missing opportunities on every other working day to boost morale and productivity.

If you'll look for and share one positive strength in a staff member per day, no matter how minuscule, the boost to that individual's morale and performance will be astounding.

➥**Reality check:** When employees are hired, they bring with them a vast array of strengths developed from their previous education, work experiences, vocational pursuits, civic or charity organizational work, and the like that, in many cases, are totally unrelated to their principal job duties. These might include skills pertaining to leadership, management, public speaking, writing, teaching, computers, artistic pursuits, or countless other areas. There are, in fact, a great many hidden talents in every person.

154 Match Skills with Interests

"Between the extremes of employed and unemployed lies a large group of workers who are misemployed," says Roger Herman, CEO of The Herman Group, a Greensboro, North Carolina, consulting firm that concentrates on workplace issues and trends. "Misemployed people," explains Herman, "are employees who are not well matched by personality or interest to their current jobs."[11]

➥**Action steps:** Seek to identify the unique strengths and talents of each staff member," says Dr. Richard A. Green, director of business systems development of the Pankey Institute. "Develop dynamic job descriptions and delegate tasks that amplify strengths and minimize weaknesses. People tend to grow more when they focus on success."[12]

Consider asking the following questions:

What interests you most? This question encourages employees to think about their core interests. You can then discuss how well their current job duties and responsibilities match their interests and, if necessary, make needed adjustments. The retention of a valued employee makes this a good investment.

What motivates you? You can't assume employees value the same work rewards that you do. If an employee puts family life first, offering alternative work arrangements may earn his or her loyalty. Another employee may express an interest for more authority or responsibility, recognition, or higher pay. Ignoring the situation either builds resentment or hastens an employee's departure.

What do you do best? "Letting top performers do what they do best will excite them and increase their productivity," says John Sullivan Ph.D., author of *Improving Productivity the World-Class Way.* "Now you might ask, who will do the unwanted tasks? Maybe someone else likes to do those," Sullivan suggests. "If so, the problem is solved. If such is not the case, give those tasks to low performers or part-time employees, outsource them, give them to interns or even hire temps to do them."[13]

What are your long-term goals? If the answer requires skills your employees don't currently have, consider appropriate on-the-job training or continuing education.

What do you need from me? How can I help? Asking these questions shows employees you're sincerely interested in their future and personal development. It builds loyalty and provides information that will make you a better manager.

155 Analyze Poor Performance

If an employee is failing to achieve the performance standards established for a given job description, the question is, Does the employee have the knowledge, skills, and motivation necessary to do the job? There are four possibilities, each of which calls for a different solution.

- He or she can do the job and is willing to do it. Solution: Learn the reason(s) for poor performance using such questions as those listed in Secrets 147 and 150.
- He or she can't do the job, but if properly trained would do the job. Solution: Provide on-the-job training or perhaps tuition-paid courses at a local college or university.
- He or she can do the job but won't do it. Solution: Learn the reason. If it is acceptable, delegate the task to another qualified person. If unacceptable, consider either revising the person's job description or termination.
- He or she can't do the job and won't do it. Solution: You've most likely hired a round peg for a square hole. Termination is the only alternative unless you're willing to keep on doing what you have been doing—and accept the loss of productivity that goes with it.

➡**Reality check:** The above assessments depend to some extent on a manager's mindset—much like McGregor's concepts of human nature that he labeled Theory X and Theory Y, as discussed in Chapter 8.

"Consider the manager who believes that with enough willpower and determination, virtually all behaviors can be changed," say Marcus Buckingham and Curt Coffman, authors of *First Break All the Rules: What the World's Greatest Managers Do Differently.* "For this manager, every case of poor performance is the employee's fault. The employee has been warned, repeatedly, and still has not improved his performance. If he had more drive, more spirit, more willingness to learn, he would have changed his behavior as required, and the poor performance would have disappeared. But it hasn't disappeared. He must not be trying hard enough. It's his fault."

"How can you have a constructive conversation with someone," ask Buckingham and Coffman, "when beneath the surface politeness, this is what you are compelled to think of him? Whatever your style, a conversation where you have to mask your true feelings is a stressful conversation, particularly when your feelings are so negative. No wonder so many managers try to avoid it."

"But great managers don't have to hide their true feelings," say Buckingham and Coffman. "They understand that a person's talent and nontalent constitute an enduring pattern. They know that if, after pulling out all the stops to manage his nontalents, an employee still underperforms, the most likely explanation is that his talents do not match his role. In the minds of great managers, consistent poor performance is not primarily a matter of weakness, stupidity or disrespect. It's a matter of miscasting."

"When an employee is miscast," say Buckingham and Coffman, "great managers use language like, **'This isn't a fit for you. Let's talk about why'** or **'You need to find a role that plays more to your natural strengths. What do you think that role might be?'** They use this language, not because it is polite, not because it softens bad news, but because it's true."

"This mind-set enables a great manager to keep two contradictory thoughts in mind at the same time—the need to maintain high performance standards and the need to care—and still function effectively."[14]

156 Provide Feedback

Chapter 9 focused on the importance of positive feedback in the form of recognition and appreciation.

"Giving feedback is the backbone of good supervision," says Ann Dohrenwend, Ph.D., director of behavioral medicine for internal medicine at McLaren Regional Medical Center in Flint, Michigan. "Provide feedback on behavior you want the employee to keep *and* behavior you want the employee to change."

"Some supervisors avoid giving negative feedback," Dohrenwend says, "because they fear that criticism will hurt their relationships with staff. However, when necessary criticism is withheld, supervisor-employee relationships remain superficial and lack the depth and resiliency needed to tackle sensitive issues. These supervisors are withdrawing from the authentic interactions that ultimately form the foundation of a trusting relationship. In addition, the supervisor's failure to confront performance problems may subsequently lead to aggressive behavior. In this case, unexpressed frustrations mount until a small error by the employee triggers an avalanche of pent-up criticism. Then, even if the supervisor's criticisms are accurate, the employee will be too overwhelmed to hear them. In the future, the employee will keep a safe distance from the supervisor and even praise will be interpreted with suspicion."[15]

➡**Hard learned lessons:**
- The six most important words about providing feedback: praise in public; criticize in private. It's common sense, but unfortunately not common practice.
- A Texas physician told me that before he criticizes an employee, he asks himself: "Will what I am about to say help this person?" If the answer is no, he doesn't say it.
- If you must criticize, criticize an employee's *performance*, not the employee. People can change what they do more readily than what they are. For example, there's considerable difference between telling a bookkeeper, "You are careless" and telling her, "The number of billing errors has risen 17 percent in the last three months." The first statement is an opinion. The second is a fact.
- Don't criticize an employee for something he or she can't change. If the person lacks the basic intelligence, talent, or personality to do a particular job no matter how hard he or she tries, criticism isn't going to help. He or she is either in the wrong job or the wrong office. Your only choices are to restructure the job for work the person is more suited for or to let him or her go.
- Criticism that becomes a personal attack not only fails to clear up mistakes, but also sometimes worsens performance. People criticized under such circumstances rarely absorb what you tell them. And in most cases, it only produces hurt feelings and hostility.

➡**Reality check:** One of the outstanding characteristics of an effective manager is the frequency and quality of feedback that he or she provides employees. Operating without feedback is like trying to learn target shooting with a blindfold. You can't improve when you don't know how you're doing.

157 Focus on Performance

"When someone makes a mistake, rather than focusing on what they did wrong, an effective manager will say something like, 'Next time maybe we ought to do it this way,'" says Ken Blanchard, Ph.D., author of *The One Minute Manager.* "Focus on what you want people to do, not on what they did wrong. People want to know when they are performing well. If they are not, they want to be helped back on the right path."[16]

Another way to focus on performance is to encourage employees to analyze problems by asking "That's an unusual number of billing errors. What happened?" or "How can we prevent this from happening in the future?" Then wait for an answer.

"Once a solution is proposed that you support," say Sam Deep and Lyle Sussman, co-authors of *What to Ask When You Don't Know What to Say,* "secure the employee's commitment with a question such as, 'May I count on you to do that?' Insist upon a yes in return. Don't accept, 'I guess' or even 'I'll try.'"

"Remember," say Deep and Sussman, "that poor performance occurs for one of three reasons: (1) Employees don't know what's expected (communication problem); (2) employees can't do what's expected (selection, training or resource problem); or (3) employees don't want to do what's expected (motivation problem). In your questioning, search for the cause in this situation."[17]

➥**Hard learned lesson:** If you're partly at fault, as you may learn from the above line of questioning, admit it. People become more willing to admit their shortcomings and mistakes if you admit yours. The fact is no one expects infallibility—so when you admit your errors, you gain rather than lose stature in the eyes of other people. It makes you more human, more down-to-earth.

158 Keep Things in Proper Perspective

Don't get bogged down in finding fault. An employee should be made aware of poor performance and strive to improve it. But to hammer away at the subject is pointless. It doesn't accomplish anything except to demoralize the person and make him or her want to give up.

Criticism should be followed by commendation—in the right proportion. It reinforces good performance. It motivates people to learn, develop, grow on the job, and utilize their full potential.

For example, in the case of an employee with a good but not perfect work record, you might say, **"I wanted to cover the negative points. There aren't many, but they are important. Now that we have taken care of them, I want to tell you how pleased I am with the overall quality of your work . . . ."**

One of the main problems with evaluations is dwelling on what's wrong and how to fix it rather than what's right and how to make it better. Conclude by discussing a strength and how to build on it.

➥**Hard learned lessons:**
- Don't bother with trivialities. If the employee's behavior isn't affecting patient care or office operations, let it slide.
- "All learning involves some 'failure,' something from which one can continue to learn," say University of Southern California professors Warren Bennis and Burt Nanus, co-authors of *Leaders*. "Indeed, we can propose a rule for all organizations: reasonable failure should never be received with anger."[18]

➥**Reality check:** "The manner in which we address mistakes and poor performance is the true test of our commitment to people, performance and professionalism," says Randy G. Pennington, president of Pennington Performance Group consultancy in Addison, Texas. "Positive performance management focuses on recognition and encouragement, coaching, counseling and corrective action."

Quoting former UCLA basketball coach John Wooden, Pennington says great managers are like great coaches. "A coach must prevent, correct, or help and not punish. He must make those under his supervision feel they are working with him rather than for him. He must be more interested in finding the best way rather than having his own way, and be genuinely concerned about the players."[19]

159 Help with Personal Problems

If an employee is having trouble at home, his or her performance at work is certain to suffer, say authors Sam Deep and Lyle

Sussman. Try one of these questions to help get the person back on track:

- "What can I do to help bring your productivity back to where it was last month?"
- "You're usually so _____, but lately that's been slipping. What's going on?"

The second question differs from the first in that it focuses the discussion on causes before asking for remedies. Use the one best suited to the occasion.

"One of the best ways to help troubled employees," say Deep and Sussman, "is by getting them to talk. Such questions may be all it takes to break the dam."

"If the response is something like, 'I wish I knew. This problem at home really has me down,' continue to listen, occasionally paraphrasing to show you're engaged. This alone may be enough."[20]

If the employee denies any problem, it's recommended you document the problem's impact on office efficiency and productivity and urge the person to take immediate steps to improve.

➡**From the success files:** George Wolff, PT, MBA, founder and co-owner of Wolff Fitness Center in Elgin, Illinois, recalls how one physical therapist (PT) entered his office, shut the door, proceeded to complain about the challenges of the managed care environment, and then rose to leave. Wolff asked, "What can I do to help?" The PT said, "Nothing. You just did it." All the PT needed, says Wolff, was to be heard.[21]

160 Agree on a Plan of Action

The improvement you want in an employee's work habits or performance can occur only when you both perceive the problem in the same way and agree on both the means and a timetable for solving it.

You can start with your recommendations—or better yet, invite your employees to tell you how they would like to develop themselves and what help, if any, they would like from you. Be specific about the changes in duties, responsibilities, or behavior that will be made. Set deadlines. Then put this action plan on paper as a form of "contract" between you and your employee. Each of you should have a copy. Such commitment will get better results than vague promises. The action plan will also serve as a benchmark against which future progress (or, if necessary, grounds for dismissal) can be measured.

➥**Reality check:** "When performance changes are requested of an employee," says consultant/speaker Julie H. Weir, "there are three questions you can ask to get an insight into whether or not the employee will be successful. **'Is this a change you want to make?' 'Is this a change you think you can make?'** and **'What kind of help do you need to make this change?'**"[22]

161 The Secrets of Great Managers

In a poll of 1,033 adults aged 18 and older, The Gallup Organization determined the respondent's level of engagement with their workplace, and then asked them to describe their managers' style. Respondents were asked to rate their level of agreement with two statements—"My supervisor focuses on my strengths or positive characteristics" and "My supervisor focuses on my weaknesses or negative characteristics" on a scale of 1 to 5.

> **Invisible managers:** "Some managers may feel they do not have the time to interact with their employees," the report states. "These invisible managers believe the best thing they can do is stay out of the way and let their staff members do their jobs—essentially ignoring them. But Gallup's data suggest that the absolute *worst* thing a manager can do is be invisible to his or her employees. Among employees who gave low scores to their managers on both of the above statements—suggesting their managers focus on neither their strengths nor their weaknesses—only 2 percent were engaged and 40 percent were actively disengaged."

> **Judgmental managers:** "Other managers always tend to 'go negative,' focusing primarily if not exclusively on what their team members are doing wrong," the report states. "When an employee sees this type of manager coming, his or her first thought is, 'I hope she isn't coming to see me.' One might think invisible managers are better than negative managers, but that's actually not true: 45 percent of workers with managers who tend to focus

on their weaknesses were engaged, while 22 percent were actively disengaged."

Great managers: "What if the manager does everything right?" the report asks. "The best managers look for employees who provide good patient care and recognize them for it. They don't avoid employees who are having a bad day, but rather seek them out and try to help them— always looking for a positive approach. It's no surprise that managers like these yield the best results. Among employees who say their managers focus on their strengths and positive characteristics, 61 percent were engaged and only 1 percent were actively disengaged."[23]

➡️**From the success files:** Lois P. Frankel, a Los Angeles consultant, and Karen L. Otazo, of the ARCO Corporation, also in Los Angeles, asked several hundred ARCO employees to enumerate the characteristics of managers who had helped them do their best work. Ten attributes topped the findings:

- Took time to listen to me
- Saw me as a person, not just an employee
- Cared about me personally and helped if I had personal problems
- Set a good example
- Let me know I could do more than I thought I was capable of; stretched me
- Encouraged me
- Never pulled rank; rolled up his or her sleeves and pitched in
- Didn't keep me in the dark; let me know what was going on
- Praised me for a job well done
- Let me know in a straightforward manner when I didn't do a job well[24]

162 The Saddest Mistake of Performance Management

The saddest mistake of performance management, one that causes endless frustration and stress, is having *unrealistic expectations.* For example, do you expect your employees to be as dedicated, hard-working, energetic, and vitally interested in your patients and the success of your practice as you are?

High expectations are fine. Studies show that employees tend to live up to their employers' expectations. It's called the Pygmalion effect. But unrealistic expectations are, by definition, unattainable.

If you have unrealistic expectations about employees, you'll be frustrated by what you perceive as unmotivated employees. They'll forever disappoint you.

Your employees, in turn, will be frustrated because it will seem as if nothing they do is good enough to earn your approval and appreciation. The result? Resentment and stress—on both sides.

Disparate expectations can also arise between HCPs in the same practice. If, for example, you're frustrated by associates who lack your desire to grow the practice, remember the drive to achieve is not uniformly distributed. Your style may be to keep pushing for higher and higher revenues, no matter what it takes to achieve them. Probably, too, when you arrive at some predetermined benchmark, it seems perfectly natural to push on to a new and even higher goal.

When you look back, however, you may find your associates lagging behind and making no special effort to keep up with you. One explanation: They may not have the drive to "climb the mountain because it's there." Some may be content to relax in the meadow part way up. Or pursue other goals such as spending more time with their families or sailing or whatever. In fact, they may think you are as strange as you think they are.

➡**Reality check:** Your expectations of employees and associates may be unrealistic. You may not have hired the right people for your practice. They may not be doing the things they do best or like doing. It may be your management style that's at fault. A one-on-one performance review may pinpoint the problem.

163 Hard Learned Lessons About Performance Reviews

- Conducting performance reviews is often stressful for HCPs and office managers as well as employees. *Avoiding* reviews, however, creates even more stress.

- To be effective, a performance review is a summary of observations and experiences that you've documented in writing since the last review—not a spur-of-the-moment evaluation of the employee.
- Allergist Robyn Levy, Atlanta, Georgia, believes quarterly performance reviews—as opposed to annual reviews—are very effective ways to reinforce the individual staffer's importance to the group, set expectations, keep employees involved in reaching the group's goals, and recognize good performance.[22]
- Performance reviews are not a substitute for day-to-day talks with employees about their work. Some HCPs save up their criticisms and commendations for these once- or twice-a-year discussions with employees. Then they deliver them broadside. For most employees, its more criticism, praise, and advice at one sitting than they can absorb or want to hear.
- New employees should be evaluated shortly after they're hired, typically after three months. If there is a problem, it's least painful, and least expensive, for you and for them to discover it early. The new hire is a "go" or "no go." Don't waste time trying to rehabilitate someone who's a poor fit.
- The goal of the performance review should be improved performance in the future. Don't make the common mistake of putting undue focus on past performance.
- Know when to quit. After discussing relevant performance issues, some managers have a tendency to go on and on. They raise new issues, rehash points that don't need rehashing, and generally get in the way of their own message.
- "Sometimes, by interviewing employees, a doctor can discover the potential burnout or boredom that results from doing the same thing over and over," says practice consultant Cathy Jameson, Ph.D., whose firm, Jameson Management Inc., is based in Davis, Oklahoma. "Often, you can defuse burnout by changing the job responsibility or switching people around. This switch may be temporary or

you may discover that an employee blossoms in the new role, and you may encourage her or him to stay in the new position. Switching roles, exchanging responsibilities or adding responsibilities, can uncover tremendous potential within team members."[26]

- "If possible, have your office manager meet one-on-one with employees every six to eight weeks," recommends Richard D. Hansen, vice president of the Medical Group Management Association (MGMA) Health Care Consulting Group. "It needn't take long. Focus on one task that's being done very well and one that needs improvement. Then use the year-end review to decide on what training to provide when skills are lagging."[27]

- "Performance reviews can help buttress your defense in the event you are sued by an employee (or more likely, a former employee)," says practice management consultant Jeffrey J. Denning, whose firm, Practice Performance Group, is located in La Jolla, California. "On the other hand," he adds, "the absence of an evaluation or adequate review can sometimes be used against you with devastating results. Juries tend to come down hard on employers who don't appear to have given an employee a chance to improve. And the employee with no bad reviews who suddenly finds herself fired, is justified in being shocked—and you may be equally shocked when she sues for wrongful termination."[28]

References

1. Indiana University. *Performance Management*, University Human Resource Services. http://www.indiana.edu/~uhrs/training/performance_management/intro.htm
2. Welch J, Welch S. *Winning*. New York: HarperCollins; 2005.
3. Zemke R. The Corporate Coach. *Training*, December 1996, 24–28.
4. Katz R. Six Steps to Successful Performance Appraisals. http://www.workforce.com/archive/article/22/14/02.php
5. Wiley MJ. Is Your Practice Staffed Correctly. *Medical Economics*, June 21, 2002, 66–73.
6. Capko J. 5 Steps to a Performance Evaluation System. *Family Practice Management*, March 2003, 43–48.

7. Farmer J. How to Get the Most from Performance Reviews. *PT Magazine*, November 1, 2004.
8. Maddux RB. *Effective Performance Appraisals,* 4th ed. Boston: Crisp Learning; 2000.
9. Bodaken B, Fritz R. *The Managerial Moment of Truth.* New York: Free Press; 2006.
10. Rogers C. *On Becoming a Person: A Therapist's View of Psychotherapy.* New York: Mariner Books; 1995.
11. Joinson C. Making a Good Match. Society for Human Resource Management (SHRM). http://www.shrm.org/ema/EMT/articles/2004/spring04joinson.asp
12. Green RA. A Great Place to Work! *Dental Economics*, July 2003, 56.
13. Sullivan J. *Improving Productivity the World Class Way.* Peterborough, NH: Kennedy Information Inc.; 2003.
14. Buckingham M, Coffman C. *First Break All the Rules: What the World's Greatest Managers Do Differently.* New York: Simon & Schuster; 1999.
15. Dohrenwend A. Serving Up the Feedback Sandwich. *Family Practice Management*, November/December 2002, 43–46.
16. Blanchard K. How to Instill Passion in Your People. *MNWORLD*, American Management Association, Spring 2004, 6–9.
17. Deep S, Sussman L. *What to Ask When You Don't Know What to Say.* Englewood Cliffs, NJ: Prentice Hall; 1993.
18. Bennis W, Nanus B. *Leaders,* 2nd ed. New York: HarperCollins; 2003.
19. Pennington RG. Presentation at the Society for Human Resource Management 57th Annual Conference, San Diego, California, June 2005.
20. Deep S, Sussman L. *What to Ask When You Don't Know What to Say.* Englewood Cliffs, NJ: Prentice Hall; 1993.
21. Coyne C. Motivational Factors for PTs and PTAs. *PT Magazine*, October 11, 2004.
22. Weir JH. Performance Reviews: How to Make Them Great! *Dental Angle Online Magazine*, Fall 2001.
23. Blizzard R. Staff Engagement Begins with Hospital Managers, September 6, 2005. http://poll.gallup.com/content/default.aspx?ci=18388
24. Zemke R. The Corporate Coach. *Training,* December 1996, 24–28.
25. Sonn B. Staff Salaries Climbing. *Physicians Practice,* October 2004.
26. Jameson C. Review Time. *Dental Practice Report*, May 2001, 37–40.
27. Pennachio DL. Let Employees Know Where They Stand. *Medical Economics,* February 7, 2003.
28. *UnCommon Sense*, published by Practice Performance Group, La Jolla, California, June 1997, 4.

Chapter Thirteen

MANAGING

Management's Most Unpleasant Task

O ne of the questions I've posed to countless seminar audiences is, What do you consider management's most unpleasant task? The most frequent response? Having to fire an employee.

No matter how well your organization deals with the hiring, management, and retention of employees, inevitably some will leave. How you handle the process of employees' departures will have a significant impact on the practice.

"In physician practices especially," says David Lewis, president of OperationsInc., a human resources consulting firm in Stamford, Connecticut, "a termination can be 'tantamount to firing a child, sister or uncle' because offices are smaller and everyone tends to work closely together, both literally and figuratively."[1]

The first thing to remember is that there's no way to make a dismissal pleasant. You can only minimize the pain and hostility—which is the purpose of this chapter.

164 Bad Apples

Every healthcare practice has a bad apple from time to time: the person who never should have been hired in the first place, the employee whose job performance has seriously deteriorated, the person who just doesn't blend in with the rest of the team.

➡**Reality check:** When *Physicians Practice* magazine asked some of the country's busiest practice management consultants what mistakes they see repeatedly made in practices, one of the major ones they identified was retaining incompetent employees. Management intuitively knows something is wrong but doesn't act on it, says consultant/ speaker Elizabeth Woodcock, based in Atlanta, Georgia. Staff members who come in late, do nothing, or simply aren't doing a good job ruin the morale of everyone else, Woodcock says. Those who do arrive on time, for example, need to cover for the employee who is always late. Worse than the extra work, everyone on the staff begins to feel like management doesn't care. If the physician owners don't seem emotionally invested in the practice, you can be sure no one else will. The only solution, Woodcock adds, is to tackle underperformance head on.[2]

➡**Hard learned lessons:**
- Attempts to salvage an employee gone bad seldom work
- Lingering dismissals occur when everyone knows a person is about to be fired (including the person about to be fired)—but the manager delays doing it. Such foot-dragging only prolongs the agony for everyone.
- "Employees don't want to work with low performers," says Quint Studer, former hospital president and author of *Hardwiring Excellence*. "Nothing makes employees as discouraged and resentful as having to co-exist with people who don't pull their own weight. In fact, low performers usually drive high performers out the door."[3]
- Employees who are not performing up to par are expensive in terms of payroll and, even worse, are at risk of alienating or possibly endangering patients.
- Low performance employees can undermine your practice in countless ways.

165 The Borderline Employee

A surprising number of successful practices are affected by a single employee who's out of step with everyone else but, for various reasons, remains on the payroll. Recent complaints I've heard include the following:

- "Our receptionist [of 11 years] refuses to change her outdated ways of doing things. The practice has grown but she hasn't."
- "My radiology technician [of 7 years] has become so overbearing and short-tempered with patients and other staff members, that it has created unbearable stress in the office."
- "Our office manager [of 9 years] thinks she knows everything. If I say anything about her work, she rolls her eyes and there's often a scene."

What typically complicates these situations is that these employees are not thought to be totally unsatisfactory. Frequently, they're passable, if not good, at some aspects of their jobs and less than satisfactory in other aspects.

The reasons given by HCPs for not firing such employees are often similar: a sense of obligation ("because of his or her many years of service") or kindness ("she needs the job") or because "I dread having to fire her."

If you're faced with such a dilemma, the question to consider is, *To whom do you owe what?* What do you owe a long-term employee who won't change? What do you owe your patients, associates, and other staff members who have to contend with such behavior? And what do you owe *yourself* in this situation? How troubling is it for you?

➡**Litmus test:** If this person were to quit, would you be relieved or upset?

If you've conducted periodic performance reviews with such employees, given fair warnings to those who need to change, documented such discussions, and have seen no improvement, it may be time to let them go.

166 Keep It Real

Have you ever conducted a performance review with the goal of changing an employee's work habits or way of dealing with people—urging him or her to be more attentive to details? Or sensitive to other people's feelings? Or helpful to co-workers?

Trying to change other people's behavior assumes their priorities and motivations are the same as yours. That's always possible, but based on the feedback I've received from countless HCPs and practice managers, unlikely.

➡**Hard learned lesson:** Accept that you can change people—but not very much.

➡**Action steps:** There are several alternatives: One is to keep trying, but perhaps with a different approach. Another is to consider switching the person to a job more suited to his or her temperament. "Most of the time," says Betty Doria, medical office manager of an eight-physician practice in Smithtown, New York, "I discuss reassignment in a way that the employee thinks she is being transferred because of her attributes rather than substandard performance."[4]

If necessary, you can adopt a "what is, is" philosophy and learn to live with the situation.

Progressive (incremental) discipline is still another option to consider before firing an employee.

167 Progressive Discipline

"Labor lawyers recommend that you use a technique called progressive discipline," says Steven Kern, a healthcare attorney in Bridgewater, New Jersey. "The first time a billing clerk is rude to patients, warn her not to do it again. A second episode generates a written reprimand. Infraction number 3 means probation, and finally she'll be out the door. Incremental discipline is especially helpful in large practices, because it makes it easier to establish standards; you can't be arbitrary and apply different rules to different groups of employees."[5]

Alec Ziss, practice administrator at Weston Pediatric Physicians in Weston, Massachusetts, thinks that small practices can also benefit from this multi-step process. "A discussion might not convince an employee that you're serious," he observes, "but being put on probation undoubtedly will."[6]

➡**Reality check:** Depending on the circumstances, you may want to issue more than one verbal reprimand before moving to the next step.

168 The Rules for Fairness

The following rules are intended for fairness when using progressive discipline:

> **Rule 1:** The employee needs to know what the problem is. (Employees are often in the dark about performance-related issues.)
>
> **Rule 2:** The employee needs to know specifically what he or she needs to do in order to fix the problem. (Employees are often unaware of management's expectations or the standards of performance by which their work will be evaluated.)
>
> **Rule 3:** The employee needs to have a reasonable period of time in which to fix the problem. (What's considered a reasonable amount of time will depend on the nature of the work performed, the length of time the employee has been with the practice, and how similar situations have been handled in the past.)
>
> **Rule 4**: The employee needs to understand the consequences of inaction. (Generic, open-ended warnings such as "further action will be taken" are subject to wide if not misleading interpretations.)

➡**From the success files:** "We have a section in our employee manual dealing with disciplinary procedures," says Dr. Dan Spencer, who has offices in Hudson and Reading, Michigan. "It is prefaced by the statement, 'The officers of the corporation reserve the right to determine if policy was violated, the significance of the violation, and what action is appropriate.' We have five levels of disciplinary action: verbal warning, written warning, one day suspension without pay, one week suspension without pay and termination."

"If any level of discipline is required," Spencer says, "this fact is documented in the employee's personnel file. We have a disciplinary form with a space allowed to detail the incident. The employee signs the form to acknowledge his or her understanding of the level of discipline received and that corrective behavior in the future is required. Having this documentation is crucial if the employee files an unemployment claim or wrongful-termination lawsuit."[7]

➥**Reality check:** An additional rule to help you administer progressive discipline fairly, says Paul Falcone, author of *The Hiring and Firing Question and Answer Book*, is to ask yourself, How would I respond if my best-performing employee committed the same error? "If you would respond the same way with your best performer as you would now with an employee who's having difficulty meeting job expectations, then you know you're responding fairly. On the other hand, if it appears that you may be acting more harshly with your current employee than you would with others, then reconsider your actions before moving forward."[8]

169 Action Steps for the Moment of Truth

- Always fire someone face to face. The job can't be delegated any more than it can be postponed.
- Come to the point within the first two or three minutes and make the reasons for termination clear. Remain firm in your decision. Do not relent.
- Adopt a low-key approach that the employee is just not right for your practice, in that job, at this time. Don't dwell on the person's shortcomings. Simply express disappointment that things have not changed since the last performance review and that you have no alternative but to terminate employment. Acknowledge the person's capabilities and strong points. If appropriate, express regret that you don't have a job opening more suited to the person's qualifications—and let it go at that.
- "Consider having a witness," advises Paul Preston, Ph.D., author of *Employer's Guide to Hiring and Firing*. "In most firings, a witness is unnecessary. If however, there is any chance that hostility will turn into a physical threat, or if

there is a chance for legal action by the employee, a witness is good protection."[9]

- Should you tell the employee the reasons for your decision
or gloss over them? Most human resources managers advocate an explanation somewhere between the two extremes.
They advise giving the employee enough information to
show your decision was not arbitrary, but not so much
detail as to destroy the person's self-esteem in the process.

- "Managers should avoid the word 'attitude' when speaking
with an employee or documenting progressive discipline,"
says Paul Falcone, director of employment and development for Paramount Pictures in Hollywood, California.
"It's simply too subjective a word and typically escalates
disagreement by fostering feelings of resentment and anger.
As a matter of fact," he adds, "courts have interpreted 'attitude problems' as mere differences of opinion or personality conflicts. It is therefore critical that you avoid that specific term in any of your disciplinary documentation. Only
behaviors and actions that can be observed and documented
may be presented as evidence in court."[10]

- Once you make the decision, "get 'em out quick." That's
the overwhelming recommendation of the HCPs, practice
administrators, and human resource specialists I've asked
about the timing of an employee's dismissal. The end of
the day is preferred to avoid embarrassment for the
employee. Mondays are preferred to Fridays so the person
can go out on a Tuesday to look for other work, rather than
stew about the dismissal over the weekend.

- Tell other employees of your decision, indicating in simple
terms the reasons for it and ask for their support until you
find a replacement. Staff members may be more aware
than you of the shortcomings of the former employee and
actually applaud your decision.

➡ **Reality check:** It's important to remember that departing employees are also "ambassadors" for your practice—whether you wish them
to be or not. Even if they encountered several months of rough going

before leaving, if the parting was amicable, they will be more inclined to speak favorably about the practice.

➡**Hard learned lessons:**

- "A disgruntled employee can do more damage to you and your practice than employees in other fields can do to their employers," says Dr. Michael Metzger, Dallas, Texas. "They could call Medicare with a complaint that you're over-billing or under-billing, or they could file an OSHA complaint. They could call a disgruntled patient and make problems for you there too. You have a liability in the medical profession that you don't have in other situations."[11]

- If your decision to fire someone is based on performance issues, you'd better have a clear and reasonable documented record that the person knew what was expected, that the employee had the tools and opportunity to succeed, and that he or she was given reasonable notice and a chance to improve. In other words: Make sure there are no surprises.

- "There are three main ways that managers get firing wrong," say Jack Welch, former CEO of General Electric, and Suzy Welch, co-authors of *Winning*. These are moving too fast (without giving the employee adequate warning), lack of candor (about the person's shortcomings during one-on-one meetings), and taking too long (which results in what Jack Welch calls a "Dead Man Walking effect.")[12]

- "Rest assured that how you treat people on their way out," say Richard Hadden and Bill Catlette, co-authors of *Contented Cows Give Better Milk*, "is being watched and noted by a lot of other folks who are simultaneously forming an opinion about how you would treat them under similar circumstances. If you are counting on their discretionary effort, you can't have them wondering if you would mistreat them."[13]

- "It's not the people you fire who make your life miserable," says Harvey McKay, author of *Swim with the Sharks Without Being Eaten Alive*, "It's those you don't."[14]

➡**From the success files:** Following a recent seminar, an HCP wrote me: "When I returned to my office, I fired our bookkeeper of 13 years.

It was without doubt, the hardest, most painful thing I've ever done. It was also the best thing—for my staff, my patients and myself. It was hard to recognize the negative impact she had on the practice—until she left."

➡**Resource:**

Rightful Termination: Defensive Strategies for Hiring and Firing in the Lawsuit-Happy 90's by James Walsh (Merritt Publishing, Los Angeles, CA, 1997). Among other important issues, this book covers job applicant testing, at-will employment, civil rights claims, wrongful termination claims, and termination methods.

170 Layoffs for Economic Reasons

Being fired from a job because of incompetence, misconduct, or negligence is invariably a blow to one's ego, not to mention the pocketbook. But what about the employee whose work is satisfactory but is nonetheless being let go for economic reasons, such as declining reimbursements by insurance companies, rising malpractice premiums, fee reductions by Medicare, a drop in patient visits, or increased overhead and a subsequent need to reduce payroll expenses? For this employee, being fired may seem even more brutal and unfair than it might for those who deserve to be fired.

➡**Action steps:** As in firing those who deserve to be fired, there's no foolproof way to deliver the message to the undeserving. The following recommendations are made by Paul Preston, Ph.D., author of *Employer's Guide to Hiring and Firing*:

- "Avoid blame. Reassure the fired person that his or her past performance is not the reason for the firing, but don't overdo this reassurance since painting a too glowing picture of the employee's worth may make the firing seem all the more undeserved."
- "Separate the action from the reason," says Preston. "Make clear to the fired person that this action in no way reflects his or her personal worth. Keep out of your conversation any mention of past errors, problems or difficulties."
- "Many managers have found that providing a 'to whom it may concern' letter of recommendation at the termination

meeting is a good approach," says Preston. "It can be an important source of reassurance."

- "Beyond recommendations, offer the fired employee real assistance in either finding other employment or in making the transition to retirement."

- "Consider the impact on those staying. Whenever there is any change in the composition of the work group, the group members want to know what is going on, how the change affects them personally, and what changes—if any—are coming next. Provide open-discussion times when employees' questions and anxieties can be aired, and be willing to frankly discuss the situation as it unfolds."[15]

➥**Hard learned lesson:** "Make any major staff and payroll revisions in one, clean move—then immediately work to restore staff morale," advises John Pinto, president of J. Pinto & Associates Inc., an ophthalmic practice management firm in San Diego, California. "If you're in a practice survival situation and find one day that you must cut staff, hours, wages, benefits or all four to stay afloat, make the needed changes all at once."

"Stretching out terminations or slowly peeling back perks is a sure path to low staff morale," says Pinto. "Instead of cutting costs, this demoralizing approach will more likely result in a hollowing out of your organization as the most capable staff start shopping out their resumes."[16]

171 Exit Interviews

Ever wonder about the level of morale among your employees or how they view their jobs, co-workers, and the day-to-day management of your practice? The answers could be helpful in improving productivity and practice growth.

Interviews with employees who voluntarily leave their jobs, called *exit interviews*, can often yield information that, for a variety of reasons, they're reluctant to tell you while still on the job.

➥**Tested tip:** To get honest feedback, assure departing employees (1) of complete confidentiality and (2) that what they say during the exit interview will not in any way be held against them (for example, if they ask for a reference).

Suggested questions:

- **Are there any specific features of your new job that you feel were lacking in your job here?**
- **What did you think about the features of your job here such as salary, benefits, supervision, and office policies?**
- **What did you like best about your job here? What did you dislike about it?**
- **What suggestions do you have for us to make our office a better place to work?**
- **Were you satisfied or dissatisfied with the office environment? Are changes needed in the working space, lighting, heating, air conditioning?**
- **How about the working conditions? Did you feel overworked? Underutilized? Were you under unusual stress?**
- **What was your real reason for leaving our office? (Consider probing for the *critical factor* with follow-up questions such as "What was the straw that broke the camel's back? When did you decide you wanted a different job?")**
- **Would you recommend our office as a good place to work?**

In her book *HR from the Heart*, Libby Sartain, senior vice president of human resources at Yahoo Inc., recommends always asking departing employees, **"Is there anything we could have done to keep you here?"** You may discover that there may still be a sliver of a chance to keep valued talent and avoid the costs of turnover.[17]

All these questions may not fit each departing employee, so pick and choose as the situation warrants. During the questioning, it's best to be empathetic and nonjudgmental. Comments such as **"I wasn't aware of that; please go on"** or **"That's an interesting point; could you give me more details?"** will encourage the employee to speak openly.

"The benefit [of exit interviews] to the practice," says consultant Linda Miles, based in Virginia Beach, Virginia, "is to hopefully avoid losing staff for the same reasons by identifying unfavorable traits in the employer or co-workers, unfair policies or unmet expectations. The benefit to the doctor is discovering weaknesses he or she may not even know exist."[18]

➥**Reality check:** Some employees may provide more detailed (and possibly more truthful) exit information if they are given the option of responding by mail. In such cases, inform them that they will receive a written questionnaire (with a stamped return envelope) in the next two weeks and that further input would be greatly appreciated.

You may receive the questionnaires back from only 50 percent of the departing employees; however, the quality of the information may well be worth the extra effort. Mailed questionnaires often contain information that people are uncomfortable saying face-to-face.

(172) One-on-One Interviews by a Third Party

➥**Reality check:** A major obstacle for interviewers is that exiting employees see no benefit in being candid when they've already left, or are in the process of leaving. If you are doing all the right things and after a reasonable trial you are not succeeding in getting meaningful information from departing employees, the problem may be that they won't talk to anyone from inside the organization.

➥**Action step:** Consider using an outside firm.

A multi-office corporation encountered sizable numbers of good employees voluntarily leaving. Employees typically stated they were leaving for better opportunities, more money, or more time with their families. Exit interviews with departing employees produced little that was helpful in identifying what management suspected were the real issues. As a result, the company engaged Langer Associates Inc., a New York market research firm, to conduct telephone interviews with those who had quit.

Each respondent was paid an incentive fee for participating in the study. Because many ex-employees were working at new jobs or were occupied with young families during the day, interviews were often conducted on evenings and weekends.

Anonymity was a serious concern, says Naomi Brody, vice president of Langer Associates. "We assured the ex-employees that we would not identify them by name, except at their own request, and that in our report to the company, their comments would be combined with those of all other interviewees so they would not be identifiable."

"From their responses," Brody says, "it was clear that we were viewed as an objective third party and that our status as an outside firm was important in getting them to open up and be honest."

"The problems of which the company had been unaware, had to do primarily with training, managerial treatment and job expectation issues, and were the most commonly cited causes of job-dissatisfaction. For example, many ex-employees felt overwhelmed by heavier work loads and a much faster pace than they had been led to expect in the job interview. Others felt they had been treated unfairly by their managers."

As a result of the study, the company is dealing with the real issues causing the departure of good employees.[19]

173 The Wake-Up Call

"The more I tried to educate my staff about promptness and perfection," admits ophthalmologist, Dahlia Hirsch, Bel Air, Maryland, "the worse the situation became. It wasn't because of the message, but how I delivered it. I often didn't appreciate what my employees did. I only noticed what they didn't or couldn't do. I was impatient. Sometimes I corrected them right in front of patients. My wake up call came one day when all four of my employees quit. We went to lunch, which became an exit interview of sorts and I asked them why they were quitting. I learned (painfully) that I was the reason. That lunch," she adds, "was the most valuable consultation I ever had. I realized that if I didn't change some patterns, I would have constant turnover."[20]

References

1. Norbut M. Be Decisive Yet Sensitive When Terminating Employees. April 24, 2006. http://www.ama-assn.org/amednews/2006/04/24/bica0424.htm
2. Moore P. Management Mistakes: Dodging Bullets. *Physicians Practice*, March 2006.
3. Studer Q. The Magic of Rounding. *Successful Meetings,* February 2006, 19–20.
4. Weiss GG. Turn a Problem Employee into a Pearl. *Medical Economics*, December 23, 2002.
5. Weiss GG. Practice Pointers: When It's Time to Give an Employee the Boot. *Medical Economics,* July 26, 2002.
6. Ibid.
7. Spencer D. Become a Recruiting, Hiring and Termination Expert. *Chiropractic Products*, January 2006, 28–30.

8. Falcone P. *The Hiring and Firing Question and Answer Book*. New York: AMACOM; 2002.
9. Preston P. *Employer's Guide to Hiring and Firing*. Englewood Cliffs, NJ: Prentice-Hall Inc.; 1982.
10. Falcone P. *The Hiring and Firing Question and Answer Book*. New York: AMACOM; 2002.
11. Smith R. When You Have to Fire an Employee. *Podiatry Today,* July 2002, 63–70.
12. Welch J, Welch S. *Winning*. New York: HarperBusiness; 2005.
13. Catlette B, Hadden R. You're Fired! http://www.contentedcows.com/200505fr.html
14. McKay HB. *Swim with the Sharks Without Being Eaten Alive: Outsell, Outmanage, Outmotivate, and Outnegotiate Your Competition*. New York: HarperBusiness; 1995.
15. Preston P. *Employer's Guide to Hiring and Firing*. Englewood Cliffs, NJ: Prentice-Hall; 1982.
16. Pinto J. Retaining and Rewarding Your Practice's Top Staff. *Ophthalmology Management*, June 1999.
17. Sartain L, Finney M. *HR from the Heart*. New York: AMACOM; 2003.
18. Miles L. Measuring the Value of Exit Interviews. *Dental Practice Report*, October 2003, 17.
19. Brody N. Why Are the Employees Leaving. *Quirk's Marketing Research Review*, December 1997, 34–37.
20. Hirsch D. How to Rediscover the Person in the Patient. *Review of Optometry*, July 1999.

Section Three

Studies show that employees leave managers more often than they leave their jobs or companies.

—Marcus Buckingham and Curt Coffman, co-authors of *First, Break All the Rules*

Chapter Fourteen

RETAINING

Secrets of Staff Retention

"There are so many organizational priorities in healthcare that retention is often overlooked," says Karen Hart, R.N., B.S.N., senior vice president, healthcare division, Bernard Hodes Group and former executive director of the National Association for Health Care Recruitment. "Everyone talks about wanting to retain employees and acknowledges that they need to do more retention work," Hart says, "but there are so many other things going on that it gets put on the back burner. To create change," Hart adds, "retention has to be a culture that is pushed by people at the top of the organization. Retention has to have a godfather or godmother in the organization who is really going to make a case for it."[1]

The question this chapter addresses is: How does one retain great employees—especially when, in many cases, they could be earning more or working an easier schedule elsewhere?

174 The High Cost of Turnover

At the outset, what's a typical turnover rate for front office staff in a small primary care group?

"It isn't unusual for the front desk staff to turn over every nine to 16 months," says Geoffrey T. Anders, J.D., C.P.A., of The Health Care Group in Plymouth Meeting, Pennsylvania. "This is a faster rate than for clinical positions because these employees are the ones who take heat, while the clinical staff sees patients' nicer side. Moreover, the pay for front office staff is usually the lowest in the office."[2]

To calculate your annual employee turnover rate, divide the number of employee departures your practice has experienced in the last 12 months by the number of staff members you've employed during the same period. Then multiply that number by 100.

"Employee turnover in the healthcare sector is extremely high; so high in fact that in some US states it is more than double the national average of 15.6%," reports Keith D. Jones in *The Internet Journal of Healthcare Administration.* "This alarming (and rapidly worsening) statistic," he adds, "costs healthcare systems billions of dollars every year and is a direct threat to the future of the healthcare sector."[3]

Estimates of turnover costs vary from 25 percent to 150 percent of annual compensation, depending on the costs of separation, recruitment, interviewing, and training—plus the time a new employee takes to reach his or her maximum efficiency level.[4]

"The average cost of turnover," says the consulting firm of Kepner-Tregoe, "is 25 percent of an employee's annual salary plus the cost of benefits. Typical benefits amount to about 30 percent of wages." As an example, assume an annual salary of $30,000 × .25 = $7,500. Add the cost of benefits ($30,000 × .30 = $9,000 × .25 = $2,250) for a grand total of $9,750. This amounts to almost a third of the position's annual salary.[5]

In addition to these substantial costs, turnover also results in a huge toll on staff morale and patient satisfaction. So focusing your attention on improving staff retention rates can accomplish much more than just improving your bottom line.

175 Why Employees Leave

In the healthcare field, surveys indicate that more than 25 percent of employees leave within the first 90 days, says Quint Studer, CEO of The Studer Group, a consulting firm in Gulf Breeze, Florida.[6]

Employees leave for a variety of unpreventable reasons: a long commute, the perception of greener pastures, partner or spouse relocation, the desire to be a full-time parent, retirement, health reasons, and so on. There may be nothing you can do about it.

Then there are the preventable reasons that people quit their jobs—about which you can do something. These include

- Boredom or lack of challenging work
- Too many repetitive problems
- Unreasonable work hours
- Too much pressure
- No leeway for balancing work and family
- Lack of appreciation
- A hypercritical boss
- Inadequate compensation (either in comparison with other newly hired, less experienced employees and/or what other HCPs are paying)
- Because something occurred that's "the last straw"

Too often, the new employee is confronted with a dramatic mismatch between the culture, the job itself, the working conditions, or his or her manager or peers described during the interview process— and the actual experience on the first day of work or during training, says Nancy S. Ahlrichs, author of *Competing for Talent.*[7]

"I've studied countless exit interviews and countless post-exit interviews [questionnaires given out six months or so after someone leaves]," says Professor John Sullivan, head of the human resource management program at San Francisco State University. "Reason number one for leaving is usually some variation on the theme, 'My boss was a jerk.' The second most common reason is, 'I wasn't challenged.'"[7]

What, then, are the "action steps" needed to improve staff retention?

176 Get Them Off to a Good Start

Onboarding, assimilation, orientation, integration, new-hire transitions—whatever term you use, it's about getting employees up to speed as quickly as possible and then to achieve long-term success.

"How new employees are treated on their first day," writes James B. Miller, author of *The Corporate Coach* "makes an indelible impression that affects long-term performance. Quite frankly," he adds, "it is the most important day in an employee's career. It sets the tone for everything that will follow. How employees are treated on their first day is something every manager should make a top priority."[9]

Regardless of a person's work history, a staff member's first day on a new job can be intimidating. For some, it is so overwhelming and confusing, they don't return for a second day. Some don't even make it back from lunch on the first day.

➡**Action steps:**
- Send a "Welcome to the Practice" letter to the homes of new employees *before* their first day. It lets them (and their families) know they're important members of a healthcare team and that you're looking forward to working together.
- If possible, avoid starting a new employee on the busiest day of the week. For most practices, it's better to start on a Tuesday or Wednesday than on a Monday or Friday.
- Make sure to let all staff members know in advance that the new employee is expected, and ask them to make him or her feel welcome.
- Conduct a tour of the facility. "The tour allows a medical group to showcase its facility and allows people to see certain parts of the facility that the employee may not normally see," say Michael A. O'Connell, MHA, FACMPE, CHE, and Deborah M. Jewell, FPC, vice president, Professional and Physician Services at Huron Hospital/Cleveland (Ohio) Clinic Health System and HR program manager, Cleveland Clinic Health System, respectively. "For example, a medical records clerk may not have the opportunity to visit the ambulatory surgery center, even though she may pull records for it daily. Seeing parts of the orga-

nization helps the employee to be connected to how her job connects to other groups."[10]

- On the first day, pair the new staff member with a co-worker who will serve as a coach and encouraging presence for as long as needed. This has two advantages: First, it gives a new staff member a one-on-one way to "learn the ropes" from someone who's been in his or her shoes. Second, the coach feels proud you chose him or her to be personally responsible for the new team member. Coaches can be any staff member who's had a couple years of experience at your practice, exhibits leadership qualities, and wants to help new employees grow in their jobs.

- "The co-worker should be in contact with the new employee even before the employee's first day on the job," says urologist/author Neil Baum of New Orleans, Louisiana. "The worst thing you can do is to talk enthusiastically to the employee about the team spirit that pervades your practice and then let him or her flounder about unaided. If you adopt a sink-or-swim policy," he adds, "your potential dream team can become your worst nightmare."[11]

- Attend to the little things. "Even little things like having the employee's desk ready and a space to hang up a coat can have an impact," says Susan Keane Baker, author of *Managing Patient Expectations*. "A call to explain housekeeping items like where to park or what the staff usually does for lunch can ease first-day jitters. It's stunning," Baker adds, "to hear people talk about how nothing was ready when they got to work. If you call the night before, the person really comes in with those little questions taken care of."[12]

- During the break-in period, the coach can monitor the new staff member's progress with such questions as: **Do you have the resources you need to do the job? Do you need any assistance in dealing with anyone in the practice? Is the job what you expected it would be? Is there anything we can do for you?**

- New employees should finish their first day feeling they've made the right decision and joined the type of practice for which they want to work.

Finally, and perhaps most important, you must decide that welcoming a new staff member is an investment in long-term retention and should be given a high priority.

➥**Follow-up:** Ask for staff input on how to improve the orientation of new employees. For example, what would they have liked (that they didn't have) when they first started working at the practice? To what activities should more time have been devoted? Less time?

➥**From the success files:** "At Byron Family Medicine, a five physician practice in Byron Center, Michigan, new employees go through an extensive orientation. New medical assistants spend time with all physicians to learn specific nuances and quirks. The practice has a checklist of items to review with each new employee, says Tim Tobolic, M.D., a family physician and partner."[13]

(177) Hard Learned Lessons About New Employee Orientation

- "The odds of a company keeping employees," say Donald O. Clifton, Ph.D. and Paula Nelson, co-authors of *Soar with Your Strengths*, "improves significantly when people are celebrated and acknowledged by name in their first hours at a new position."[14]
- Make orientation and training a priority. Good employees will want to give their best from day one if you give them the tools and resources to do their jobs. Have an agenda outlining the specifics.
- "We strive to make people feel welcomed immediately," says Ann Miller, vice president of workforce strategies at Children's Healthcare of Atlanta, recognized by *Fortune* as one of the top 100 employers in the country. "Once a potential hire accepts an offer, a personalized letter is sent welcoming him or her to our organization. All new hires go through a two-day orientation that reinforces their importance as a stakeholder in Children's while covering the essential information for them to be successful."[15]
- "As a leader," says Mike Poskey, VP of Zerorisk HR Inc., a Dallas-based human resources risk management firm, "your

participation in new employee orientation sends a vital cultural and leadership message: 'We're all involved here in the drive toward what we want to be in the future.'"[16]

- During the orientation and/or initial training phase, be attuned to a new person's need for information and individual capacity for learning. Some new employees may want to move quickly beyond the basics to learn about the broader issues such as the core values and philosophy of the practice.

- "When people come on board, set up a realistic training regimen," says Alec Ziss, practice administrator at Weston Pediatric Physicians in Weston, Massachusetts. "Save the most difficult things for later, when they understand the flow of the office and what their main responsibilities are."[17]

- Watching others helps new employees get a handle on the office's priorities and how the workflow is managed. "Sometimes new employees fall behind because they're spending too much time on unessential tasks and letting critical duties slide," says Sam Platia, administrator of the five-clinician Northwestern Medical Center in New Tripoli, Pennsylvania. "I'll sit with them—or have a seasoned employee sit with them—and work hands on."[18]

- "Based on my research, a new hire is most influenced during the first 30 days and will base his or her decision to stay with a firm long-term within the first 90 days," says Tim Augustine, director of human resources for Atwell-Hicks, Ann Arbor, Michigan. "If you structure your new employee orientation program and include those current employees and leaders who will help the new employee become acclimated to your way of doing things, the return on your investment of time and money will be realized within the first six months."[19]

178 Employee Handbook

Another must-have item for a new employee's orientation is an employee handbook with such information as your philosophy of practice, office policies, the importance of patient confidentiality, employee benefits, and a checklist of personnel issues to ensure the smooth operation of your practice.

Having office policies in writing helps to eliminate misunderstandings when employees know up front what's expected of them. "A typical employee handbook," says Gail Garfinkel Weiss, senior editor of *Medical Economics,* "covers job performance standards, training periods, termination policies, severance pay, benefits and your rules regarding substance abuse, smoking, safety, sexual harassment, confidentiality, overtime, performance evaluations, salary reviews, dress codes, computer policies, work schedules, lateness, absenteeism, vacations, sick leave, and family and medical leave."[20]

➡Resources
- Professional Association of Health Care Office Management (PAHCOM): http://www.pahcom.com
- *Group Practice Personnel Policies Manual,* by Alys Novak and Courtney Price, available from the Medical Group Management Association: http://www.mgma.com
- *Create Your Own Employee Handbook: A Legal & Practical Guide,* by Lisa Guerin and Amy DelPo, available from the publisher, Nolo: http://www.nolo.com

➡Hard learned lessons
- If your employees don't know what you expect from them, how can they live up to your standards?
- No policy manual can anticipate every circumstance or question. As your practice continues to grow, the need may arise to revise, supplement, or rescind policies.
- "I think it's critical to have an employee manual," says orthopedic surgeon Greg D'Angelo of Bluegrass Orthopedics in Lexington, Kentucky. "It's very nice when things are written down and there's no ambiguity. It's also a good reference tool. If you have a question about something, the answer is right there at your fingertips."[21]
- "Don't make the rules too rigid, because even your best employees may occasionally break them," says Catherine Kocher, a practice management consultant with Clayton L. Scroggins Associates in Cincinnati, Ohio. "Leave some flexibility in the interpretation and administration of your

office policies so that you'll have some options when dealing with individual cases."[22]

- The services of an attorney are recommended to ensure
that your office policies are in compliance with all federal
and state regulations.

179 Get to Know Your Team

"One of the first steps to successful retention is getting to know your
staff," says Susan Osborne, R.N., M.S.N., M.B.A., director of inpatient services at Children's Healthcare of Atlanta, Georgia. "Building
relationships is very important. You can learn a great deal about what
motivates your staff and what produces job satisfaction," she says, "by
understanding their 'real life' outside of work, such as their interests,
family, and children. What are their childrens' ages and names? Do
they have pets? On a professional level, why did they choose nursing?
What do they like about their current position? What are their long
term goals and how can you help them achieve them? Ask them what
is working well and what needs to be changed. This is a great way to
start getting to know your team. Direct managers who know employees by their first name and something about them show the staff members they are valued."[23]

180 Get New Employees Up to Speed

Some companies find the best way to bring new employees up to
speed quickly is to have veterans share their "secrets."

"Michael Watkins, an associate professor at Harvard Business
School and author of *The First 90 Days,* worked with one company that
accomplished this by selecting 10 employees who had been with the firm
for two to three years," says Joe Mullich, writing in *Workforce Management.* "This was long enough to know the terrain, but short enough so
they remembered what it was like to be the new kid on the block."

"The 10 employees, all of whom were articulate and successful in
their jobs," Mullich says, "were videotaped candidly answering the
kinds of questions that new employees have, like 'What do you wish
you had known about this place before you started?' The responses
were edited into a 30-minute video that was handed to each new
employee immediately after hiring."[24]

➥**Reality check:** When HCPs fail to put much effort into helping new employees acclimate to the workplace, employees either leave or take longer to reach what economists call the "break-even point," the point at which a new employee becomes productive.

181 Ask for Commitment, Not Loyalty

"At Brush-Wellman Inc., we are asking for the commitment—not loyalty of employees," says Daniel Skoch, vice president of human resources. "Commitment requires an agreement to do something; loyalty implies being blindly faithful to a duty or obligation. Thus we have begun to tell our employees:

"We will help you grow and develop. We will provide you opportunities to learn, to be involved, to practice new skills, to have responsibility, to be respected and valued, and to be rewarded and recognized for your contributions. In return, we seek your commitment to our company's mission. We cannot guarantee what is going to happen in the future, but if it doesn't work out, you will leave here a more talented, responsible, self-confident and employable person."

"As a result," Skoch says, "we believe that our employees recognize that their personal needs for security, growth opportunities, and job satisfaction can link up very well with the company's need for employees who are willing to continually learn, and be adaptable and self-supervising. This linking will provide us with a competitive advantage and our employees with their best opportunity for personal security."[25]

182 Measure Before You Manage

How do you know whether a newly hired team member is right for his or her job and, equally important, right for your practice? Many HCPs evaluate a new hire's job performance during a probationary period, which can last from 30 to 90 days. Some parameters you might use:

- **Goal completion**: It helps to agree on some clear goals for measuring an employee's on-the-job success during the first few months. These objectives can involve quantity or quality of work, or a combination of the two. Keep in mind, the clearer these goals are, the less chance you and your new hire will disagree on whether he or she achieved them.

- **Action steps:** "You need to set performance standards based on how long it has traditionally taken your employees to master certain tasks," says management consultant Judy Capko, Thousand Oaks, California. For example, with a new telephone operator: "How many calls per hour is she expected to handle? At what point should she be able to triage calls on her own? How long is she permitted to keep a caller on hold?" Such standards, says Capko, give both you and the employee goals to aim for and a clear yardstick to measure whether the employee is working out satisfactorily.[26]
- **Motivation:** Does the person come to work on time and appear motivated and energetic? Is he or she eager to learn and take on more responsibility?
- **Problem-solving skills:** Almost every job requires some ability to analyze and solve problems. If the employee continually asks basic questions and doesn't seem to learn, he or she may lack required problem-solving skills.
- **Compatibility with co-workers:** Getting along with others, pitching in when needed, and meshing with the culture of the practice are critical to morale and efficiency. A person may have the right skills and experience, but if he or she doesn't fit with the team, major problems can ensue.
- **Compatibility with patients:** In a service-oriented practice, you really need to tune in to patients' complaints about new employees. Don't be the last to know if a newly hired team member is undermining your practice.

Admittedly, such evaluations tend to be subjective. Keep in mind that we sometimes expect new employees to accomplish more than their predecessor. Ask yourself whether this is reasonable.

Consider also asking other team members to rate the new staff member. This approach helps eliminate any bias you have and gives your team members an important role in a decision that affects their work.

➡**Reality check:** No matter how adept you are at interviewing job applicants, a few won't make the grade. And the longer you delay confronting the issue, the more damage you'll wreak on your practice.

(183) Think 30/60/90

The first 90 days of an employee's tenure can be the difference between an employee who stays for a decade and one who's gone before the year is out.

Many HCPs discontinue recruiting at precisely the wrong time. In actuality, finding and hiring the right person is only the beginning, not the conclusion, of the recruiting process. Even before the ink is dry on the employment paperwork, you immediately need to launch another phase of recruiting (sometimes called re-recruiting) as part of a long range retention strategy.

"The concept of re-recruitment has been most widely adopted, consultants say, by service industries like restaurants and hotels, where turnover is both high and costly. A report by the American Hotel and Lodging Association found that it takes about 90 days for a new employee to reach the level of productivity of an existing worker. If new hires don't receive proper training and support early on, 47 percent leave their jobs within the first six months."[27]

Sonesta Hotels, a family-run chain of 18 properties on the East Coast of the United States as well as abroad, has developed a formal program to continuously acclimate new hires to their jobs throughout the first 100 days. The purpose? To boost performance and lower turnover. The main thrust at Sonesta is to re-recruit employees on their 30-, 60-, and 90-day anniversaries.

At 30 days, the human resources director sits down with new employees to see if their expectations are being met, and whether they have all the tools they need to perform their work. "This time period is far enough into the job so the employee has an idea what it's like, but not so far down that adjustments can't be made if necessary," says Grace Andrews, president of Training by Design, a Melrose, Massachusetts, company that runs the program.

"At 60 days, new employees receive a second orientation, called 'the Booster.' The focus is in developing the worker's communication and service skills. The company also solicits feedback about the employees' training and asks them what else they need to be successful," Andrews says.

At 90 days, employees have a formal review with their manager, which focuses primarily on joint goal-setting for the rest of the year.

"It's more of a conversation than a review," Andrews says. "People don't want to be graded. They want to know what their future is."[28]

184 Crunch Time

Somewhere between 30 and 90 days, the honeymoon for a new employee ends and reality starts to set in, says Quint Studer, a former hospital president and CEO of the Studer Group in Gulf Breeze, Florida. Schedule several one-on-one meetings during this period, he recommends, with a structured list of questions such as the following, to find out what is really on the minds of your new employees:

- **How do we compare to what we said we would be like?**
- **Tell me what you like. What is going well?**
- **Which employees have been helpful to you in the first 30 days?**
- **Are there things you did in your last job that might be helpful to us?**
- **Do you know anyone who might be a valuable addition to our team?**

"Not only do such meetings go a long way toward securing long-term relationships with your hard-won new talent," Studer says, "they can also serve as a vehicle for gaining insight into your organization."[29]

➡**Hard learned lesson:** If an employee's performance has not been up to par, the probationary period should either be terminated or perhaps extended. It makes no sense to let the probationary period of an unsatisfactory employee end without taking some action. If the person is not working out after three months, chances are, what you see is what you've got. Replace him or her and start the process all over. Life's too short to have problem employees in your practice.

185 Focus on the Top 20 Percent

"Many managers have the mistaken impression," says John Sullivan, a recruiting expert and professor at San Francisco State University, "that they should treat all workers equally. The opposite is true. Great managers have figured out how to treat top, average and poor performers 'differently.' If you want to give your company a competitive advantage and increase employee productivity," he says, "you should dedicate more time and resources to the top 20 percent of your employees. This doesn't mean you should ignore the rest of your employees. It just means you shouldn't treat all employees equally."[30]

His advice is aimed at industry; however, the principle involved is also applicable to a healthcare practice. The first step is identifying high performance employees. These include individuals who

- Contribute valuable new ideas to help the practice
- Provide formal or informal leadership to others
- Require little or no supervision to accomplish their tasks
- Have the highest productivity and/or effectiveness at what they do
- Facilitate the work of others
- Have unique knowledge or skills
- Have excellent rapport with patients
- Are essential to the operation of your practice and who would be difficult to replace
- Would create the most disruption if they were to leave

➥**Action step:** One way to increase productivity (and retain the best employees) is to let key people and top performers spend most of their time doing what they like—and what they do best. Redesign their jobs if necessary. It's unlikely you can do this for all employees, but to the extent you can do it for your top performers, it will exponentially increase their job satisfaction and loyalty.

➥**Reality check:** Top performers differ significantly from the average employee in what they expect from an employer and the job itself. If you offer top performers the same level of challenge and reward as average employees, you'll frustrate them and, in many cases, they will leave. "Top performers," says Sullivan, "want differentiation, not equal treatment. They expect different treatment for different performance."[31]

186 Reduce Work-Related Stress

"One of the reasons older nurses leave the profession is physical stress," says Lee Ann Runy in *HHN Magazine*.

"Tampa [Florida] General Hospital," she reports, "implemented a patient-lift initiative to reduce back and other types of injuries among nurses and support staff. A dedicated lift team assists nurses and other staff when they cannot safely move patients. Since the initiative was launched in 2002, lift-related injuries have fallen 60 percent."

"The team consists of 12 specially trained personnel who are available 21.5 hours per day, seven days a week," says Runy. "When a nurse needs assistance, he or she pages the team. Response time is about 15 minutes and the team averages about 100 calls per day. The team can lift a patient in five to seven minutes; it takes a lone nurse about 20 minutes to lift a patient. The hospital spent between $250,000 and $300,000 on lifting equipment and training the team on its use. That money has been recouped because of the need to hire fewer agency nurses, reduced worker's compensation claims and decreased rate of pressure ulcers among patients." "It's had a big impact on nurse morale,'" says Manon Short, the hospital's injury prevention coordinator. "Among other things," she adds, "the nurses credit the team with providing them more time for other nursing duties, allowing them to leave work on time."[32]

➥**Action steps:** What innovations or investments might you make in your facility to reduce work-related stress for your employees?

187 Prevent Employee Burnout

Job burnout is a form of work-related stress that affects the disposition and productivity of everyone in the office. Burned out employees grow more and more negative about their jobs, doing the bare minimum required to get the job done. They become actively disengaged from their work, and often are irritable toward co-workers, employers, even patients. They're late for work, call in sick more often, and may quit their jobs.

On the surface, burnout looks like an employee problem.

Christina Maslach, Ph.D., professor of psychology at the University of California, Berkeley, says burnout is caused as much by the job and the way people are managed as by an employee's personality.[33]

The first step in preventing burnout is to understand what causes it. The following are several stress-producing scenarios commonly found in healthcare practices:

> **Work overload:** With the ever-increasing demands of paperwork, patients to see, tasks to complete, and the need

for greater productivity, it's not uncommon to hear employees say, "There's just too much work to do and never enough time. I don't know where to start." In many practices, the pressure never lets up, and neither does the workload.

What exacerbates the problem, in many cases, is the quantity of low-level work (paperwork) required of people trained for far higher-level work (patient care). As one NP described it to me, "It becomes a soul-destroying situation."

Practice management consultant Elizabeth Woodcock, based in Atlanta, Georgia, recalls being in a practice in which the billing office was flooded with piles of claims. The manager said her staff were simply drowning in work and didn't have the resources to keep up. "When I did interviews," she says, "the staff had tears in their eyes. When you have good employees who care—but have too much work to do, you'll see that emotion come out. It's just classic."

Woodstock stresses "the importance of staffing around provider productivity instead of staff per full time equivalent (FTE) physician benchmarks. Busy physicians produce more calls, more claims, and more work for staff than less-busy physicians."[34]

Role conflict: Mixed messages are the problem in this case. An example is an HCP who stresses that employees should be friendly and helpful to patients *while at the same time*, expects them to handle an increased workload. That's a tough assignment. If a bottleneck occurs on a busy day, which "role" takes precedence?

Role ambiguity: When employees are uncertain about exactly what's expected of them on a day-to-day basis, they experience stress. "My job has not turned out to be the way it was described to me when I was hired" is a common complaint.

Inadequate compensation: When employees feel underpaid for what they do, they tend to become demotivated and resentful. If, in addition, an employee believes her or his job is more difficult or demanding than that of a co-worker who is paid the same, let alone a higher salary, a sense of inequity is experienced that often turns to outright anger.

Low job control: This occurs when intense work demands are placed on an employee who has little say about how his or her work is performed. It's not the difficulty of the work itself, but rather the employee's lack of input into how it is performed that causes stress.

"My view of burnout," says Dr. Mitchell T. Rabkin, past president of Beth Israel Hospital in Boston, "is that it has less to do with hard word and more to do with powerlessness. It can come from working hard and seeing things that are incongruous and inappropriate—and being utterly unable to do something about it. The first task in addressing and preventing burnout is to identify situations in which employees feel that way and to deal with those situations. You need to encourage people to voice their concerns and questions, their suggestions for change, and to give good answers."[35]

Rabkin's views highlight the need for dialogue between management and employees, which may range from one-on-one discussions between employees and their supervisors to more formal techniques such as those discussed in Chapter 12.

➥**Action steps:** "Emotional support is vital," says Krista Gregoria Lussier, R.N., M.S.N., writing in *Nursing Management.* "Take the time to talk to staff members individually about their concerns. Make your employees feel comfortable about coming to you with problems or grievances. Have an open-door policy. Offer support groups or hold group meetings, if they will reduce workplace stress. Ensure that the staff is kept abreast of new information or changes that will be occurring. Informed employees are less anxious and hopefully more satisfied."[36]

➥**Reality check:** Organizations that overlook the needs of their employees will run into greater retention risks in the long term, says Brian Stuhlmuller, CEO of Mission Control Productivity, a Yardley, Pennsylvania–based company that designs productivity programs. "Employers are so focused on the bottom line that they have been downsizing and downsizing. There is more work to get done by fewer people to the point it is not possible. People are constantly overloaded. They feel like they're not accomplishing anything," says Stuhlmuller. "Instead employees just go through the motions to get a paycheck, and then go home feeling overwhelmed and frustrated. Organizations are paying attention to profit at the cost of their employees' well-being. It eventually contributes to burnout and turnover."[37]

188 Hard Learned Lessons About Retention

- The old-school belief that "employees should consider themselves lucky to have a job" reflects a blind spot about the importance of employees to your services, say Wendy Leebov and Gail Scott in their book, *The Indispensable Health Care Manager.* "Perceiving your team members as *individuals* worthy of respect and care, and also as your organization's most precious resources, is pivotal to retaining talented people, and through them, attracting even more."[38]

- Asked for the number one reason employees leave a practice, consultant Marilyn Moats Kennedy, a specialist in healthcare workplace issues, says: "The younger ones leave because the grass is greener or they get bored. The older employees leave because they say to themselves, 'Is that all there is?' Doctors have to expect some turnover and be willing to take nurses back. Don't beat them to a pulp on the way out the door. If you treated them right, they'll be back if there's an open-door policy. This is the only sensible attitude for an employer to have."[39]

- "If the supervisor is interested in a candidate we offer him or her the opportunity to spend a half-day (unpaid) with one of our nurses or secretaries to see what working for AAIR (Allergy Asthma Immunology of Rochester [NY]) may be like," says, Robert J. Holzhauer, M.D., M.B.A. "The readily apparent camaraderie of our staff has often convinced job candidates that our practice might be a fun and interesting place to work. On the other hand, we have had some who have decided our practice was not for them and some that, on more extended observation, were not for us. This process sometimes saves us from making the mistake of hiring the wrong person for a job and wasting time, money and resources training her, only to have her leave shortly thereafter."[40]

- "Finding and keeping great employees has never been so critical," says Pam Withers, co-author of *Values Shift: The New Work Ethic and What It Means for Business,* "but the way to get the job done has changed dramatically in the past few years. That's because employees view their work differently than they used to, a fact that has given rise to an overall shift in workplace values. Understanding this shift is essential to building a strong company while saving on payroll. Ignoring it will cast you on the other side of the divide."[41]

- A successful retention strategy for nurses is the "Magnet Hospital" designation awarded by the American Nurses Credentialing Council (ANCC), an affiliate of the American Nurses Association. The magnet program is the result of research conducted by the American Academy of Nursing that analyzed how hospitals can attract and retain qualified nurses. "Applicants must meet 14 standards that address such issues as collaboration, research and clinical outcomes," says Jan Greene in an article in *Trustee.* "More specifically, hospitals meet the standards by having a flatter organizational structure that allows nurses more say in both patient care and how their jobs are designed; making the chief nursing officer part of the executive team; hiring more staff RNs and supporting top nurses in pursuing research and advanced degrees. Research indicates," Greene says, "that magnet hospital nurses are more satisfied with their jobs and that patient outcomes do improve with the program."[42]

- Helena Dahan, office manager for Lawndale Internal Medicine in Philadelphia, Pennsylvania, attributes the high staff retention rate at her office to cross-training. "With the exception of the receptionist, whatever one of our staffers can do, they all do," she says. "They do desk duty and sign-in-window duty, work with the physicians in various clinical capacities, and do phone triage. That way, they don't get burned out or lose any skills."[43]

- "The bottom line," says Susan Genrich, office manager of Selden Medical, a solo family practice in Selden, New York, "is that people want to be treated nicely, and they want to be appreciated for a job well done. If you do that, you'll have whatever staff you want, and they'll stay as long as you want."[44]

- One of the financial benefits of turnover is that it provides a rare opportunity to reset salaries. "Driving turnover among employees who have reached the high end of the pay structure generates substantial cost savings because the company can typically bring in a replacement at a lower rate or promote from within and lower the rate for that employee's replacement," says Jamie Hale, senior consultant and leader of the workforce management practice for Watson Wyatt in Dallas.[45]

- "Talk to your employees," say Roger Shenkel, M.D., and Cathy Gardner, manager of a 56-employee office in Grand Junction, Colorado. "I may go a week and hardly speak to my physician partners. They could care less, but with employees such behavior is a real mistake. Physicians should always speak to their employees. When you see them, address them by name. (Institute name tags, if you have to.) It's fairly easy to visit with your medical assistant or nurse, but go out of your way to say 'hi' to your front-office employees and your business staff."[46]

- Since launching their Web site, North Suburban Dental Associates in Skokie, Illinois, has found that *staff longevity* has proved to be an important element to the people who visit the site before showing up at the office. "We have found," says Dr. Barry Freydberg, "that staff longevity has been a major confidence builder in new patients we haven't met yet. We didn't know that this would have an influence on new patients but it has. Our credibility gets a boost based on staff longevity."[47]

- "Although retention is an indicator of employee commitment and the consequences of turnover are very real (high costs of hiring, lost intellectual capital, psychological toll on remaining team members, etc.) retention is not the grand prize," states the *Employee Engagement Report*, published by the global consulting firm of Blessing/White in Princeton, New Jersey. "Sticking around might actually mean stuck in the mud. Retention doesn't automatically deliver stellar performance or discretionary effort towards business-critical goals. That's where employee engagement comes into play."[48]

- Employee retention is not the same thing as employee loyalty. If there's a tight job market, you'll retain your employees. Suppose, however, there are more jobs than there are employees (as there are now in numerous sectors of the healthcare field)—will your employees remain loyal? Loyalty implies a *choice*. It's a very important distinction.

- Maybe you're a glass-half-empty person and think your current employees are captive in a sluggish economy. If so, here's a simple test. Do nothing. And see what happens.

References

1. Jackson K. Employee Retention in an Era of Shortages. *For the Record,* 2004, 30.
2. Practice Management Q&As. *Medical Economics*, September 16, 2005, 75.
3. Jones KD. The Impending Crisis in Healthcare. *The Internet Journal of Healthcare Administration,* 2001. http://www.ispub.com/ostia/index.php?xmlFilePath=journals/ijhca/vol1n2/crisis.xml
4. Webber AM. Firms Will Pay When Workers Make Escape. *USA Today*, April 12, 2004, A-21.
5. To Conquer Turnover, First Calculate Its True Impact. *The HR Specialist*, National Institute of Business Management. www.hrspecialist.net
6. Mullich J. They're Hired: Now the Real Recruiting Begins. *Workforce Management Online,* January, 2004. http://www.workforce.com/archive/feature/23/59/60/index.php
7. Ahlrichs NS. *Competing for Talent*. Palo Alto, CA: Davies-Black Publishing; 2000.
8. Imperato G. How to Hire the Next Michael Jordan. *Fast Company*, December 1998, 212–216.
9. Miller JB. *The Corporate Coach*. New York: HarperBusiness; 1993.
10. O'Connell MA, Jewell DM. Human Resources Management in Group Practice. Chapter 6 in *Physician Practice Management*. Sudbury, MA: Jones & Bartlett Publishers; 2005.
11. Baum N. *Take Charge of Your Medical Practice . . . Before Someone Else Does It for You*. Gaithersburg, MD: Aspen Publishers; 1996.

12. Norbut M. Employee Orientation Key to Transition. September 22/29, 2003. http://www.ama-assn.org/amednews/2003/09/22/bica0922.htm
13. Ibid.
14. Clifton DO, Nelson P. *Soar with Your Strengths*. New York: Dell Publishing; 1996.
15. Lauter VZ. The Welcome Wagon. May 2, 2006. http://www.hhnmag.com/hhnmag/hospitalconnect/search/article.jsp?dcrpath=HHNMAG/PubsNewsArticle/data/2006April/060502HHN_Online_Lauter&domain=HHNMAG
16. Poskey M. Seven Steps to Increase Employee Retention. http://www.zeroriskhr.com/ZeroriskhrCom/Articles/SevenSteps.aspx
17. Weiss GG. Turn a Problem Employee into a Pearl. *Medical Economics,* December 23, 2002.
18. Ibid.
19. Augustine T. Building a Solid Orientation Program. http://hiring.inc.com/columns/taugustine/20051003.html
20. Weiss GG. Turn a Problem Employee into a Pearl. *Medical Economics,* December 23, 2002.
21. Printz C. By the Book: Rules of the Worker's Road. August 15, 2005. http://www.ama-assn.org/amednews/2005/08/15/bisa0815.htm
22. Rice B. Practice Pointers: What Goes into an Employee Handbook. *Medical Economics*, January 6, 2006.
23. Osborne S. The Art of Rewarding and Retaining Staff, Part 2. *Nurse Leader*, August 2004, 2–4.
24. Mullich J. They're Hired: Now the Real Recruiting Begins, *Workforce Management Online.* January 2004. http://www.workforce.com/archive/feature/23/59/60/index.php
25. Skoch DA. Ask for Commitment, Not Loyalty. *Industry Week*, November 21, 1994, 38.
26. Weiss GG. Turn a Problem Employee into a Pearl. *Medical Economics*, December 23, 2002.
27. Mullich J. They're Hired: Now the Real Recruiting Begins, *Workforce Management Online.* January 2004. http://www.workforce.com/archive/feature/23/59/60/index.php
28. Ibid.
29. Studer Q. *Hardwiring Excellence*. Gulf Breeze, FL: Fire Starter Publishing; 2004.
30. Sullivan J. The True Value of Hiring and Retaining Top Performers. *Workforce Management Online.* August 2002. http://www.workforce.com/archive/article/23/27/12.php
31. Ibid.
32. Runy LA. Nurse Retention: An Executive's Guide to Keeping One of Your Hospital's Most Valuable Resources. January 17, 2006. http://www.hhnmag.com/hhnmag/hospitalconnect/search/article.jsp?dcrpath=HHNMAG/PubsNewsArticle/data/backup/0601HHN_FEA_Gatefold&domain=HHNMAG
33. Maslach C, Leiter M. *The Truth About Burnout: How Organizations Cause Stress and What to Do About It*. San Francisco: Jossey-Bass; 1997.
34. Moore P. Management Mistakes: Dodging Bullets. *Physicians Practice*, March 2006, 33–38.

35. Lovelock CH. *Product Plus.* New York: McGraw Hill; 1994.
36. Lussier KG. Taming Burnout's Flame. *Nursing Management,* April 2006, 14.
37. Tansiri JC. Misery & Company. *Incentive,* November 2004, 28–33.
38. Leebov W, Scott G. *The Indispensable Health Care Manager.* San Francisco: Jossey Bass; 2002.
39. Treat 'Em Right. *Physicians Practice Digest,* July/August 2001.
40. Holzhauer RJ. Secrets for Recruiting and Retaining Employees. *American Academy of Allergy Asthma and Immunology News,* August 2004.
41. Withers P. *Values Shift: The New Work Ethic and What It Means for Business.* Vancouver, B.C., Canada: FairWinds Press; 2001.
42. Greene J. Attracting Nurses: Why Magnet Hospitals Succeed. *Trustee,* April 2003, 20–23.
43. Weiss GG. How to Find and Keep Top-Notch Clinical Staff. *Medical Economics,* March 8, 2002, 36.
44. Ibid.
45. Hansen F. The Turnover Myth. *Workforce Management,* June 2005, 34–40.
46. Shenkel R, Gardner C. 5 Ways to Retain Good Staff. *Family Practice Management,* November/December 2004, 20–22.
47. Spaeth D. Winning Web Sites. *Dental Practice Report,* January/February 2002, 36–40.
48. *Employee Engagement Report, 2005.* Princeton, NJ: Blessing/White; 2005.

Chapter Fifteen

RETAINING

Retention-Friendly Compensation Strategies

"Employee compensation is the 800-pound gorilla of retention," says Michael McLaughlin, managing director of Deloitte Consulting in Chicago, Illinois. "It's easily, and obviously, the most powerful weapon in the arsenal. As with any powerful weapon, though, its misuse can cause severe and unintended damage."

"One common misuse of compensation," McLaughlin says, "is glibly known as the 'peanut butter' approach—salary increases and other incentive payments are 'spread' evenly across groups of employees rather than clearly differentiating and rewarding the accomplishments of the top performers. The predictable result is that a group of high-performing employees feel slighted and a larger group of employees have, in essence, received an unintended message that the organization pays you for showing up."

"Retention-friendly compensation strategies on the other hand, center on providing an incentive that is based on truly differentiated performance—not politics, self-promotion or peanut butter strategy."[1]

255

➥**Reality check:** It's no secret that staff salaries account for a health-care practice's highest operating expense. At the same time, staff is your most valuable asset. A finely tuned balance is needed.

(189) Conduct Separate Salary and Performance Reviews

In many practices, it is standard procedure to combine an employee's performance review with his or her salary review. Joining the two procedures, however, compels a manager to justify a salary increase (or lack thereof) in terms of the performance evaluation, something that can be difficult to do when other factors have entered into the decision-making process.

To keep this problem from developing, the salary review should be conducted separately from the performance review. The primary advantage is that during the performance review, the discussion can then be about performance only. When the salary review is later conducted, there can be more open discussion of other factors that determine a salary increase.

If you set clear, agreed-upon goals and benchmarks during performance reviews, and have follow-up, one-on-one discussions with each employee during the year, salary reviews should simply be a wrap-up of what has transpired. There should be no surprises for either side. Basically, it's an assessment of how well employees have met their goals and demonstrated new skills, and what, if any, raises are appropriate for these accomplishments.

"That implies an organized way of deciding whether performance has improved," says Jeffrey Denning, a management consultant with the Practice Performance Group, a practice management consulting firm in La Jolla, California. "Employees who are good workers this year but who aren't materially more valuable than last year, shouldn't be earning much more this year. And it may be necessary to bypass raises for employees who are being paid above the market rate for their jobs."

"It's best to take the initiative in your compensation reviews," Denning says, "even if there are going to be no raises. You need to let everyone know how carefully you consider salaries every year. Hold private interviews with each employee where you restate the main points of your prior performance reviews and how your employee's progress, or lack of it, influenced your thinking about the base pay rate for the next year."[2]

➡**Reality check:** A pay increase below the level of inflation is not a real raise because it does not keep pace with the eroding value of the dollar.

190 Satisfaction with Pay Depends on Perception

The degree of satisfaction that employees have about their pay depends on their perceptions of a number of factors. Based on detailed case studies and employee attitude surveys with hundreds of companies, consultants David Sirota, Louis A. Mischkind, and Michael Irwin Meltzer, authors of *The Enthusiastic Employee,* found the following (in order of importance) to be the major determinants of pay satisfaction:

- How well the organization pays relative to what employees believe other organizations pay for similar work
- Tenure with the organization
- The extent to which pay increases are believed to reflect the employee's actual contribution (performance)
- The extent to which pay increases reflect increases in the cost of living
- The perceived generosity of non-wage benefits, especially medical insurance
- How well the employee is paid compared to what other employees in the organization, especially those at similar skill levels, are believed to earn
- Organizational profitability (i.e., how much the organization is believed to be able to pay)

➡**Reality check:** "Pay affects the fundamental credibility of an organization in the eyes of its employees. Is it putting its money where its mouth is?" ask the authors. "For example, is an organization that does well and claims that its employees are 'its most important asset' seen as nickel-and-diming its employees when it comes to pay? Is a stated emphasis on quality and service made real with rewards for those staff members who provide it? Our surveys frequently reveal large gaps between words and deeds, with employees often defining 'deeds' in terms of how an organization pays."[3]

191 Do Your Employees Realize How Much They're Paid?

Many healthcare employees I've interviewed look at their compensation strictly in terms of *take-home pay*—without considering the substantial *fringe benefits* they also receive. Knowing all the facts makes employees realize how much they're actually paid and often has an immediate and highly positive impact on morale, motivation, and staff retention.

To make employees aware of the total compensation they receive, provide them annually with a *year-end benefits statement* like the following, with their W-2 form. List the dollar value of the many extras your practice offers that otherwise may be overlooked or taken for granted.

Delete those benefits that are not applicable and add others such as 401(k) plan benefits if they are part of an employee's salary package.

Year-End Benefits Statement

This statement is a summary of the various forms of compensation you receive as a staff member of this practice.

Benefit	*Value ($)*
• Gross base salary	
• Overtime and bonuses	
• Health insurance premium (for employee and dependents)	
• Pension/profit sharing plan	
• Employer's contribution to Social Security	
• State unemployment insurance premium	
• Workers' compensation insurance premium	
• Free health care	
• Paid holidays	
• Sick leave	
• Uniform allowance	
• Continuing education costs (tuition, transportation, lodging, and meals)	
• Professional dues and subscriptions	
• Other	

Then total up the *total dollar value* of each employee's salary and benefits. In most cases, it will be substantially higher than the person's take-home pay.

➡**Reality check:** Many healthcare practices suffer from above-average staff turnover. Although some turnover is related to factors beyond an HCP's control (transfers, retirement, pregnancies, etc.), in many cases, it is due to employees accepting other positions with a higher perceived value to them.

In reality, the perceived value of the new position often turns out to be less than the total compensation actually paid by your practice. As a result, this failure to communicate may cause costly, disruptive, and perhaps unnecessary turnover in your practice.

The year-end benefits statement is meant to close that gap. It's also an excellent tool for employee recruitment and retention.

➡**From the success files:** In Dr. Robert J. Holzhauer's practice, Allergy Asthma Immunology of Rochester, New York (AAIR), a total compensation report provided shortly after each year end is viewed as a useful retention tool. "This report," says Holzhauer, "shows employees that they are being paid more than just the hourly pay that they are most likely to think of as their compensation. This report includes AAIR's employer share of Social Security, life insurance, worker's compensation, 401(k) and profit-sharing contributions, health and dental care insurance, as well as the annual holiday gift. As an aside," he adds, "dental insurance is relatively inexpensive and is a popular benefit with our employees."[4]

192 Equity Theory

Equity theory states that when employees feel underpaid, they will find a way to rectify the situation. The most obvious ways are to quit or ask for a raise. Other more devious ways include attempts to make one's job more rewarding in *nonfinancial ways* such as socializing with co-workers, taking long breaks, surfing the Internet, text messaging or emailing friends, or making personal phone calls. It may include slowing down at work, taking more sick leave, or becoming less attentive to details. (Telltale sign: Three people are needed to do the job of two.) If feelings run deeper, it may result in white collar crime such as stealing—just to "even the score."

What employees do, according to equity theory, is compare what's called their *job inputs* (education, skills, experience, responsibility, productivity, years on the job) and *job outputs* (salary and benefits) with *those of co-workers*. When this ratio is out of balance, a sense of inequity is experienced. It happens, for example, when an employee thinks his or her job is more difficult or demanding than that of a co-worker who's paid the same, let alone a *higher salary*.

➡**Action steps:** "The lack of *written job descriptions* often results in some employees doing more (or less) than they were initially hired to do," says consultant Dr. David Goodnight in Kerrville, Texas. "For a variety of reasons," he adds, "it just happens and in time, the over-worked person is likely to sense an inequity. The solution is to adjust workloads, salaries or benefits and if necessary, hire additional people—even if it means increasing overhead. In the end, you'll have greatly improved employee morale, productivity and practice growth."[5]

➡**Reality check:** "The degree of active behavior that under-rewarded employees will take, is largely dependent on how equity-sensitive they are," says Stephen P. Robbins, Ph.D., faculty member at San Diego State University (Emeritus). "Some employees are very good at ignoring inequities or adjusting their perceptions to make them less bothersome. But many professional and technical employees are equity-sensitive. They're likely to move quickly to correct any perceived inequity."[6]

➡**Hard learned lesson:** The perception of fairness is reality when it comes to employee satisfaction and loyalty.

193 Offer Concierge Services

"Vanderbilt University Medical Center, in Nashville, Tennessee is among a growing group of hospitals nationwide that have begun offering concierge services to physicians, nurses and other workers. The services save employees time by taking care of personal chores such as dropping off cleaning, shopping for groceries or coordinating car repairs. And the hospitals can use the services to recruit and retain employees by touting them as a luxurious perquisite."[7]

Concierge services have been offered in some corporate sectors for more than a decade as a way to boost employee satisfaction and productivity. They only recently have begun to catch on in healthcare as workforce shortages have sharpened competition for staff.

Central DuPage Hospital in Winfield, Illinois, began offering concierge services to its employees several years ago as a means of improving the quality of their workdays. "The hospital also recognized the service's potential to help in recruiting and retention efforts," said Eileen Belokin, director for volunteer and guest services at the hospital. "There are some key positions in health care where there are shortages, and this helps differentiate us. If all other things are equal, this might be the deal breaker," she said.[8]

➥**Reality check:** "Vanderbilt consulted attorneys before rolling out its concierge services to ensure that it would not be seen as an illegal inducement," says Charlotte Chaney, assistant hospital director.[9]

194 Use PTO Plans to Control Absenteeism

Paid sick leave was originally intended to provide salary continuation while employees were ill. But according to a survey conducted by Chicago-based Commerce Clearing House (CCH), a provider of human resources and employment law information, personal illness accounted for only 45 percent of unscheduled absences. Other reasons cited were family issues (27 percent), personal needs (13 percent), and stress (6 percent). "Entitlement mentality," in which employees believe "time is due me—whether I'm sick or not," accounted for 9 percent.[10]

The solution that an increasing number of healthcare organizations are utilizing is called a paid time off (PTO) plan. Employees receive a bank of time to be used for absences (short-term sick leave, vacation, emergency leave, and personal days). Legal holidays are typically excluded. Other time-off benefits such as jury duty, bereavement leave, and military leave are also excluded because not all employees use them.

Every time employees need time off, they dip into their reserve of days, although most organizations retain the right to grant approval for leaves of absence. So if employees have 20 days off in the bank, they are empowered to use those days however they wish. PTO programs also afford employees more privacy about their reasons for taking a day off. They may need the day to care for children, to wait for delivery of an appliance, or simply to preserve their mental health.

Unplanned absences tend to decrease with PTO plans because employees have an incentive to use less sick time so they'll have more vacation time. This benefits the employer greatly because he or she doesn't have to deal with the chaos and expenses of unexpected absences.

On the other hand, there are those who believe that PTO plans cause sick employees to come to work when they really should stay home. Such employees would rather risk annoying their co-workers (and even contaminating them) than to have their boss question their motives for staying home. This situation not only makes it uncomfortable for employees, but also hurts the practice, because ailing employees are unlikely to perform at their best.

➡**From the success files:** "When the types of leaves were separate, people used sick leave because they had it," says Robin Wilkinson, senior vice president of HR for 6,400-employee Mercy Hospital in Des Moines, Iowa. "When we put in the PTO bank, we found that the utilization of unscheduled time off changed drastically. People saved their time and used it for vacation."[11]

➡**Hard learned lesson:** "The value of PTO banks as a recruitment and retention tool is especially vital in the health care industry, which is facing one of the most competitive recruitment markets in the American economy," says attorney Diane Cadrain. "Because its 24/7 operation requires flexibility, health care remains the industry most receptive to the PTO concept."[12]

➡**Reality check:** As with all personnel policies, PTO plans should be spelled out in writing in a personnel manual and all employees should be familiar with its contents. Changes in policies should be updated in the manual and employees should be notified of the changes—either in a short staff meeting or in a memo if yours is a larger office.

195 Avoid the "Cycle of Failure"

Declining reimbursement rates, rising malpractice insurance premiums, and increasing overhead and equipment costs have prompted many HCPs to cut corners not only on what they pay their staff, but also on the number of support staff. "Lean and mean" is their thinking.

Leonard Schlesinger and James Heskett capture the potential implications of such a strategy in what they term the "cycle of failure."[13]

The consequences of this cost-containment strategy include stressed employees who are forced to carry a heavier workload and/or disgruntled employees who feel underpaid and unappreciated. The inevitable result is errors, inefficiencies, and high employee turnover.

Not surprisingly, patients become dissatisfied with the poor service they receive, fail to develop any loyalty to the practice, and turn over as rapidly as the staff.

Management justifies these actions, say Schlesinger and Heskett, by claiming, "To get good people would cost too much and you can't pass on these cost increases to patients" or "High turnover is simply an inevitable part of our business. You've got to learn to live with it."

Part of the problem, say Schlesinger and Heskett, is a failure to measure all relevant costs. Left out of the equation are three cost variables: the cost of constant recruiting, hiring, and training; the lower productivity of inexperienced new employees; and the time, effort, and expense of constantly attracting new patients.

Also ignored are two revenue variables: future revenue streams that might have continued for years but are lost when unhappy patients leave the practice, and potential income from prospective patients who are turned off by negative word of mouth.

➡**Reality check:** Employees may stay on the job for a variety of reasons, but if they feel overworked, unappreciated, and resentful about being exploited financially, they are unlikely to be highly productive or provide good service.

➡**Hard learned lessons:**
- More than anything in your practice, your investment in support staff is likely to pay the highest dividend. HCPs need to think of it as just that—an investment, rather than an expense.
- If you underpay your employees, you will attract either less competent people whom you probably will let go or those who are just starting out, who will learn all they can from you, gain some experience, and move on to better paying jobs. Either way, your salary policy will generate more staff turnover than loyalty.

- Howard Schultz, CEO of Starbucks, said it well in his book, *Pour Your Heart into It: How Starbucks Built a Company One Cup at a Time*: "I know in my heart, if we treat people as a line item under expenses, we're not living up to our goals and our values. Their passion is our number-one competitive advantage. Lose it, and we've lost the game."[14]
- Better performing practices tend to have more staff than the norm, not fewer. More support staff can mean HCPs are better able to focus strictly on patient care—even if costs are higher. Better patient care in turn leads to greater patient satisfaction, referrals, and practice growth.

196 The Overcompensated Employee

This is the other side of the coin and is more common than most HCPs care to admit. This occurs when a good employee has been on the job so long that a simple compounding of reasonable yearly raises has increased that employee's salary to the point where it is unreasonably high.

The employee expects an annual cost of living increase, but from your perspective his or her compensation has become excessive. This problem can be resolved in part by giving smaller increases and by using tax-free fringe benefits. These can include, but are not limited to, group insurance (medical, dental, life, etc.); child care; sick leave; vacation; tuition reimbursement; uniform allowance; and other specialized benefits. Dr. James Steinberg, Tampa, Florida, is among those who have provided employees with a mileage allowance to help offset the current high price of gasoline.[15]

This arrangement also benefits the practice, says John K. McGill, M.B.A., JD, CPA, of Charlotte, North Carolina, since there are no federal or state income or matching payroll taxes on the value of tax-free fringe benefits provided. Nor are retirement plan contributions required on the value of such benefits.[16]

Once you reach the point of overcompensation, however, you have a business decision to make: risk losing the person if you fail to grant an increase *or* overpaying the employee.

If you were to lose such an employee, could he or she get another job at an equal salary? If the person is truly overpaid for what he or she does, the answer is probably "no," in which case, the employee will most likely stay on the job unless, of course, there are other considerations.

If, however, you do lose the employee, have you lost or gained in the long run?

197 Psychological Paychecks

"The old tools for rewarding employees—competitive wages, benefits, and incentives—are still important," says Dianne Michonski Durkin, author of *The Loyalty Advantage*. "But more than ever, they are just the price of entry for hiring or retaining the employees you value. If your organization relies solely on a compensation and benefits package to attract and retain loyal employees, over time there's a good likelihood that you'll be caught in a price war for the talent you want. When your only leverage is financial, you can either choose to outbid your competitor or let a good employee choose another home."[17]

"If you can't compensate your employees with more cash, how do you reward good performance?" ask Price Pritchett and Ron Pound, co-authors of *Team Construction: Building a High Performance Work Group During Change*.

"The intangible rewards you have to offer are limitless," they say. "Words of encouragement, compliments, empathy and understanding, a note of appreciation. Stopping to share a cup of coffee, or taking an employee to lunch. Bigger titles or special assignments. More decision-making authority. A sincere thank you. Asking about the family, celebrating small victories, soliciting opinions and suggestions. Listening . . . really listening. A mere smile, or calling the person by name. A warm handshake or pat on the back. Taking the person into your confidence. Even asking an employee for help—'needing' the person—is gratifying because it validates one's worth."

"Psychological paychecks," say Pritchett and Pound, "have an intrinsic value that hard currency can never touch."[18]

198 Is a Counteroffer the Answer?

The dilemma: A key employee gives notice that he or she is leaving to take another job for more money. Do you make a counteroffer to persuade the person to stay?

In speaking with HCPs and practice managers, the consensus seems to be: No. The reason: The problems caused by counteroffers often outweigh the benefits. For example, if concessions are made and the employee stays, it may lead to resentment among other employees who feel they too deserve a raise, additional perks, a change in work schedule, or whatever. Worse yet, a counteroffer to a departing employee may lead to a chain reaction, prompting other employees to use the same tactic to gain concessions.

In addition, if the departing employee has repeatedly asked for a raise and been denied it, she may resent the lengths to which she had to go to get it. At the same time, the HCP may resent having to make such concessions under duress. Resentment on either side, let alone on *both sides*, is sure to erode employer–employee relations and the spirit of teamwork so necessary in a successful practice.

➡**The one exception:** a key employee who is critical to the day-to-day operation of the practice. In the long run, it may cost more to replace the person than to *retain* him or her. Consider making a counteroffer in such a case, and take a chance that the aftermath will be smooth sailing.

➡**Reality check:** In many cases, salary counteroffers have proven to be ineffective at keeping key employees after they announce they are leaving for employment elsewhere. "Within a year, 50 percent of those who accept such offers, end up leaving the company anyway," says Jacques P. André, writing in *Financial Executive*. The reason: Money usually is not the primary reason a valued employee considers leaving. Rather, it is a morale problem or personal conflict. If the root problem isn't resolved, the employee will still be motivated to look for work elsewhere.[19]

199 Benchmark Salaries

Knowing how much to pay your staff is a delicate balance. Pay too little, and your staff will feel underpaid and underappreciated and may jump to a practice with a better salary. Pay too much, and you'll spend too much of your hard-earned revenue on salary and wages.

Several resources are available to help you find appropriate salaries for your medical assistants, receptionists, billing clerks, and practice managers.

➨**Action steps:** "To determine if your salaries are in line with industry standards, it pays to ask around," advises Michael Beirne, associate editor of *Review of Ophthalmology.* "You can obtain survey data from statistical databases that are often backed by the vast resources of national societies. Salary comparisons can also be done locally by consulting the local chamber of commerce, your state labor department, and even your hospital's human resources department."

"Localized surveys often give the better comparison," adds healthcare consultant John Pinto of J. Pinto Associates in San Diego, California. He urges office managers to communicate with other office managers in their regional marketplace to learn what back office and front office staffers make, and what the comparable benefits are. Although it used to be that you could do that every year or two, in today's dynamic market, he advises checking more frequently.[20]

Keep in mind that the job descriptions for the positions in your office may not exactly match those of colleagues' practices—and what they pay their staff may not be appropriate for your staff.

➨**Resources for Salary Surveys**

- Medical Group Management Association, Englewood, CO: http://www.mgma.com/surveys/
- *The Health Care Group's Staff Salary Survey,* published annually by The Health Care Group, Plymouth Meeting, PA: http://www.healthcaregroup.com/servlet/catalog. ProductDetails?pid=1

➨**Reality check:** If you're not paying your staff a fair salary, you'll probably quickly find out through high staff turnover. Turnover rate, in fact, is one way that Austin Heart, a 26-physician group in Austin, Texas, keeps tabs on whether the staff salaries it's paying are competitive.

"We do a turnover report, and if we find the reason why people are leaving is because of better compensation elsewhere, we will adjust it upward. Or we look at the amount of time that a position goes unfilled," says Steve Gornik, practice manager for Austin Heart.

The group tries to pay a bit above the average salaries in order to attract and keep good staff, Gornik says. Salary, however, is only one component of the overall compensation package. "You have to be careful," he adds. "You can be paying a market rate in salary, but a below-market rate in benefits."[21]

200 Base Employee Raises on Merit

"Your way of compensating employees sends a strong message about the culture of your practice," says Amy Morgan, CEO of the Pride Institute in Novato, California. "If you never give raises, even if your productivity keeps rising, you'll convey the message that it's futile for the staff to work harder because their efforts go unrewarded and they have no control over their compensation. On the other hand, if you give raises just because a year has passed and an annual increase is expected, you'll convey the message that employees are rewarded without having to work toward new levels of productivity and excellence. Both of these approaches are de-motivating and encourage lack of accountability and substandard performance. In stark contrast is a compensation model that expects, recognizes and rewards achievement, making a statement that you want employees who are hardworking, strive for excellence, and take your practice to new levels."[22]

"Base raises on merit to reward excellent and good performers," advises The Health Care Group in Plymouth Meeting, Pennsylvania. "Giving everyone a flat raise, for example 3.5 percent of the previous year's salary, across the board, tells your best performers that no matter how hard they work, it doesn't matter and tells your poorest performers that they can continue to generate inferior results and still be rewarded."[23]

➡**Reality check:** "The net effect of merit pay raises should be that, individual employees will each receive different percentage pay raises," says attorney Mark E. Kropiewnicki. "Thus if the average pay increase is 3 percent, the 'good' employee will merit a pay raise greater than 3 percent (perhaps significantly greater), an 'average' employee will receive 3 percent and the 'poor' employee will receive less than a 3 percent (and sometimes no) increase."[24]

➡**From the success files:** The "clinical ladder" at Children's Medical Center in Dallas, Texas, is an example of merit-based compensation. Salaries increase based on how much an employee does. "If you want to give in-services on your unit or question/answer projects or do nursing research, you can earn more money," explains emergency room R.N., Joan McGuigan. If a nurse has an interesting case or if she wants to research a new diagnosis, he or she can gather data and present it. This not only encourages career development, but also develops the entire staff. "If I weren't a single parent with two jobs, I'd do more," she says. "There are nurses who love it."[25]

➥**Hard learned lesson:** Base raises on merit, not only to encourage those who work hard and learn well, but also to show others what they are missing by not performing well.

201 Four Criteria for a Pay Raise

"Base the first 25 percent of a merit increase on personal attitude," advises practice management consultant Linda Miles, CEO of Linda Miles and Associates in Virginia Beach, Virginia. "Is the employee cheerful, caring and a pleasure to work with? Is the person negative? Does he or she speak negatively about the practice to others? Is the staff member a team player?"

"Use your overall evaluation form to determine the second 25 percent of the employee's merit increase. An overall evaluation should include a self-evaluation, your evaluation of the employee and an evaluation by the employee's peers."

"The next quarter of the merit increase," Miles says, "should be based on the employee's scope of responsibility and volunteerism. When there are projects to make the practice better, does this employee volunteer to implement each step which may take some personal time? What new task has the person mastered that makes him or her worth more this year?"

"The final 25 percent of the raise should be based on what Miles considers the most important criterion—the health of the practice since the last performance increase."[26]

202 Skills-Based Compensation

Skills-based compensation is an effort to pay employees for the number of skills they possess, rather than for the specific job they may be doing at any given time. Pay increases are given when the employees add to or improve their skill sets, rather than when they have achieved a certain level of seniority. This gives employees a tangible incentive to acquire new skills.

➥**Action steps:** "This type of compensation works only if both you and the employee agree in advance on what you want to accomplish and by when," says consultant Dr. Jerry Hayes, Vicksburg, Mississippi. "Then put it in writing. When staff members successfully master new skills to your satisfaction, congratulate them on their achievements and then follow through on the promised raise. Otherwise, you're going to have some less-than motivated employees on your hands."[27]

Those failing to acquire the agreed-upon skills must, by definition, be denied the raise.

➥**Reality check:** As one might expect, HCPs must make training opportunities available to employees for a skills-based pay system to work. "But only pay for skills that bring value to your practice," says management consultant Kurt Oster, Haverhill, Massachusetts. If you do this, it's a safe bet that as training goes up, so will the quality and efficiency of work output.[28]

➥**From the success files:** Dr. Sandy Seamans, Sugar Land, Texas, points to three direct benefits of skills-based compensation. "Empowered employees possess higher skills for patient care; cross-training means less downtime because a staff member can step in for a coworker and perform at the same level; and employees with goals are more motivated and happier, which translates into a more rewarding work environment."[29]

203 Hard Learned Lessons About Compensation

- Coddle your employees. Without them, you may not have a practice. If necessary, pay them before you pay yourself. Give them benefits you would not take for yourself. Spoil them and empower them in every way possible.
- As Bob Townsend, former CEO of Avis, has said, "Thanks" is a really neglected form of compensation.[30]
- "Too many doctors trying to cut costs don't care about staff. They just want a warm body standing there," says Vicki Seibert, administrator for a solo medicine and gastroenterology practice in Clearwater, Florida. "It's important to keep good staff long-term, no matter what it takes in terms of salaries and benefits."[31]
- "A cash-only incentive plan generates mercenary loyalty, not emotional loyalty," says Dianne Durkin, author of *The*

Loyalty Advantage. "In the long run, people will not stay if the culture and environment are not congruent with their values and beliefs."[32]

- "Don't give raises to marginal employees," says consultant Jeffrey J. Denning. "Raises never motivate workers to improve. To the contrary, a raise in pay signals the employer's satisfaction with status quo. Further, if the employee is terminated and sues, she has simply to point to the history of pay raises to show she was doing a good job. Judgment for the plaintiff."[33]

- "The rule of thumb is that in a healthy market an unhappy employee will bolt the company for a 5 percent pay increase, but it will take at least an increase of 20 percent to compel a satisfied employee to jump ship," says W. Michael Kelly, director of research at The Saratoga Institute, a division of PriceWaterhouseCoopers. "Of course, pay is more important to some than others," says Leigh Branham, Founder/Principal of the consulting firm Keeping the People Inc. in Overland Park, Kansas. "We know that many employees who struggle to pay their bills can understandably be enticed to leave for increases of less than 5 percent."[34]

- It would be nice to offer your employees a world of benefits," says Dr. Pamela Miller, Highland, California. "Unfortunately, that's not realistic. So find out what they need most."[35]

- "Many doctors are overly concerned that one or more of their top employees has reached or surpassed some arbitrary ceiling for their position," says management consultant Dr. Charles Blair of Charlotte, North Carolina. "We're more concerned with the effectiveness of individual employees in helping the practice grow profitably and thus focus on the ratio of staff payroll costs to practice gross income. As a result, we often find that paying top dollar for truly stellar employees can result in a more profitable practice."[36]

- "Employers have to realize that salary and benefits alone, are only a small part of an employee's 'value equation,'" says Michael Lowenstein, managing director of Customer Retention Associates in Collingswood, New Jersey. "Employees want enrichment. They want inclusion. They want communication and participation. They want training. They want recognition. They want to have pride in where they work."[37]

References

1. McLaughlin M. Four Ways to Lose Your Best People, *Workforce Management Online*. http://www.workforce.com/archive/article/22/14/15_printer.php
2. Denning JJ. Practice Pointers, Staff Pay Policies That Work. *Medical Economics*, July 25, 2003.
3. Sirota D, Mischkind LA, Meltzer MI. *The Enthusiastic Employee*. Upper Saddle River, NJ: Wharton School Publishing; 2005.
4. Holzhauer RJ. Retention Plan Worth Effort. *Academy News,* published by the American Academy of Allergy Asthma & Immunology, December 2004.
5. Personal communication.
6. Robbins SP. *The Truth About Managing People . . . And Nothing but the Truth*. Upper Saddle River, NJ: Financial Times Prentice Hall; 2003.
7. Vogt K. Hospital's Latest Perk: Running Your Errands. *AMNews,* June 20, 2005.
8. Ibid.
9. Ibid.
10. Markowich MM, Eckberg S. Get Control of the Absentee-Minded. *Personnel Journal*, March 1996, 115–120.
11. Cadrain D. Employers Increasingly Willing to Test the PTO Waters. http://www.shrm.org/hrnews_published/CMS_013549.asp#P-11_0
12. Ibid.
13. Schlesinger L, Heskett J. Breaking the Cycle of Failure in Services. *Sloan Management Review,* Spring 1991.
14. Schultz H. *Pour Your Heart into It: How Starbucks Built a Company One Cup at a Time*. New York: Hyperion; 1999.
15. Personal communication.
16. Staff Raises for 2005: How Much? *The McGill Advisory*. Charlotte, NC: John K. McGill & Company Inc.; January 20, 2005, 2–3.
17. Durkin DM. *The Loyalty Advantage*. New York: AMACOM; 2005.
18. Pritchett P, Pound R. *Team Constru.tion: Building a High Performance Work Group During Change*. Dallas, TX: Pritchett Publishing Co.; 1992.
19. André JP. Salary Counteroffers Are Ineffective. *Financial Executive*, March 1998.
20. Beirne B. Does It Pay to Pay More? http://www.visionweb.com
21. Jacob JA. Keep Staff by Keeping Salaries Competitive. October 28, 2002. http://www.ama-assn.org/amednews/2002/10/28/bica1028.htm
22. Morgan A. Compensation: Do You Feel Hijacked? *Woman Dentist Journal,* May 2005, 38–44, 57.

23. How to Establish an Employee Evaluation Process. The Health Care Group. http://www.healthcaregroup.com/archive.jsp?PageID=21239

24. Kropiewnicki ME. Basing Employee Raises on Merit. http://www.healthcaregroup. com/archive.jsp?PageID=54088

25. Solomon CM. The Loyalty Factor. *Personnel Journal*, 1993, 52–62.

26. Spaeth D. Speaking of Staff Salaries. *Dental Practice Report*, April 2004, 28–32.

27. Hayes J. Dealing with Review Time. *Optometric Management*, November 2003, 20.

28. Grubb D. Raises for a Reason. *Trends Magazine*, August/September 2003, 9–12.

29. Ibid.

30. Townsend R. *Further Up the Organization*. New York: Harper & Row; 1984.

31. Walpert B. Tips for Finding and Keeping a Good Receptionist. *ACP Observer*, January 1998.

32. Durkin DM. *The Loyalty Advantage*. New York: AMACOM; 2005.

33. How'm I Doin' Boss? *Uncommon Sense*. La Jolla, California: Practice Performance Group; June 1997, 4.

34. Branham L. *The 7 Hidden Reasons Employees Leave*. New York: AMACOM; 2005.

35. Black A. Benefits: Money Well Spent? *Review of Optometry,* June 2001, 37.

36. Avoid Arbitrary Salary Ceilings for Top Employees. *Blair/McGill Advisory,* October 1999, 3.

37. Lowenstein M. Nurse Retention Wars: Who Wins, Who Loses, and Why— Part 2. http://www.hr.com

---

Chapter Sixteen

RETAINING

Training and Skills Development

There are numerous benefits of employer-sponsored training—the subject of this chapter. Among them:

- **Aids in recruitment:** Studies conducted by The Gallup Organization indicate that employer-sponsored training is a major attraction for employees entering the workforce or deciding whether to remain in their current position.[1]
- **Encourages employee retention:** Trained employees who have the skills to deliver needed services, who feel they are contributing to the organization, and who are recognized by management are less likely to look for another job.
- **Spurs innovation:** Untrained employees seldom look for better ways of doing things. By giving your employees the training needed to hone their skills and boost their efficiency, they'll be more likely to seek innovative ways of making your practice more successful.

- **Highly appealing:** "Training as a perk appeals to employees who value professional development and excellence—the ones who will be especially important to your organization's success in a talent-driven economy," says Lin Grensing-Popal, author of *Motivating Today's Employees*.[2]
- **Justifies higher salaries:** Training enables employees whose salaries have "maxed out" for their current position to move up to higher paying positions.
- **Projects a positive image for your organization:** Knowledgeable, well-trained employees are highly effective "ambassadors" for your practice.
- **Improves profitability:** Companies listed in *Fortune* magazine's annual 100 "Best Places to Work" provide an average of 40 days of training per employee per year. As far as impact to the bottom line, firms in the top quarter of training expenditure per employee (averaging $1,595 per year) had profit margins 24 percent higher than those in the bottom quarter (averaging $128 per year).[3]

This chapter will discuss the needed action steps to reap these benefits.

204 Provide a Positive Learning Culture

"By providing a positive learning culture, you can motivate employees to apply their talents and expertise to help your practice and their careers," say Courtney Price, Ph.D. and Alys Novak, M.B.A., co-authors of *The Medical Practice Performance Manual: How to Evaluate Employees,* 2nd edition.

They make the following recommendations:

- Cross-train employees to learn new jobs and skills.
- Give them new, challenging responsibilities.
- Provide financial support to employees interested in continuing their formal education.
- Send them to seminars to enhance or learn new skills.
- Allow employees to explore memberships in trade and professional associations to meet, interact with, and learn from other professionals.

- Have them train others in areas where they have strength or expertise.
- Offer learning materials for personal and professional growth by establishing a library of books, audiotapes, videos, and periodicals on a variety of job-related and non-job-related topics.
- Encourage employees to borrow learning materials from local libraries.
- Contact local bookstores to inquire about new books on topics of interest to your employees.[4]

➥**From the success files:** Dr. Nancy Torgerson of Lynwood, Washington, schedules in-office training for her seven vision therapists. These are held once a week, for an hour and a half (9:30 to 11:00 a.m.). Among the topics: amblyopia, strabismus, visual thinking, visual memory, directionality, laterality, and spatial relationships.

"This training pays off in many ways," Torgerson says. "The staff is more knowledgeable, able to do more for patients and provide better care. This in turn delights patients and parents and makes them excited about the office."

"Hearing patients rave about the practice," she adds, "is great for our team spirit. Staff morale is great."[5]

205 Make Your Office Staff Tech-Savvy

When you hire or promote employees, in many cases you must train them to use billing systems, electronic medical records, and other software applications used to run your practice.

➥**Action steps:**
- **Designate an in-house trainer.** "After your office staff has been trained by a vendor to use practice management software, EMR software or both, it's a good ideas to designate someone to train new employees," says Tim Ward, computer trainer for Northeast Cardiology Associates, a 20-doctor group practice in Bangor, Maine.
- **Standardize the training.** "When I do the training," Ward says, "I do it the same way each time so that depending on

the department the person is training for, they are trained the same way as others who have the same job." To foster standardization, Ward says he creates and hands out written material because it makes classes go more quickly than teaching on the fly.

- **Pair trainees with experienced employees.** After Ward finishes training employees, he has them "shadow" and work with someone else in their department for about a week. "If there are specific issues," he says, "we retrain."[6]

- **Break it down.** When St. Joseph Regional Medical Center, a health system in South Bend, Indiana, began implementing EMR at 20 outpatient sites, it broke down the training into four phases—scheduling, messaging, prescribing, and clinical documentation—and taught each phase on separate days instead of cramming them all into one day. "It's a great deal of information," says Margaret Lynch, St. Joseph's director of technology learning. "Sometimes learning even one step can be overwhelming."[7]

➡️**Hard learned lessons:**
- Solicit existing employees for tips related to their jobs and incorporate them into training.
- Schedule classes in the morning rather than later because employees will be fresher and more alert.
- Keep classes short. Ideally they should be 60 minutes long but not longer than 3 to 4 hours. Daylong sessions should be broken into 3 to 3½ hour sessions with at least an hour break for lunch.
- Studies reveal the following:
  - *Reading* training materials generates about a 10 percent comprehension rate.
  - *Hearing* yields a 20 percent comprehension rate.
  - *Seeing* increases comprehension to around 30 percent.
  - *Watching* someone perform the task brings about 50 percent comprehension.
  - Actually *participating* in the task produces a 70 percent comprehension rate.
  - And *doing* the actual task or performing a simulation alone results in a 90 percent comprehension rate.

206 Improve Your Billing Operation

A four-physician OB/GYN group in Germantown, Tennessee, brought in an extra $250,000 by getting more aggressive about billing, reports Deborah Grandinetti, former senior editor of *Medical Economics*. Among the winning strategies: replacing three billing employees with more capable people, investigating why claims were denied instead of simply refiling them, and training the front desk people to capture all information needed for claims at the time of scheduling, including verification that the requested service would be covered.

Grandinetti goes on to say, "Help your billing people become even better at what they do by investing in training." This will help retain them, too, because they'll have the satisfaction of a job well done, adds practice management consultant David C. Scroggins of Clayton L. Scroggins Associates in Cincinnati, Ohio. Certainly, you'll want to send staffers to coding seminars. He also recommends sending them to off-site training with the makers of your billing software. Even though that will cost more than in-house training, they'll get "a more comprehensive grasp of the whole process," says Scroggins. "After nine months, send them back for a refresher course. Send the office manager too," says Scroggins. "If he or she picks up a nugget that improves collections by just one-half percentage point, it's worth it."[8]

207 Role Play Training Sessions

What does your receptionist say to a patient who, when told the charges for the visit, replies, "I forgot my checkbook"? How does a business office person respond to an irate patient? In such cases, is everyone following a similar script and is what they're saying the best response? If not, role playing may be of help.

Role playing is a training technique in which a facilitator sets up a scenario where two participants are assigned different roles (such as receptionist and patient) that mimic everyday occurrences (such as those above). The two then act out the situation, improvising as they go along, while the rest of the group observes. Later, everyone critiques what was said and brainstorms for improvement. As a follow-up, the roles can be reversed or assigned to others.

Your staff can role play any number of scenarios such as a disgruntled, demanding, argumentative, or extremely anxious patient. Consider, for example, the following scenario: "An obviously annoyed patient calls to complain that he just waited more than half an hour in the pharmacy only to find out that his refill had not been called in. How would you respond?"

A few ground rules: Make critiques impersonal by using fictitious names for the individuals or by simply referring to them as "the patient" and "the staff member." After the role play, ask the person playing the patient how he or she felt about the staff member's response. Also, ask the group how they might have handled the situation differently. Vote on the best ways to respond in these situations and then use them as models for future encounters.

The objective is to make everyone aware of the skill and diplomacy needed in these situations, agree on the best response, and then practice saying it in a nonthreatening environment. Done properly, it can be a lot of fun and a great learning experience.

208 Diversity Training

The changing demographics of our increasingly multi-cultural population have challenged healthcare providers to consider cultural diversity as a priority. In response to this trend, many healthcare organizations, such as Cincinnati's Children's Hospital Medical Center, have initiated diversity awareness and skills training. The objective is to present actual employee, patient/parent, and visitor situations that include diversity-related issues to the trainees and to teach them how to react and respond appropriately.

During the training, real incidents of diversity conflict are discussed, along with what actions were effective and ineffective in dealing with the various situations.[9]

The following training goals are among those recommended by Kathryn Hopkins Kavanagh and Patricia H. Kennedy in their book, *Promoting Cultural Diversity: Strategies for Health Care Professionals*:

- Promote a feeling of acceptance.
- Understand what members of the cultural or subcultural group consider as "caring," both attitudinally and behaviorally.

- Anticipate diversity, and avoid stereotypes by sex, age, ethnicity, socioeconomic status, and other social categories.
- Understand the other's goals and expectations.
- Know the traditional, health-related practices common to the group with whom you are working, and do not discredit any of them unless you know specific practices are harmful.
- Learn to appreciate the richness of diversity as an asset rather than as a hindrance to communication and effective intervention.[10]

➥**Reality check:** There are numerous examples of misinterpretations of actions. Native American Cultural Consultant Art Shegonee says the way young people receive information from their providers may appear disrespectful, when in fact, it is respect that the young people may be demonstrating. "Many cultures do not condone looking into the eyes of elders or people of authority," says Shegonee. "This is out of respect for the person's position. But a lot of physicians or lawyers or judges don't realize that and are quick to conclude the young person isn't listening to them."[11]

➥**Hard learned lesson:** Cultural competence is rapidly becoming a major quality issue for healthcare systems, a risk management issue for hospitals, and a necessary skill set for clinicians who wish to provide the best possible care to an increasingly diverse population.

➥**Resources**
- Society for Human Resource Management (SHRM): http://www.shrm.org
- American Society for Training & Development (ASTD): http://www.astd.org
- *Promoting Cultural Diversity: Strategies for Health Care Professionals* by Kathryn Hopkins Kavanagh and Patricia H. Kennedy, Newbury Park, CA: Sage Publications, 1992.
- *Caring for Patients from Different Cultures* by Geri-Ann Galanti, Baltimore, MD: University of Pennsylvania Press, 2003.
- *Culture & Nursing Care: A Pocket Guide* by Pamela A. Minarik, San Francisco: University of California San Francisco Nursing Press, 1996.

209 Cross-Training

"We train all of our front desk people at all of our offices to have the ability to make appointments, register people as they come in, manage the medical records area, and get the physicians' claims into our business office," says Dr. Carol Reynolds, medical director of Potomac Physicians, a multi-specialty primary care group with 10 practices in the Baltimore, Maryland, area. "They all have primary functions in one area or the other, but if they want to, they can move around—or if we have an urgent issue, we ask them."

"By cross-training its front desk staff to perform in other areas of the practice," Reynolds says, "it adds variety to staff members' days, builds their professional credentials and gives the practice some flexibility. The results have been solid."

"Statistics I've read suggest that practices have an annual turnover rate of 20 to 25 percent at most front desks or medical record operations," Reynolds says. "We've been lucky. At our practice, turnover is around 12 percent, and we're really happy with that."[12]

➡Additional benefits

- "It's a quality improvement tool," says Chris Kelleher, administrator of a one-physician OB/GYN practice in Columbia, South Carolina. "When one employee sits in for another, there's a fresh mind in that job. We get many ideas and suggestions from cross-trained people, such as how to do a job more efficiently."[13]

- "It uncovers hidden talents," says Helena Dahan, office manager for a four-physician internal medicine practice in Philadelphia, Pennsylvania. "Someone who's hired as a receptionist might find she has a knack for coding, or a biller might turn out to be a crackerjack medical assistant. The more a staffer learns, the more she's worth as an employee. Cross-training is also a patient pleaser," adds Dahan. "Patients are less likely to experience insurance snafus, difficulty in reaching your office via telephone, or long in-office visits if cross-trained employees are on hand. With cross-training, you're always going to be as fully staffed as possible."[14]

- It avoids being "held hostage" by a key employee who considers him- or herself irreplaceable, and consistently makes demands that must be met in order to retain his or her services. Being able to replace such an employee, even temporarily, with a properly cross-trained employee allows HCPs to effectively negotiate and/or replace this staffer whose attitude has soured.

- Cross-training all clerical and some clinical staff can help your practice avoid costly overtime and the need to hire temporary employees when regular staff members are out due to illness, vacation, continuing education, or other reasons.

- Cross-trained employees gain an understanding of other jobs in the practice. As a result, they better appreciate the difficulties and demands of their co-workers' jobs, thus helping to promote teamwork.

- "The ability to make an employee's work life more interesting by cross training in varied functional areas is an advantage that we offer as a fairly large allergy, asthma, immunology and rheumatology practice," says Dr. J. Holzhauer about his practice, Allergy, Asthma Immunology of Rochester, New York (AAIR).[15]

➥**Reality check:** Take the billing office and front office staff for example: "If each of them understands what the other does and is trained to do either job, you'll see greatly improved performance," says consultant Elizabeth Woodcock, founder and principal of Woodcock & Associates in Atlanta, Georgia. "Sure it may cost you more per hour to staff the front desk with someone who can also do medical billing, but because that person understands the importance of getting the correct registration information, they will make fewer errors, and you'll probably see higher collections—outweighing the higher salary cost. Plus, because denials will drop, the practice can cut insurance follow-up staff and improve cash flow."[16]

➥**Hard learned lessons:**

- "Cross-training starts with hiring the right people—folks who can multitask, want to learn new skills, and can shift gears quickly and effectively," says *Medical Economics* senior editor, Gail Garfinkel Weiss.[17]

- "Nobody should perform the same task all the time," says author/speaker Dr. Marvin H. Berman, Chicago, Illinois. "Beware the employee who says, 'I'm the only one who knows how to do that.'"[18]

210 Coding Credentials for Your Staff

"Most legal worries physicians face regarding billing lie in coding," says Elizabeth Woodcock, editor of *Physicians Practice Pearls*. "Large practices often have a robust billing and coding team, but small practices tend to lack experienced in-house coders. They may give that responsibility to an unqualified office manager or a data-entry employee."[19]

"Every medical practice can increase efficiency and profitability by certifying its billing staff," writes Michael D. Brown in *Medical Economics*.

"Keeping up with the most current coding is essential," Brown says, "and more and more healthcare organizations are raising the educational bar for billers and coders. In fact, a growing number of large practices won't even grant interviews to noncertified applicants for these positions."[20]

"But the increased emphasis on credentialing is hardly universal, 'It's amazing to me how many practices rely completely on underqualified office staff to handle today's complex billing issues,' says Robert Liles, an attorney in Washington, DC, who specializes in healthcare fraud. 'If your practice gets audited, those employees are just going to say they were doing as they were told, putting you at risk under the False Claims Act'—adding that if an audit uncovers billing errors, you'll need to prove that you've taken steps to train your staff properly."[21]

"Attendance at credentialing programs provides that proof. The certification process helps refine an employee's knowledge of current documentation and coding issues, and provides an official designation that demonstrates professional achievement. In addition, an accredited professional will be able to train others in the practice."

"Certification also provides your staff with the opportunity to network with other certified professionals," Brown says, "and gives them access to continuing education, reference materials, and newsletters on the latest regulations."[22]

➥**Reality check:** "Financial self-interest motivates a growing number of physicians to send members of their billing and collection department to coding classes," writes Robert Lowes in *Medical Economics.* "More accurate coding usually leads to higher reimbursement since doctors tend to undercode, experts say. A bevy of groups offer this schooling—MGMA, PAHCOM, Medicare carriers, large consulting companies, and organizations that credential coders."[23]

➥**Resources**
- Medical Group Management Association: http://www.mgma.com
- American Academy of Professional Coders: http://www.aapc.com
- Professional Association of Health Care Office Management: http://www.pahcom.com
- American Health Information Management Association: http://www.ahima.org
- Practice Management Institute: http://www.pmimd.com

211 Safety Training

"Too many practices make the mistake of assuming an experienced medical office employee knows how to recognize, prevent and deal with safety hazards or emergencies," says healthcare consultant Karen Childress, based in Scottsdale, Arizona. "Just as bad is presuming that when staff has been trained once, that's the end of the story."[24]

"The best run groups set aside regular staff training hours," says Dr. G. Steve Rebagliati, director of medical affairs and quality management at the Oregon Health Sciences University in Portland. "They'll create a training roster and over the course of a year cover subjects that will give them the biggest return on the investment of time, depending on the patient population. Developing something like this," says Rebagliati, "takes just a few hours of thinking, and then creating a plan that fits your budget and that you'll follow through on."[25]

Sandra Adams, OSHA compliance manager for West Clinic, an oncology/hematology practice in Memphis, Tennessee, has instituted a comprehensive online training program for staff. "It's on our intranet," she says. "I let managers know when training is due so that during a slow time, staff can log on and do the program and answer the questions. They then enter a code word to move on to the next training." Adams says her staff members are trained every year around their anniversary dates.[26]

➡**Reality check:** "If you don't have technical capabilities to provide online training," says Childress. "There are plenty of low-tech ways to keep staff up to speed: presentations at staff meetings, hands-on practice sessions, video training and sending staff to seminars are all good options."[27]

212 Customer-Service Training

"I purposely use the term 'customer service' as opposed to 'quality patient care,'" writes consultant Michael Malley in *Ophthalmology Management*. "It is possible to provide outstanding patient care and substandard customer service."

"Customer service," Malley says, "really has more to do with how you interact with a patient than how you make a diagnosis or treat a disease. It has more to do with the method in which you answer the telephone than the information you dispense on it. It is the gentle, empathetic nature of your technicians versus their technical prowess."[28]

➡**From the success files:** "Which comes first—happy nurses or happy patients?" asks Maggie Rauch, senior editor of *Incentive* magazine. "Whatever the answer, it seems hospitals have a labor pool that, for the most part, is hardwired to understand the value of customer service. But far from assuming that nurses automatically understand customer service, smart administrators work hard to keep service top of mind. At award winning Griffin Hospital in Derby, Connecticut, every employee learns about patient care on a retreat to a convent on Long Island sound. They bunk up together and spend two days doing exercises simulating the hospital experience through the patient's eyes."

"We sometimes have to drag people there kicking and shouting," says Bill Powanda, vice president at Griffin, "but they come back with a much different appreciation for how intimidating and scary the hospital experience can be. We think that contributed the most to changing the culture of the organization."

In 2005, *Fortune* magazine ranked Griffin Hospital fourth on its "Best Places to Work" list, the highest ranking ever for a hospital and the seventh time it has made the list.[29]

➠**Reality check:** "Regardless of your health care institution's financial condition, you have the capability to improve patient satisfaction and to build patient loyalty," says Jim Davis, vice president, Workforce and Service Development at DDI in Pittsburgh, Pennsylvania. "While technology, physical appearance and atmosphere are important factors, teamwork, communications and responsiveness are shown to matter more. Creating a service culture that places patients first enhances your institution's reputation in the community and can lead you to a clear, sustainable, competitive advantage."[30]

➠**Action steps:** "The most important thing," says J.W. Marriott, founder of the Marriott Corporation, "is to serve the hot food hot— and the cold food cold."[31]

He's talking, of course, about the importance of basics—and it's as true in healthcare as it is for food service. If you and your team don't deliver on what patients consider the basics of good service, you've missed the boat. Big time.

What are the basics? They're the fundamental things that decide whether or not your patients have a positive experience at your facility, remain loyal to your practice, and refer others to you.

Decide with your team what basic services (other than clinical) matter most to your patients. Use the following statement and fill in the blanks:

"Nothing else matters if we don't _____ or aren't _____."

This is one of the exercises I have seminar audiences do. What's surprising is the diversity of answers—often from people within the same practice.

If this also happens when your staff completes the above statement, discuss their various answers, and reach a consensus. It's the best way to get everyone "rowing in the same direction."

213 Empathy Training

"Empathy," says Dr. Dick Barnes, Rialto, California, "is the key to both understanding and influencing others. Empathy is letting people know you understand what they have said or what they are feeling, or both. If you want to be understood, then you have to understand. You have to have both the right attitude and proper technique to understand the heart and mind of another person."[32]

➡**From the success files:** At the Hunterdon Medical Center in Flemington, New Jersey, medical residents spend three hours learning how it feels to be old. "A makeup artist deepens the lines on their face, adds gray to their hair and powders a pallor onto their skin. They are given yellowed contact lenses with a smearing of Vaseline to blur their vision, they don rubber gloves to dim their sense of touch and they wear wax earplugs to diminish their hearing. Splints are fastened to their joints, making it difficult to move. Raw peas in their shoes simulate corns and calluses."

"With their limitations in place, they are sent to several departments in the hospital. In the X-ray clinic, the residents are sent into small changing rooms and told to undress then redress. At the pharmacy, they are required to fill out Medicaid insurance forms in order to receive a variety of prescriptions. They then return to the program training room where they are assigned a variety of seemingly simple tasks: thread a needle, read the label and open the child-proof caps on the medicine vials, open an orange juice container, unwrap the plastic from a bran muffin."

"In addition to increasing the sensitivity of those who work with the elderly," says Linda F. Bryant, coordinator of the program, "this training has brought visible changes to the hospital. Signs have been made easier to read, registration counters have been lowered to wheelchair height and elevator doors have been altered to allow slower moving patients more time to get on and off."[33]

214 Lunch-and-Learn Programs

Lunch-and-learn programs are typically organized as a way of introducing other HCP's staff members to your office and scope of practice. It combines networking with training and skills development.

"All that is necessary," says urologist Neil Baum, co-author of *Marketing Your Clinical Practice Ethically, Effectively, Economically,* "is for your staff to invite a referring physician's staff to lunch in order to exchange ideas, resources and friendship."

"We host these luncheons on a monthly basis," Baum says. "They are an effective means of solidifying relationships between medical staffs and often lead to increased referrals."

"Our office manager usually begins the luncheon with a brief welcome," says Baum. "All our office staff then take turns introducing themselves, giving their job descriptions, and providing brief biographical sketches. The office manager then asks the visiting staff to do the same."

"During lunch, several of our staff members give 'mini-lectures,' two to three minutes in length, about some area of medical interest that our office specializes in, such as impotence, urinary incontinence, urinary tract infections, or infertility. I have found that when I encourage my staff members to give the mini-lectures, they make an effort to become more knowledgeable about the assigned subject or topic. As a result, they can also better explain the procedure or subject to our patients."

"Our staff members also try to learn about the interests and areas of expertise that are unique to the guest staff and their office. Our staff then encourages an exchange of ideas about issues such as insurance billing, coding, patient scheduling, dealing with HMO approvals, and computer technology."

"We have been conducting monthly luncheons for nearly ten years," Baum says. "Everyone in our office really likes the program, and we have received glowing letters thanking us for being gracious hosts."[34]

215 Training Options and Resources

➡Options

"Off-site conferences and seminars, distance learning, and self-study courses can all supplement your in-house training," says Dr. Karen E. Felsted, a consultant with Brakke Consulting in Dallas, Texas.

"Self-study programs," says Felsted, "may be as simple as a staff member borrowing a manual or a video, or as complicated as a distance-learning program that leads to certification."

"Distance learning is a broad term that describes a number of educational formats that don't involve face-to-face interaction between the instructor and students. The program could involve written correspondence, audio and videotapes, audio and videoconferencing, CD-ROM, online learning, interactive television or fax."

"E-learning is an internet-based distance learning option," Felsted explains. "For example, the program might provide online sessions with a live instructor scheduled at a particular time; recorded sessions online; Web-based text and slides; e-mail conferences with the instructor; and so on. More programs offer certificates and some offer degrees."

With all distance learning, off-site seminars, or self-study programs, Felsted recommends that attendees bring the knowledge back and share it with the rest of the practice team. "As a minimum," she suggests, "require a two-minute informal presentation at the next in-house meeting about the most interesting thing the employee learned."[35]

➡Resources

Do your people need to learn more about HIPAA? Front desk skills? Coding? Electronic health records? Do they need certification or recertification as a medical assistant? The following groups offer continuing education on a wide variety of topics through national, state, and regional conferences; online and on-site classes; and in some cases, touring workshops.

- American Medical Association:
  http://www.ama-assn.org
- Medical Group Management Association:
  http://www.mgma.com
- Professional Association of Health Care Office Management:
  http://www.pahcom.com
- American Association of Medical Assistants:
  http://www.aama-ntl.org
- American Medical Group Association:
  http://www.amga.org
- Healthcare Finance Management Association:
  http://www.hfma.org
- American Health Information Management Association:
  http://www.ahima.org
- The Medical Records Institute:
  http://medrecinst.com
- The Bayer Institute for Health Care Communication:
  http://www.bayerinstitute.org
- MedLearn:
  http://www.medlearn.com

216 Hard Learned Lessons About Training

- "All development is self-development," says Jay Beecroft, former director, education and training for the 3M company. "It suggests that in the final analysis, every individual determines how much he or she gets from any program. It recognizes that the best a company can do for employees is to give them the opportunity to learn, expose them to the course, and encourage their use of a program. Management must provide regular on-the-job coaching, skillfully administered. But, in the final analysis, a company cannot make a person grow. The self-interest of an individual is the greatest factor in getting value from an educational opportunity. But it is not the only factor. Management must also provide guidance, stimulation, and motivation which can stretch a person and get him (or her) to reach beyond his (or her) grasp."[36]
- "Be sure to send all employees to workshops on a rotating basis, so one employee doesn't become Ms. Know-It-All, and everyone gets a chance to get out of the office," says practice management consultant Judy Capko, based in Thousand Oaks, California.[37]
- Don't send your ducks to eagle school. Training someone who wishes only a paycheck is as pointless and self-defeating as placing someone with a desire for professional growth in a repetitive, dead-end job.
- Surprisingly, some HCPs say they can't afford to train because of the expense and because better-trained, more highly skilled employees may decide to leave for better opportunities. That's true. But training new employees and having them leave is not nearly as bad as *not* training them—and having them stay.

References

1. American Society for Training & Development. *Trends Watch.* Alexandria, VA, 1999.
2. Grensing-Popal L. *Motivating Today's Employees,* 2nd ed. Bellingham, WA: Self-Counsel Press; 2002.

3. Wells SJ. Stepping Carefully: Attention to Staffing Levels, Compensation, and Training Will Help Ride Out a Slowdown. *HR Magazine,* April 19, 2001.

4. Price C, Novak A. *The Medical Practice Performance Manual: How to Evaluate Employees,* 2nd ed. Englewood, CO: Medical Group Management Association; 2002.

5. Personal communication.

6. Chin T. Train Without Pain: Doing What It Takes to Make Your Office Staff Tech-Savvy. July 12, 2004. http://www.ama-assn.org/amednews/2004/07/12/bisa0712.htm

7. Ibid.

8. Grandinetti D. Scoop Up Every Dollar You've Earned. *Medical Economics,* September 3, 2001.

9. Flynn WJ, Mathis RL, Jackson JH. *Healthcare Human Resource Management*, 2nd ed. Mason, OH: Thomson South-Western; 2007.

10. Kavanagh KH, Kennedy PH. *Promoting Cultural Diversity: Strategies for Health Care Professionals.* Newbury Park, CA: Sage Publications; 1992.

11. Richards B, Yasiri J. *Putting the Patient First.* Englewood, CO: Medical Group Management Association; 1997.

12. Keaveney B. 5 Keys to a Better Practice. *Physicians Practice,* November 2004.

13. Weiss GG. Practice Pointers: The Benefits of Cross-Training Staff. *Medical Economics*, July 8, 2005, 42–45.

14. Ibid.

15. Holzhauer RJ. Retention Plan Worth Effort. *Academy News,* published by the American Academy of Allergy Asthma & Immunology, December 2004.

16. Woodcock E. Creative Cross-Training. *Physicians Practice Pearls,* July 29, 2004.

17. Weiss GG. Practice Pointers: The Benefits of Cross-Training Staff. *Medical Economics*, July 8, 2005, 42–45.

18. Berman MH. Tips from a Fellow Traveler, Part 1. *Dental Economics,* February 2000.

19. Woodcock E. *Physician Practice Pearls,* May 4, 2006.

20. Brown MD. Coding Credentials for Your Staff: Why and How. *Medical Economics*, February 6, 2004.

21. Ibid.

22. Ibid.

23. Lowes R. Practice Pointers: Your Staff Needs CME, Too. *Medical Economics,* June 18, 2004.

24. Childress K. Play It Safe. *Physicians Practice,* March 2005.

25. Ibid.

26. Ibid.

27. Ibid.

28. Malley M. Does Your Customer Service Need a Check Up? *Ophthalmology Management*, June 2005, 41–42.

29. Rauch M. RN: Retention Necessary. *Incentive,* April 2006, 18–23.

30. Davis J. Loyal Patients Will Make Yours a Healthier Hospital. October 16, 2003. http://www.ddiworld.com/directions/healthcare_content.asp?id=283

31. Dow R, Cook S. *Turned On: Eight Vital Insights to Energize Your People, Customers and Profits,* New York: HarperCollins, 1996.

32. Barnes D. Why Using Empathy Can Lead to Greater Case Acceptance. *Dental Products Report*, October 1998, 124–129.

33. Murray K. Make Nice and Make It Snappy: Companies Try Courtesy Training. *New York Times*, April 2, 1995.

34. Baum N, Henkel G. *Marketing Your Clinical Practice Ethically, Effectively, Economically*. Sudbury, MA: Jones & Bartlett; 2004.

35. Felsted KE. Develop an Effective Training Program. *Veterinary Economics*, July 2004, 65–76.

36. Beecroft J. *Motivation, Training and Development of Salespeople Through the Management by Objectives Concept*. Syllabus for a course presented to the New York Sales Executive Club. August 5, 1976.

37. Lowes R. Practice Pointers: Your Staff Needs CME, Too. *Medical Economics*, June 18, 2004.

Chapter Seventeen

RETAINING

Upward Communication

"It is my belief," said Harold S. Geneen, former CEO of ITT and author of *Managing*, "that the worst disease which can affect business executives in their work is not, as popularly supposed, alcoholism; it's egotism. Whether in middle management or top management, personal, unbridled egotism blindsides a man to the realities around him; more and more he comes to live in a world of his own imagination; and because he sincerely believes he can do no wrong, he becomes a menace to the men and women who work under his direction. He becomes unwilling to accept information which is contrary to some preconceived notion of himself. The supreme egotist in corporate life believes he is smarter then everyone else around him, that he is somehow 'ordained' from on high to know the answer to everything, that he is in control and everyone else is there to serve him. That kind of egotism," Geneen writes, "will demean and destroy the collective effort of a company's management team. People become wary of bringing such a boss any kind of bad news. He is too likely to shoot the messenger. In turn, that will have a curdling effect upon any degree of open communications in a company. Ultimately, this attitude will catch up with the egotist in the performance of his department, his division or his company."[1]

Gender bias aside, Geneen makes a point that's also applicable to the healthcare professions. One way to avoid the problems he raises is *upward communication*—the subject of this chapter.

217 Encourage Upward Communication

The fact that you never hear job-related complaints from employees doesn't necessarily mean everyone is happy. Many employees are reluctant to speak up when they dislike something about their work or the way they're treated by their boss. Some are timid or afraid. Others think speaking up would be a waste of time because nothing would change if they did. So they talk among themselves and their families, perhaps with patients as well, about the things that bother them about the practice. And the problems continue.

Eventually this lack of communication takes its toll. Unhappy people do not perform as well as those who like their jobs. They're not as interested in what they do or how well they do it. They tend to be slower, perhaps more careless. And, they're not as pleasant. In time, it begins to affect everyone's morale, patients included.

Firing unhappy employees isn't the answer. Effective management and motivation of people depends on good communication—*upward* as well as downward. Downward communication takes place when the HCP does the talking and the staff listens. Upward communication is just the opposite. The staff talks. The *HCP* listens.

➡**Reality check:** "After more than 40 years in business," says J.W. Marriott, chairman and CEO of Marriott International Inc., "I've concluded that listening is the single most important on-the-job skill that a good manager can cultivate. A leader who doesn't listen well, risks missing critical information, losing (or never winning) the confidence of staff and peers and forfeiting the opportunity to be a proactive, hands-on manager."[2]

Upward communication is the only way HCPs can ascertain the level of staff morale and job satisfaction—and what changes, if any, are needed to improve it. It's also the key to discovering what impact their management style has on others.

Upward communication is only meaningful if employees are free to tell it like it is, and confident the HCP will listen with an open mind. If they're concerned their job security or future raises might in any way be threatened by what they say, it's understandable (and predictable) they'll say only what they think the HCP *wants* to hear. And the problems will continue.

This chapter describes some of the tools and techniques used to facilitate upward communication in a healthcare practice. Adopt or modify them to suit the circumstances of your practice.

218 The "Stay Interview"

Many HCPs want to know the secret of retaining their best employees. Yet most overlook the obvious: asking what's important to their employees, why they like working for the practice, and what, if anything, might lure them away.

Rather than conducting exit interviews with departing key employees, stop guessing what keeps them happy and use what's called "stay interviews" to head off potential problems and cement early retention.

Asking such questions has many positive benefits. The people you ask feel valued and important, which often engenders stronger loyalty and commitment to the practice. In other words, just asking the questions is by itself a retention strategy

➟**Action steps:** Beverly Kaye, co-author of the book, *Love 'Em or Lose 'Em: Getting Good People to Stay,* says it's critical that retention *be* viewed as an individualized process. She recommends that stay interviews should be a one-on-one meeting, ideally in a neutral environment, where you can sit and talk with an employee who reports to you and have uninterrupted time.

Kaye's recommendations in this case, are made to nurse leaders.

"Start by telling a nurse that it's important to you to keep her on your team," Kaye advises, "and you want to know how you can best accomplish that." Kaye suggests that leaders say, **"My hands might be tied in many ways, but let's look for ways in which my hands aren't tied."**

"Nurse leaders might then ask questions to gain insights into what makes that nurse stay. Examples include:

- **"What might keep you here and what might entice you away?**
- **What do you love about your work?**
- **Am I fully using your talents?**
- **What can I do to make your job more satisfying?**
- **What makes for a great day?**
- **Do we suppose your career goals? How could we do better?**
- **Do you get enough recognition? What kind would you like?**
- **What can I do differently to make this a place you really want to stay at?"**

➡**Hard learned lesson:** "Conducting stay interviews," says Kaye, "is only as valuable as your intentions. Actions and follow up are what make these meetings work."[3]

➡**Reality check:** "One of the ground rules of good questioning is that when a question is asked and an answer is given, the questioner does not (and often should not) respond," says Chris Clarke-Epstein, author of *78 Important Questions Every Leader Should Ask and Answer.* "Given an answer, you should simply acknowledge the information, clarify any ambiguities, and assure the person that his or her opinion is valuable and will be considered. If you express an opinion or make a promise based on a single response to your question," Clarke-Epstein says, "you might find yourself in the middle of something more complex than that one answer indicated. This is especially problematic when a response to your question points a finger at an individual. An emotional reaction from you may satisfy the answerer but cause great difficulty for the other person mentioned. Your best response to this situation is **'Thank you for bringing this to my attention. As I understand it, your situation is [restate the problem]. You have my word that I will look into this matter and will get back to you with a resolution. Please know that I appreciate your efforts to make our organization better.'** Now your job becomes one of detective. By asking more questions and listening to the additional answers carefully, you'll be able to fulfill your promise to deliver a resolution to the original answerer. It may not be exactly what he or she wanted or envisioned, but the person will appreciate the fact that you kept your word and followed through."[4]

Some staff members will jump at the chance to discuss these issues. Others may be more hesitant. Encourage the latter by saying, **"That's interesting. Tell me more."** Or simply repeat or paraphrase the final words of their last sentence—and pause. To someone who complains about a co-worker, your response might be, **"How did you feel about that?"** or **"What can I do to help?"**

If a staff member is talking about an especially emotional situation, statements of empathy work well to help him or her continue to ventilate. Try this: **"That must have been difficult/frustrating/upsetting for you."**

➡**Benefits:** These discussions will give your staff an outlet for their gripes—perhaps for the first time. They'll enable you to learn your staff's needs, expectations, priorities, likes, and dislikes. And by being a good listener, you'll earn their respect and appreciation.

219 Initiate an Employee Survey

Another more comprehensive technique for initiating upward communication is the employee survey. It's widely used as a management tool in industry to learn what employees (in general) think of their jobs, working conditions, quality of supervision, compensation, co-workers, opportunities for advancement, and other factors.

The advantage of the employee survey is that many employees are more comfortable expressing themselves *anonymously* on paper than they are in person. Make sure that employees feel comfortable in the knowledge that their responses are and will remain anonymous, and that nothing they say, whether positive or negative, will come back to haunt them. This will greatly improve the chances of getting truthful results.

The following is a composite of employee surveys used in a wide variety of healthcare professions. Use or modify it for your particular situation. Add additional questions. And leave space for employees to elaborate on their answers.

Employee Survey

	Strongly Agree	Agree	Strongly Disagree	Disagree
1. The people I work with help each other out when someone falls behind or gets in a tight spot.				
2. When changes are made that affect me, I am usually told the reasons for the changes.				
3. The doctor really tries to get our ideas about things.				
4. The doctor's review of my performance gives me a clear picture of how I'm doing on the job.				
5. The practice could benefit from more frequent staff meetings.				
6. My job is a satisfactory challenge to me.				
7. Our staff meetings are a waste of time.				
8. If I have a complaint, I feel free to tell the doctor about it.				
9. The doctor has always been fair in dealing with me.				
10. I look forward to coming to work.				
11. The doctor lets us know exactly what's expected of us.				
12. There's too much pressure in my job.				
13. Some of the working conditions here need to be changed.				
14. I'm paid fairly compared with other employees.				

continues

	Strongly Agree	Agree	Strongly Disagree	Disagree
15. My job has not turned out to be as it was described to me when I was hired.				
16. I have all the authority I need to perform my job properly.				
17. I have been properly trained to do my job.				
18. I am very much underpaid for the work I do.				
19. I have the right equipment and materials to do my job well.				
20. The office policies are clearly spelled out.				
21. I am given the opportunity to learn and grow in my job.				
22. I feel my efforts to do a good job are appreciated.				
23. I enjoy working with the people here.				
24. The doctor lets me know in a fair and constructive manner when I have done something wrong.				
25. The hours of work are satisfactory.				
26. Our productivity sometimes suffers from lack of organization and planning.				
27. I think some good may come out of completing this survey.				

Optional: The reason I feel as I do about question # _____ is:

_____

_____

What I think should be done about it is:

_____

_____

Signatures are optional.

➡**Reality check:** Will such a survey open a can of worms? Create more problems than it solves? The answer is no. Problems either do or do not already exist. Ignoring them won't make them go away. It may, in fact, make them *worse*, lead to deep resentment, and cause a capable person to quit.

Evidence indicates that the attitude of employees tends to improve when they're given an opportunity to speak their minds. It's why such surveys are so widely used in industry.

220 A Shorter Litmus Test

Here's a shorter, slightly different version of an employee survey designed to take a reading on employee morale and job satisfaction. Although this tool is certainly not a comprehensive assessment instrument, it may help identify critical issues that you may have overlooked or underestimated. As with the longer survey, allow employees to share their input anonymously with the same assurances that nothing they say will come back to haunt them.

➡**Reality check:** As mentioned in the Introduction to this book, the first step to solving a problem is *recognition*. If employee morale or

	Strongly Agree	Agree	Strongly Disagree	Disagree
1. I understand the core values and philosophy of the practice.				
2. I know exactly what my job responsibilities are.				
3. The amount of work I'm expected to do is reasonable: It's not too much and it's not too little.				
4. I have the decision-making authority I need to do my job effectively.				
5. I'm given the recognition and appreciation I deserve for the work I perform.				
6. I recommend the practice to others as a good place to work.				

job satisfaction problems do exist in your organization, hopefully one of these surveys will help get the issues out in the open where they can be addressed.

221 Submit to an Upward Appraisal

A Texas physician thought of himself as good humored and easy-going until he learned that his staff was, in fact, *terrified* of him. A Florida office manager who thought of herself as efficient discovered staff members thought her a *control freak*. Needless to say, neither of these impressions was conducive to good employee morale, motivation, and productivity.

The discoveries each made about their management styles was a result of what's called in industry an "upward appraisal." This is a process by which employees evaluate their managers—a switch on the usual, *downward* performance appraisal that managers make of employees.

An upward appraisal enables you to learn how your day-to-day behavior and management style is perceived by your staff members. If you receive high marks, you'll want to stay on course. If not, you'll want to make changes.

Regardless of the outcome, an upward appraisal will make you a better manager. To get started, consider the form on page 304. It's a synthesis of many I've seen. Use it as is or modify it to suit your needs. Then distribute it to everyone on your staff, emphasizing that no signatures are required. It will encourage your staff to tell it like it is.

➡**Benefits:** Upward appraisals enable you to discover your strengths and shortcomings as a manager. There's also another, more subtle benefit. The performance criteria represented by each of these statements in the evaluation form *define and promote an internal code of behavior for all employees* (e.g., being punctual, a good listener, thoughtful and considerate of others). In effect, it's saying, this is what this practice is all about.

➡**Hard learned lesson:** Some HCPs describe their personal style in forceful terms: "What you see is what you get" or "I'm not going to change the way I behave just to make other people comfortable." Their

Upward Appraisal Evaluation Form

Ratings: 1 = poor   2 = fair   3 = good   4 = excellent   x = no opinion

Doctor _____   Office Manager _____

(write in name of person being evaluated)

	1	2	3	4
1. Personal appearance	1	2	3	4
2. Conducts himself/herself in a professional manner	1	2	3	4
3. Has a likable personality	1	2	3	4
4. Is a good listener	1	2	3	4
5. Is good at giving feedback to others	1	2	3	4
6. Is open to other people's ideas and opinions	1	2	3	4
7. Is thoughtful and considerate of staff members	1	2	3	4
8. Looks for win/win solutions to disagreements	1	2	3	4
9. Has good self-control when under pressure	1	2	3	4
10. Will admit mistakes and apologize when wrong	1	2	3	4
11. Is punctual	1	2	3	4
12. Leaves personal affairs at home	1	2	3	4
13. Is good at giving compliments and positive feedback	1	2	3	4
14. Provides on-the-job training	1	2	3	4
15. Willingly answers questions for staff members	1	2	3	4
16. Makes me proud to work in this practice	1	2	3	4
17. Lets me know when I have done something wrong in a fair and constructive manner	1	2	3	4
18. Keeps his/her promises	1	2	3	4
19. Delegates the authority I need to do my job	1	2	3	4
20. Has good people skills	1	2	3	4

(Use reverse side for comments. Signatures not required.)

declarations are meant to convey honesty and integrity. Instead, they reveal an inflexible and insensitive leadership style that's out of date and smacks of the egotism to which Harold Geneen referred at the beginning of this chapter.

222 The Problem That Has No Name

"We live in a culture, especially at work, that prefers harmony over discord, agreement over dissent, speed over deliberation," says Leslie A. Perlow, associate professor at the Harvard Business School and author of *When You Say Yes But Mean No.* "Whether with colleagues, friends or family members, the tendency to paper over differences rather than confront them is extremely common. We believe the best thing to preserve our relationships and to ensure our work gets done as expeditiously as possible is to silence conflict." She dubs it: "The problem that has no name."[5]

Healthcare practices are not immune to what Perlow calls "the vicious spiral of silence." Examples include team members who stifle their feelings about being underpaid or underappreciated or who are bored by their work. HCPs, too, have their reasons for failing to confront employees who are often late for work or who are careless about keeping the office spotlessly clean or perhaps socialize too much with patients.

"If no one expresses their thoughts," Perlow writes, "people will likely continue thinking and behaving in the same way and nothing will change. Problems are likely to persist and may even get worse because corrective actions are not taken."

One of the costs of silencing conflict, Perlow says, is the effect it has on employee motivation and engagement. When work relationships are marked by pent-up frustration, work suffers and it is hard to be motivated as a result. "We don't experience a reason to put much of ourselves into our job, be creative or go above and beyond the call of duty. Instead we may lose interest in our work and start to disengage from it and our organization—psychologically, at first, and then often physically, by quitting. This is highly costly for both individuals and organizations."

"The best advice for anyone caught in this bind," says Perlow, "is to speak up and seek mutual understanding. Employee Surveys and Performance Reviews are two ways to start the process. Talking things over may not solve all the problems. It may however, clarify them; enable you to learn each other's needs; make needed adjustments; and improve the productivity of your practice."[6]

➡**From the success files:** Sam Platia, administrator of the five-clinician Northwestern Medical Center in New Tripoli, Pennsylvania, says he periodically meets with employees and asks for their ideas and how their jobs can be modified. "They know their jobs better than anyone," he says. "Feedback from them and making them feel part of a team increases the likelihood of a successful staff and smooth-running practice."[7]

➡**Action step:** What's the one thing your employees complain about the most? The one single thing? Maybe it's the same thing that got dinged the hardest on your last employee survey. Can you do something to provide relief where that one thing is concerned? If so, do it. Forget all the reasons it can't be done. If it's a problem, and it's interfering with your employees accomplishing your mission, and you have the power to fix it, fix it.

References

1. Geneen HS, Moscow A. *Managing.* New York: Avon Books; 1993.
2. Marriott Jr. JW, Brown KA. *The Spirit to Serve.* New York: HarperBusiness; 1997.
3. Hilton L. 'Stay' Interviews—Because the Exit Interview Is Too Late, *Nursing Spectrum/Nursing Week,* April 7, 2004. http://www.helpatnursingspectrum.com/recruiters/load_article.html?AID=882
4. Clarke-Epstein C. *78 Important Questions Every Leader Should Ask and Answer.* New York: AMACOM; 2002.
5. Perlow LA. *When You Say Yes But Mean No.* New York: Crown Business; 2003.
6. Ibid.
7. Weiss GG. Practice Pointers: Turning a Problem Employee into a Pearl. *Medical Economics,* December 23, 2002.

Epilogue

The prologue of this book stressed the pivotal role that staff have as ambassadors for a healthcare organization or practice—and the importance of hiring, managing, and retaining the right people for the right jobs.

But it goes beyond that.

"Employee satisfaction and retention have always been important issues for physicians," say J. Michael Syptak, M.D., David W. Marsland, M.D., and Deborah Ulmer, Ph.D., writing in the journal of *Family Practice Management*. "After all, high levels of absenteeism and staff turnover can affect your bottom line. But few practices (in fact, few organizations) have made job satisfaction a top priority, perhaps because they have failed to understand the significant opportunity that lies in front of them."

"Satisfied employees tend to be more productive, creative, and committed to their employers," the authors say, "and recent studies have shown a direct correlation between staff satisfaction and patient satisfaction."

"Family physicians that can create work environments that attract, motivate and retain hard-working individuals will be better positioned to succeed in a competitive health care environment that demands quality and cost-efficiency. What's more, physicians may even discover that by creating a positive workplace for their employees, they've increased their own job satisfaction as well."[1]

In short, hiring, managing and retaining great employees is a win/win situation—for your employees, your patients, your practice and yourself.

Reference

1. Syptak JM, Marsland DW, Ulmer D. Job Satisfaction: Putting Theory into Practice. *Family Practice Management,* October 1999.

About the Author

B ob Levoy, a former corporate executive, is an internationally acclaimed seminar speaker on human resource and management issues. In the course of his career, he has conducted more than 3,000 seminars for business and professional groups, *Fortune* 500 companies, and leading colleges and universities throughout North America and overseas. Among them have been hundreds of healthcare associations in a wide range of disciplines and specialties.

He holds three degrees from the University of Connecticut and Columbia University; has written six best-selling books and hundreds of articles on management topics for business and professional journals, and he has recorded numerous audio programs. Currently, he is a monthly columnist and Editorial Board member for various publications in the healthcare professions and can be reached via email at b.levoy@att.net.

Index